A NEW BIRTH OF FREEDOM?

A NEW BIRTH OF FREEDOM?

*

World Communism
after Stalin

by

K. ZILLIACUS

MONTHLY REVIEW PRESS
New York 1958

Contents

Introduction

THE PURPOSE of this book is to help in understanding the phenomenon of the twentieth century—the Russian Revolution, the society that has grown out of it in the boundaries of the former Russian Empire, and its *sequelae* in Europe and Asia. For our understanding of and consequent attitude to the social revolution—both as an accomplished fact in nearly two-fifths of the world and as movements for social change in most of the rest—is quite literally a question of 'to be or not to be' for humanity.

My reason for believing I may have something to contribute to this subject is that most of my life has been mixed up with it, in one way or another. My father was a 'Finlander'—that is, he belonged to the Swedish minority in Finland. He was the founder and leader of the so-called 'Activist' party. This was a radical party which thought that Finnish national resistance to the Russification policy of Tsar Nicolas II need not be confined to constitutional methods only, nor refuse to have any dealings with the Russian revolutionary parties.

He was so good a patriot indeed, that he had to live most of the time in exile, including some time in this country—which is why, "in spite of all temptations to belong to other nations, I became an Englishman." But part of my childhood memories is of our house in Finland—during the brief period after the 1905 revolution that my father could stay legally in that country—as an underground station for Russian revolutionaries escaping from Siberia to the West. My mother was American, of Scottish descent, and a strong liberal and supporter of women's suffrage.

I emerged from this childhood background with two ideas and a piece of unconscious knowledge lodged firmly in my mind: first, that some day there was going to be a revolution in Russia, and this would be something great and good to which all liberal and civilised people looked forward. Second, that the Russians were a backward, barbarous and semi-Asiatic people, from whom the rest of the world had nothing to learn politically, although the Revolution should free the Finns and the Poles and enable the Russians to start catching up with the West.

The piece of subconscious knowledge, that in after years rose to the surface, was of the abyss between the attitude of a democrat or 'reformist', and that of a revolutionary (or counter-revolutionary). The former thinks in terms of political opponents, with whom he shares certain fundamental loyalties. The latter is dealing with enemies, against whom anything goes. This difference is so fundamental that each side has the greatest difficulty in understanding the position of the other.

The next stage was two years (1917-1919) as Intelligence Officer in the British Military Mission in Siberia, from start to finish of intervention. Here I learned more about revolution and counter-revolution, shed my early 'Vansittartism' (to use a word that was coined in the Second World War) about Russia and acquired an enduring affection and admiration for the literature and people of that great country. I also found out that the restraints and decencies of democracy did not apply, in the eyes of our Tories, to their dealings with a class enemy such as the Bolsheviks.

After that came nineteen years in the Information section of the League of Nations Secretariat at Geneva. Here the connection became plain between the search for peace and the struggle for a new social order, or to put it the other way around, between the drift to war and defence of the old order. I lived through all that, took part in the fight, and did my puny best to help the Labour Party—which I joined on demobilisation in 1919—to understand. One of my jobs was to follow Soviet affairs. I read Soviet reviews and papers, saw Soviet delegates and journalists who came to Geneva, received whatever information became available to the Secretariat from other sources, and visited the country.

Geneva drove home the lesson learned from Finland and Siberia, the sense of the Russian national background and content of the new society in the Soviet Union. I can understand the point of view of Western Communists and anti-Communists who regard Soviet Communism as a promise or threat for their own countries. But to me the Russian revolution has always seemed too Russian to spread except to countries that missed the French Revolution, and even then only in their own national versions.

What I learnt in those years I have preached in a series of books and other writings from 1925 until to-day, and tried to practise as a Labour Member of Parliament between 1945 and 1950 and again since returning to the House after the last election. In 1946, '47 and '48 I visited the East European countries and talked with their leading men. In 1947 the visit was extended to the Soviet Union and included long talks with Stalin and Molotov. These visits were made easier by the fact that I had learnt Russian in the First World War; Polish soon after; and became fluent in Serbo-Croat and acquired a fair understanding of Czech after the last war.

But my efforts to win friends and influence people for a Socialist foreign policy and against the Tory 'bi-partisan' foreign policy being pursued by the Labour Government to its own despite, were not conspicuously successful. They ended in my being thrown out of the Party (and shut out of the U.S.A.), and almost at the same time violently denounced in the Soviet Union and the 'People's Democracies'.

The charge on which I was expelled, as formulated by Transport House, was that "over the last three years Mr. Zilliacus's speeches and writings have, for the most part, taken the form of violent attacks on the Labour Government's foreign policy. He is recognised in Cominform literature as the leading British exponent of 'left-wing Social democracy', i.e. those Socialists whose substantial agreement with Cominform policies must ultimately lead them into complete agreement with the Communists." (In fact, I stuck all the way through to the pledges I had given in an election address approved by Transport House.)

The reason I was almost simultaneously subjected to a drum-fire of denunciation in the Cominform Press and wireless was that I had said that Tito in his controversy with Stalin was defending the all-important principle that the relations between Socialist states should be based on equality, mutual respect for each other's national independence, and non-interference in each other's internal affairs, and that Tito should be supported because it was a matter of concern to the whole civilised world that he should win his fight. Invitations to visit those countries were withdrawn, and I became a pariah and outcast all round—except in Yugoslavia. In the great Prague treason trial of 1952 I figured as the chief Anglo-American-Titoist-Fascist foreign agent, who had engineered the conspiracy of the 'Slansky centre' to overthrow Socialism and restore capitalism in Czechoslovakia, tear that country out of the Socialist peace camp and thrust it into the American war camp, etc., etc.

After Khrushchev had paid his penitential visit to Tito in October 1955 I knew it was only a question of time until I would be 'rehabilitated', particularly since in the meantime I had again become a Member of Parliament, and so someone of whom it might be politically worth while to take notice. What was more important, that visit, together with many other signs of the times, made it plain that something fundamental was happening in the Soviet Union, something that looked like the beginning of the next phase in the social revolution under Communist leadership.

I soon had unofficial 'feelers' through friends as to whether I would accept invitations from the Soviet and Cominform Embassies. I said I would, but in the case of the Czechs only after they had publicly withdrawn the grotesque charges against me made in the Slansky trial. This they eventually did.

From November onwards I was treated with great friendliness at Soviet Embassy receptions and by visiting Soviet journalists, technicians and statesmen. Prime Minister Bulganin's first remark when we met at the reception in the Royal Gallery of Parliament in April 1956 was: "I want you to know that we are very sorry about the things we have been saying about you for the last few years." That summer I was invited to visit the U.S.S.R. by the Institute of World Economy and International Relations of the Academy of Science.

All this meant that when I visited Eastern Europe and the Soviet Union in the autumn of 1956 (to be exact, between October 10th and November 8th) to gather material for this book and to pick up the threads where they had been dropped in 1948, I came not as an unknown but as someone whose record was familiar over the previous ten years, in some cases even from Geneva days, and was regarded not as a Communist or fellow-traveller but as an inconveniently awkward and outspoken, but on the whole consistent Labour friend, whose views had been broadly confirmed by events.

The sensible reader of a book on any controversial topic tries to discount the bias of the writer. That is why I have ventured to wax somewhat autobiographical in this Introduction. But to make my point of view still clearer, let me say that I am a radical who evolved into a Socialist as he became convinced—soon after the First World War—that Socialism is now the only way to fulfil the promise of liberalism, the only possible economic underpinning of a society delivered from want and fear in which equality, freedom and democracy are realities enjoyed by all, and where there is respect for human rights and belief in human brotherhood. By Socialism I mean a society where the great concentrations of irresponsible, private economic and financial power that threaten to stultify democracy by becoming States within the State are replaced by public ownership, planning and control, with workers and employees sharing in management and the good of the community instead of private profit becoming the mainspring of our economic system.

Those who reject Socialism, including the latter-day Liberals, more and more tend to line up with the die-hard defenders of the old order. They pin their faith to arms, alliances and power politics as the way to deal with the forces of social change, which they identify with the, in my view, wholly mythical danger of Soviet military aggression in order to impose Communism by force of arms on other countries. This is the road to creeping Fascism at home, to nuclear war and to the extinction of the human race, in a vain attempt to defend the old order that has become indefensible because it is rotten-ripe for change.

This book supplies the raw material, I hope, for a more realistic assessment of the nature and extent of the Communist challenge to liberal civilisation. It should give some idea of what are the vast changes in the Communist world that became perceptible on the death of Stalin and have been gathering momentum at breakneck speed (in spite of checks and pauses) ever since the 20th Congress of the C.P.S.U. in January 1956.

K. ZILLIACUS, M.P.

June 1957.

CHAPTER ONE

Moscow Re-visited

THE LAST TIME I visited Moscow, in 1947, there was great official friendliness too, but a pervading sense of an iron régime that had put up an impenetrable barrier between the Russian people and foreigners. The Soviet Union was still bleeding from the fearful wounds inflicted by the war and anxious about the tremendous tasks of reconstruction that lay ahead and the signs that their Western allies were preparing to get tough with them. There was a sense of strain and apprehension.

Moscow in 1956 looked like what it has become—the capital of a world power. "After visiting Prague and Warsaw, I feel I'm in the big time now," said an American friend I came across. "This is like London, or Paris, or New York."

Gone are the anxiety and strain, and in their place is a great confidence and sense of power. Gone too is the old barrier between foreigners and Muscovites. I met many Russians and their families and found friendliness and readiness—nay, eagerness—to talk wherever I went. Moscow was full of foreign visitors (including a young Ethiopian dignitary I first met on the 'plane). They had had a big tourist season and expected a lot more next year.

There was far more traffic, including plenty of *Pobeda* taxis and private cars, as well as a fair number of *Zims*, medium-sized cars, and of big *Zis*, which are for the higher regions of the official world and Soviet literary, theatrical and film stars. A car smaller than the *Pobeda* is coming on the market, and these four models are available in different colours. But anyone who wants something different is just out of luck—unless he happens to be a foreign journalist or diplomat and can import a car from abroad.

Moscow had expanded enormously in the nine years since I saw it last. It is now a city of eight million, and the over-crowding is fearful, although blocks of flats are being built in impressive quantities and at high speed. The main streets are so enormously wide that even the increased traffic is only a trickle on them. But traffic discipline is strict now, and there is no more of the death-defying fury on green lights that I remember from 1947 (when the idea seemed to be to charge any pedestrians who lingered on the crossings after the lights had turned). The places where a car may cross from one side to the other of the 200-300-yard-wide streets are marked, and although the road may be empty, people will drive some way along before turning and coming back to the address on the other side of the street, rather than cross directly at an un-licensed spot.

The shops have much more to sell than before and are always crowded. I noticed carved ivory powder boxes and other luxury articles from China and Northern Vietnam. Prices for most goods are still high, even when calculated at the purchasing power exchange rate of 40 roubles to the £1 (the official rate is eleven to the £1). But that does not seem to deter the shoppers.

The Leningrad Hotel where I was put up was completed in 1953. It is a vast structure (my room was on the tenth floor, and I was only halfway up) in the style fashionable a few years ago. I disturbed a Soviet friend by describing it as a cross between a skyscraper and a church. It is luxurious, but with heavy red-plush curtains, chandeliers, Empire furniture, in the style of a glorified nineteenth-century grand hotel. Against such a background it seemed incongruous but human that the staff—maids, porters, lift attendants and those in charge of the offices on every floor where you deposit your key on going out—were in their own clothes and not in any kind of livery.

In Moscow these baroque skyscraper-cum-church buildings —so out of place in Warsaw, for instance—do fit in with the whole tradition and atmosphere, and make the city look like a larger and modernised edition of its old self. They have made a new skyline of spires and pinnacles to replace the old, which is now hidden by the taller blocks of flats and offices. But they are so costly to build and to heat, and so extravagant in wasted space, that no more like them will be erected.

The Kremlin and the big Cathedral in Red Square have been repainted and decorated and look like a Diaghilev *décor* in strawberry red, blue, green, white, gold and a forest of glittering onion-shaped domes. The Kremlin is now open to the public and has become a great tourist attraction with loudspeakers and guides. It was another measure of the great change to be wandering round freely with the crowds and remember the strictly guarded and secluded Kremlin of 1947, when eight Labour M.Ps. were taken round to see the sights as a special favour, and later had our interview with Molotov. But through wars and revolutions, through the police state of Stalin and the more genial climate after his death, the Kremlin remains full of the beauty and strangeness and dark violent history of old Russia. Napoleon's armies destroyed or carried away much of the treasure of the great cathedrals, but what is left is still an illuminated page of Greek Orthodox religious history.

Another part of the Moscow scene I found impressive and fascinating was the permanent exhibition on the outskirts of the town. It is divided into the agricultural and industrial sections. The latter includes a model of an atomic energy plant; the former a 'zoological' pavilion with exhibits covering the fur industry. In addition, each of the sixteen republics has its own pavilion, built in its own characteristic architecture and displaying its chief products. The exhibition is kept up to date and is a kind of show window of the Soviet world and a popular university for visiting collective farmers and industrial workers, who are given lectures on their own subjects illustrated by the exhibits.

The exhibition is so vast that it would take several days to visit it properly, and is beautifully laid out, with fountains, gardens, orchards, an observatory, restaurants, cinemas and so forth. It gives an overwhelming impression that this really is a different world, a Eurasian world with a strong Russian flavour persisting in what is now the second industrial power in the world.

The academic world gave me a further insight into the difference that Stalin's death had made. I had been invited to visit the Soviet Union by the Institute of World Economy and International Relations of the Academy of Science, so that one of my first visits was paid to what I might describe as my ultimate host, the President of the Academy of Science, of which the Institute is a branch.

Niesmieianov, a non-party man who had recently been re-elected President of the Academy, was an impressive and forceful figure. But he submitted with good grace to answering questions, and this soon became a conversation in which I had to satisfy his curiosity as well as he mine.

The Academy of Science is the intellectual dynamo which drives the tremendous machine for research and higher education that is turning out annually some 60,000 scientists and technicians in the Soviet Union. The sheer scale of the enterprise was breath-taking. The Academy of Science, he explained, has under it the following main divisions (each composed of several institutes) for Moscow alone: Physical and Mathematical; Chemical; Biological; Geological and Geographical; Technical (including Engineering); Historical and Economic. The Institute of World Economy and International Relations is part of this last division. Originally it was a section of the Economic Institute, but has now set up as an institute in its own right studying the economies and commercial and financial relations of capitalist states, whereas the Economic Institute concerns itself with the Socialist states, mainly, of course, the Soviet Union itself. Like the amoeba, these institutes and divisions tend to multiply by fission. Other divisions include Philosophy and Jurisprudence; Etymology and Literature. Out of a total of 2,500-3,000 Scientific institutes in the U.S.S.R. (some of them very small), 120 are under the direct control of the Academy of Science. The Ministry of Health has its own Academy of Medical Science, and the Central Committee of the Communist Party of the Soviet Union controls an Academy of Social Science.

The total staff working in the Academy numbers 40,000.

Its job is research. In addition, there are over 2,000 post-graduate students taking courses in the various Institutes of the Academy, which has 150 members and 250 corresponding members (of whom less than thirty are foreign).

One of the Institutes in Moscow belonging to the Technical Division is the Institute of Scientific Documentation. It takes 10,000 scientific and technical journals from all over the world, makes abstracts and *précis* of the information they contain, and publishes them in volumes, classified according to subjects, for the use of Soviet scientists, research workers, technicians, etc. President Niesmieianov told me with pride that nowhere else in the world was this kind of thing done on the same scale, although the United States *Chemical Abstracts* and a similar publication in Germany cover the field in much the same way in their own subjects.

I asked whether the Institute of Scientific Documentation had ever considered issuing its publications in other languages than Russian. He replied they would like to, but it was a task beyond even their resources. However, he said, the Russian volumes were being increasingly used far outside the Soviet Union.*

In reply to a further question he said that the end of the 'Personality Cult' had meant there was no longer political interference with research work in the Institutes of the Academy. The kind of situation that led to the famous Lysenko battle over genetics could not happen to-day. No scientist could or would invoke party aid to support his scientific views against those of a colleague. The whole conception of a fount of scientific wisdom and infallibility in the person of the leader of the party had gone with Stalin, and the new collective leadership neither could nor wanted to revive it.

A whole new quarter of the rapidly growing capital is being set aside for the many buildings of the Academy of Science

---

* I have since learnt that U.N.E.S.C.O. is now in touch with the Institute of Scientific Documentation, and that there is a good chance that U.N.E.S.C.O. may make the Institute's unique work available in other languages. The U.S.S.R. did not join U.N.E.S.C.O. until 1954, but since then its representatives have won golden opinions from their colleagues for the high quality of the delegates and their spirit of co-operation.

and Moscow University. The Moscow State University has 20,000 students and 2,659 professors, lecturers and science assistants; 12 faculties and 12 chairs. It has 3 science research institutes, 281 laboratories, 3 museums, 3 astronomical observatories, a botanical garden, many blocks of lecture rooms, students' dormitories, and a vast and beautiful main building with fine lecture halls, laboratories, a cinema, theatre, shops, restaurants, a swimming pool, a gymnasium, recreation rooms and accommodation for various games as well as students' dormitories. Most of the students' rooms are in pairs sharing a common vestibule, shower bath and tiny kitchen. Each room has a bed that folds into the wall, cupboard space, a bookshelf, reading-lamp, central heating, a table with chair, and an easy chair. The men and women students are not divided up into different blocks (although, of course, they do not share the same 'pairs').

Only a few months earlier—June 6th—a decree of the Soviet Government had made university education free for all students who could pass the entrance examinations. The great majority of students receive State scholarships of 290 roubles (just over £70 at the 'purchasing power' rate of 40 roubles to the £1) for the first term. To get this scholarship a student must have passed his entrance examination with 'Excellent' or 'Good' in all subjects. The scholarship is continued for successive terms only so long as the student maintains this scholastic standard, and varies according to the course of studies being pursued. Students who have 'Excellent' in all subjects get a 25% increase in their scholarships, and exceptional students receive special scholarships named after prominent scientists, writers or other public figures. There were 223 such students at the time of my visit. The courses of study are over a period of five years. The students are made up of every nationality of the Soviet Union (over sixty). There are also students from the various People's Democracies and from other countries, including a few from Western Europe.

The President of the University, who received me with great kindness, had with him his assistant, a young economist. The President told me he had followed my speeches and writings for years. "So have I," said the assistant. "I particularly like the way you stood up for Tito from the beginning."

I asked my inevitable question: how the ending of the 'Personality cult' had affected their jobs. The President made the same point as his colleague, Niesmieianov of the Academy of Science, but young Glushkov, the assistant, gave the answer in terms of his own experience: "My job is to study the economies of capitalist countries. I found trade between them had increased substantially since the war and wrote a paper on the subject. I was advised not to publish it and to keep my mouth shut, because Stalin had just produced a vast dissertation proving to his own satisfaction that trade between the capitalist countries was bound to decrease. An article I did for one of our economic journals was cut to the point where it became meaningless.

"Now no one would dream of interfering with my reports. I am a research worker, and it is my job to learn as much as I can and say what I think about these things. If anyone disagrees with me, he will put a contrary view and we will have an argument about it in speech or writing. But there is no longer such a thing as political interference with my researches."

The President told me that Professor Bernal had just been lecturing there and was now regarded as virtually a visiting member of their staff and came over every year to give a course of lectures. Professor Hookham had also been lecturing on economics, including a great deal about J. M. Keynes and on John Strachey's new book, *Contemporary Capitalism*. They were anxious to get the book and were thinking of inviting Strachey to lecture to them next autumn. I found Professor Hookham was also staying at the Leningrad Hotel, and asked him about his lectures. He said he found many of his audience knew Keynes' works (which have nearly all been translated into Russian) better than he did, and gave him a hot and close argument based on detailed knowledge and some pretty basic thinking on the problems raised.

The President asked me whether I would give a lecture on the "Parliamentary Path to Socialism", which I undertook to do most willingly. But it was cancelled when the Academy of

Social Science invited me to address them on the Labour Party, and the students who were to attend my original lecture went to that one instead.

After the couple of hours' talk with the President and his assistant, who had a lot to ask about life in the West, came an entertaining but all too brief gossip with a group of twenty students, including some Poles, a Roumanian and youngsters from every part of the Soviet Union. This was meant to be only a first contact, but time was too short and crowded to see more of them. But even that brief hour was enough to get the "sense of the meeting". They were certainly enjoying and making the most of the new freedom, and looking forward to its broadening out from innovation to innovation. They had as much idealism and friendliness and intellectual curiosity as their counterparts in the West. But of course most of them took as the starting point for their conscious thinking the national and social background and framework into which they had been born, and in which the whole of their lives had been spent. If there were any basic rebels about, they were not saying anything drastic on this occasion.

In fact, one lad was taken aside and given a dressing down (which I heard out of one ear) by my Russian companion, an earnest man in his early forties, strong in the faith, for making some sort of crack (in reply to my "church and skyscraper" jest) about that kind of Soviet architecture being a left-over from the Stalinist 'Personality cult'. He was being told that this was a silly and irresponsible thing to say, that it amounted to denigrating their great Socialist heritage, etc. My companion was indignant about it to me afterwards, saying that some of these youngsters took much too frivolous an attitude toward life.

A fairly recent graduate told me that the old professors, who had been their teachers when it was still fashionable to think, and had been retired or jailed in the Stalinist heyday, were being brought back. I asked about the teachers who had been brought in during the Stalinist time? "Oh! they're still around," he said, "but they are *sierye lichnosti* (literally 'grey personalities', that is, featureless mediocrities). Nobody pays any attention to them. They don't count." This young man's hero and *maître* was the economist Varga, to whom he introduced me. He also mentioned casually that he had heard one of my broadcasts on the B.B.C. Russian service and found it highly interesting (it was about the Tito-Cominform quarrel). At first I was surprised at the openness with which people mentioned listening to the B.B.C. and talked appreciatively of its objectivity and value as a news service. But I soon got used to it. The representative of the B.B.C. Russian Service had in fact visited Moscow a few months before and established friendly relations with the Soviet broadcasters and 'jamming' had ceased (it was resumed again after the Soviet suppression of the Hungarian rising). There was a village outside Moscow, I was told, which was a centre for writers and artists. They used to gather every evening to listen to the B.B.C. and discuss what they heard. On the other hand, the propagandist and hostile nature of broadcasts from the Voice of America and Radio Free Europe was deplored.

I had two round-table discussions with the staff of the Institute of World Economy and International Relations at which they and I asked each other questions and then everyone argued about the answers. The conversation largely centred on such topics as the British Labour Party, the British Communist Party, the relations between the two, the possibility of advancing to Socialism by Parliamentary and constitutional means, and the standards of life of the British workers. The Central Office of Information had kindly furnished me with a good deal of data on the latter subject, and on our social services, so that I was reasonably well equipped for giving definite answers—and it was just as well, because I found those I was talking with exceedingly well informed.

A remark from one of my hosts has stuck in my mind, the more significant because it was made *en passant*: "Now that we have finally come round to admitting that India really has been given her freedom," he said, "we have begun to take a more sophisticated and less *simpliste* view of your Empire". This remark of course arose out of a discussion of how the Empire was changing into a Commonwealth, and what were Labour's views on colonial policy. In this, as in other talks, there were many questions about the Labour Party, and particularly its views on foreign and defence policy and the hydrogen bomb.

I had a similar round-table discussion with the editorial board of the *Literary Gazette*. Among other things I asked about the circular letter that had been sent out by the Secretariat of the C.P.S.U., not only to Soviet Communists, but also to some of the Communist parties in the People's Democracies, criticising the Yugoslav Communists and warning the others to beware of following their example. The senior member there said, it was true that they did not consider that the Yugoslavs were altogether Marxist-Leninist Communists in the same sense as the other People's Democracies. As for the Poles, they had an anti-Russian national tradition which put them in an exceptional position *vis-à-vis* the Soviet Union. He also spoke of Russians being less nationalistic than people in other countries, readier to accept foreigners as human beings first and foreigners second.

From there he was led by his enthusiasm into saying that Soviet citizens had a firm belief that the very structure of their society guaranteed that they would get justice from their government.

This I thought a bit thick, and pointed out that Soviet citizens had suffered a monstrous amount of injustice and arbitrariness from their government during the "cult of personality" era. I suggested that perhaps our more disillusioned attitude to government was on the whole safer, and quoted the old Liberal saying that there is no such thing as a good government or a bad people. "Eternal vigilance is the price of liberty" also seemed apposite!

I noticed that the man I was speaking to seemed put out by this rejoinder, but the younger people obviously enjoyed and agreed with it. Again my main impression was how friendly and openly everyone behaved. Partly this was personal. For instance, I met Professor Lemin, the specialist on British Commonwealth Affairs in the Academy of Science, who said he had followed my political campaign, read my books (part of my 1935 *Inquest on Peace* had been translated into Russian), and particularly liked the fact that, even after being attacked by the Cominform and Soviet Press, I had gone on advocating "peaceful co-existence". Partly, there was a hopeful and friendly interest in the Labour Party, of which I was getting the benefit. But over all these things was a friendliness and desire to talk with and understand the point of view of people from the West that had been there all the time, repressed into silence under Stalin, and now rising to the surface.

CHAPTER TWO
Gaol Delivery and Law Reform

IT DID NOT TAKE many hours in Moscow to discover that the 20th Congress of the Communist Party of the Soviet Union, held in February 1956, was looked on as a watershed in Soviet history, a great divide separating the Stalinist past from a brighter present and more hopeful future. Moreover, the changes that meant most to Russians were the internal changes promised or already taking place.

Everything is done to make the people conscious of the importance of international relations. You need not talk much with people in Moscow to find out how strong and urgent is the desire for peace.

Nevertheless, to most people, the political centre of gravity is in home affairs. And in this field Soviet folk think of the present reforms and changes solely with reference to the conditions that existed before in the Soviet Union, and not in terms of comparison with other countries. For Soviet society is forty years old. Only the elderly and aged can remember anything different—and there was nothing much about the Czarist régime, during or even before the First World War, for formerly land-starved peasants or ruthlessly exploited workers to remember fondly.

Hence there is no such thing as a challenge within the Soviet Union to the foundations of Soviet society, although there may be, and I believe there is, a widespread and growing demand for more political and intellectual freedom and democracy. Unlike their colleagues in the 'People's Democracies', Soviet Communists have no sense of being engaged in an experiment that is still on trial and fundamentally challenged by large sections of the people.

For this reason, Russian (i.e. Soviet) Communists are the Conservatives of Communism. They cannot imagine the Communist order of things being so unsuccessful and unpopular anywhere as to provoke revolt. And so any upheaval in a People's Democracy—East Berlin, Poznan, Hungary—is immediately denounced in the Soviet Press as due to anti-Communist infiltration and subversion by Western agents. This view is the exact counterpart of the Anglo-American conservative belief that social and colonial unrest anywhere is due to Communist infiltration and subversion by Soviet agents. The one is as much a conditioned reflex with its roots in subconscious minds moulded by a way of life as the other.

The factor of national pride in the achievements of the revolution is also important. The Russians say: "Czarist Russia was poor and backward. It was largely dependent on foreign capital and enterprise. Most of the people were illiterate and the standard of living was miserably low. When the Bolsheviks took over the country was ruined and in chaos. To-day the Soviet Union is a world power, on the same footing as the United States, and second only to that power as an industrial country. All this in spite of the terrible destruction wrought by the Hitlerite invasion, the tremendous part the U.S.S.R. played in winning the war, and the major diversion of resources necessary to enable the Soviet Union to keep militarily strong in the face of capitalist hostility. This shows the vast superiority of our socialist economy over the disorder and waste of capitalism."

True, the Soviet intervention in Hungary and the successful Polish semi-revolution have since then undoubtedly weakened the Soviet position in Europe and may be causing internal difficulties. But the overall strength of the Soviet position remains impressive and their economic achievement since the Revolution has no parallel in history.

National pride in Soviet power and economic success therefore has a pretty solid foundation in reality. And for the reasons indicated, the demand for more political freedom, although it exists and is growing, is in general relative to Soviet standards and conditions and not, as in the People's Democracies, influenced by comparisons with the West.

Nor is it easy to meet the point, which was made to me in many conversations, that it is much harder for the Soviet and other Communist régimes to democratise themselves with the West listening at the door and eager, like the pantomime policeman, to take down everything they say, alter it and use it against them. "If you in the West would not show so much ill-will and try to hustle us so roughly, we should get on faster," said one young man who had left me in no doubt about his own anti-Stalinist views.

The only observation that seemed reasonable in reply to these arguments was that whereas the cold war was inimical to the spread of democracy and freedom, it was also true that the more the Communist régimes yielded to the demand of their own peoples for democracy and political freedom, the more difficult it would be for the West to carry on with the cold war, and the sooner those who were determined to negotiate political settlements and disarmament agreements would prevail. For the two blocs lived by fear and by taking in each other's dirty linen, and the more one side did its own washing in public the greater the effect on the other.

That was why, I explained, the Soviet domestic reform that had attracted the greatest attention in the West was the whittling down of the powers of the secret police, the wholesale release of political prisoners, the revision of the criminal code, and the new position of the courts. That led to an invitation from the Deputy Chief Justice of the Supreme Court of the Soviet Union, Judge Tarassov (originally the invitation was from the Chief Justice, but he went down with 'flu).

The Supreme Court is lodged in a Moscow version of the Law Courts in London or the Palais de Justice in Paris. There seems to be a family resemblance about law courts everywhere. They all contrive to look gaunt, bare, solemn, ponderous and portentous.

But there was none of that about Judge Tarassov. He was young—only about forty, which I imagine is well under bogey for a judge of the Supreme Court in most countries, let alone a Deputy Chief Justice. Nor could anyone have been more patient in listening to my questions and comments and franker in replying than Judge Tarassov.

I had prepared myself for this talk as best I could by read-ing the references at the 20th Congress to these subjects and the articles on them in the *Kommunist** of May, July and September (Nos. 7, 11, 14). I knew, of course, that the amnesty of March 28th, 1953, three weeks after burying Stalin, had (*a*) cut by half all sentences over five years, (*b*) released all those sentenced for less than five years, as well as all under eighteen, the sick and aged, pregnant women and women with children. But it did not extend to those sentenced for 'counter-revolutionary activities'.

Since the death of Stalin, however, most of those condemned for alleged counter-revolutionary activities have also been re-leased. Judge Tarassov did not say how many, but according to other sources the number runs into millions—some say as many as five—and in the opinion of the British Embassy the job has been done so thoroughly that there are few prisoners left in this category.

These releases had taken place as a result of reviewing the sentences passed on such prisoners, in the Courts in which they had been sentenced. That was in 1954. Now, said Judge Tarassov, a travelling commission was going about interview-ing on the spot the few that were still left and finding out from them why they were still serving a sentence. He said he thought that this procedure would result in freeing any and everyone still imprisoned without just and sufficient cause.

Henceforward there would be no condemnations except by due process of law, based on the principle that the accused must be held to be innocent unless and until he should be proved guilty, and that no one should be kept in gaol for more than twenty-four hours without a Court order. These reforms were looked upon as restoring the rule of Soviet law, which had been ignored and abused. The so-called "Special Advisory Council" attached to the Ministry of the Interior, which had in fact conducted political trials and condemned people with

* The Party review that explains, discusses and develops official policy statements for the guidance of Party members. Since the 20th Congress most of its articles have dealt with the problems raised by, and the ways and means of implementing, the resolutions of the Congress and the Central Committee in these various fields.

scant regard for law, had been abolished and the courts were now given the entire responsibility. Confessions were no longer accepted as sufficient evidence. There was to be no more "guilt by association" or vague political charges. The charges must be definite and the verdict must be based strictly on evidence that the law had been broken and must give the accused the benefit of any doubt.

The legal system was being revised on an autonomous basis, i.e. each of the fifteen republics that compose the Soviet Union was drawing up its own code. But they would all be based on the general rules and principles of Soviet jurisprudence and the Supreme Court of the Union was the final Court of Appeal for every republic.

The first step in reforming the penal code was the preparing of drafts, and this work was already well advanced. On completion the drafts would be presented for popular discussion. After that they would be put into final form and submitted for approval to the legislature (Supreme Soviets) of the various republics and finally to the Parliament of the U.S.S.R.*

A Soviet citizen who is not satisfied with the verdict of the Court before which he appears may exercise the right of appeal either by petition or by being legally represented. But if he chooses to be represented he has to pay for the lawyer's services. For only an appellant who is physically or mentally incapacitated or is a minor is entitled to free legal aid. I told Judge Tarassov that this did not go so far as we do in Britain under the Poor Man's Free Legal Aid Law!

One of the recent reforms, instituted by the decree of the Supreme Soviet of the U.S.S.R., issued in May 1955, applied 'Leninist' ideas about the functions of the Attorney-General's office. It made the Attorney-General and his representatives responsible for seeing that the law was being applied correctly and with uniformity throughout the Soviet Union and its constituent republics and autonomous districts. It is now their duty to see that the laws are being observed and to take appropriate steps against those, whoever they may be, who violate

* This revision of the penal code, I learned later, has been going on so long without any visible, i.e. public, results that it may be hanging fire.

legality. The representatives of the Attorney-General's office are entirely independent of all local authorities and responsible only to the Attorney-General himself. They cannot interfere in any way with the working of the Courts, but should assist the Courts to maintain their independence and conduct their trials strictly according to the law.

This measure, it may be remarked parenthetically, is a good example of why one should judge post-Stalinist developments in the Soviet Union, not by comparison with the West, but by what existed before in the U.S.S.R. For this reform to Western eyes still indicates an inadmissible degree of influence by the Executive on the Judiciary. But in Soviet eyes it means safeguarding the Courts against the gross interference and bullying by Party bosses at local, regional and Republican levels that used to prevail, as Judge Tarassov made clear. That is also the view taken by the Soviet jurists discussing how to reform, or rather, as they put it, restore, the legal system after the death of Stalin and particularly after the 20th Congress of the C.P.S.U.

The spate of articles about all this in Soviet journals reveals what an Augean stable the whole legal system had become before the great clean-up began. It shows the admirable intentions of the would-be reformers and is itself proof of the more genial political climate in which they are tackling the job. But it leaves open the question of whether they will succeed in their Herculean task, whether indeed it is possible for the Soviet legal system to safeguard justice and the rights of the individual as they desire, unless and until the Soviet political system allows more scope for democracy than is so far contemplated.

But the stage the discussion had reached by the autumn of 1956 is worth summarising. For the very frankness with which the evils of the past are described shows how vast is the change that has already taken place, and the views expressed show a conception of what the rule of law should be that is not so different from our own. Here are the main points made in the discussion, expressed or quoted in the magazine *Kommunist*, and with the minimum of comment of my own:

The 'personality cult' of Stalin was responsible, say the

Soviet writers on the subject, for gross violations of Soviet legality and wholesale condemnations and savage punishment without just cause. As early as December 1934 Stalin introduced an extraordinary procedure for dealing with cases of the commission of terrorist acts against servants of the Soviet Government, that nullified the rules of law in the criminal code and opened the door to every kind of arbitrary action and punishment of the innocent. This procedure was later taken advantage of by Beria, as head of the Secret Police, for the most flagrant violations of the rights of Soviet citizens and for the application of illegal methods of investigation, for the manufacture of evidence and for the persecution of decent and innocent people.*

"In 1937 Stalin developed a false theory that the class struggle was bound to become more acute," say the Soviet legal commentators, "as the building of Socialism advanced. Whereas in fact the intensity of the class struggle depends on the balance of forces between the classes, and the new Soviet constitution adopted in 1936 had already proclaimed the existence of a new Socialist society in which the exploiting classes no longer existed. It is true that the capitalist world that surrounded the Soviet Union in those days was using spies, wreckers and agents of one sort or another to make things more difficult for the Soviet régime. That is still the case— the United States Congress appropriates $100,000,000 annually for hostile activities of this sort against the socialist countries. But all this should not be confused with the question of the class struggle within the country becoming more acute."

"This false proposition of Stalin's," the argument continues, "was used for introducing more severe penalties into the law and above all into the practice of the Courts when dealing with a whole series of offences against the State. To-day that has been changed by a decree issued in 1955, which reduced the penalties for minor offences such as small thefts, allows for suspended sentences, for release of prisoners before serving their term, for indulgence to first offenders, fines instead of imprisonment, and in general for more elastic and humane

* Beria in fact did less than and began the clean-up after the holocaust of murder and torture under his predecessor, Yezhov.

procedures which aim primarily at educating the convicted person so that he will be a better citizen in future."

The *Kommunist* articles I have referred to further point out that the practical abuses that followed from Stalin's 1934 extraordinary procedure and 1937 false theory about the sharpening of the class struggle, were developed into wrong principles of jurisprudence and dangerous and undesirable ideas by a number of Soviet jurists, headed by the then Attorney-General (Public Prosecutor) Vyshinsky. For one thing, Vyshinsky and his like insisted upon the importance of extorting confessions from the accused. This idea goes back a long way in the legal history of Russia: the military code of Peter the Great declared that confession was the best evidence in the world, and that once a confession had been obtained no further evidence was required. It was common practice to extort the required confession by torture.

This conception, say the Soviet commentators, coming up after their dive into history, is clean contrary to the spirit and letter of Soviet law. But Vyshinsky, following in the footsteps of Stalin, declared that cases of conspiracies or other anti-State activities should be exceptions to the usual rule, and that in such cases confessions should be adequate evidence. Article 282 of the existing Criminal Code in the Russian Soviet Federal Republic allows a judge, if the accused has pleaded guilty and made a confession, to dispense with further evidence. This article has not, in fact, been relied upon to any extent by Soviet judges. But it should be repealed. For relying on confessions may lead to judicial errors: the accused may confess in ignorance, because he does not realise that he has not in fact committed any crime. Or he may be trying to shield someone else. Or he may think that by confessing to a minor offence he has not committed he can escape punishment for something worse that he actually has done. Or, of course, he may have been compelled to confess under duress.

Some Soviet jurists, says a *Kommunist* article, have gone even further than Vyshinsky. For instance, in an article in *Socialist Legality* (the organ of the Ministry of Justice, of the Supreme Court and of the Attorney-General's office of the U.S.S.R.), entitled "Tactics in Interrogating an Accused Person", A. Vasiliev* argued that obtaining a confession was of great importance, but that it was also necessary to get the confession so fully confirmed that the accused would feel himself bound by it and could not "easily go back on it under further interrogation by the examining magistrate or in Court; the latter would be particularly tragic for those charged with making a case".

According to this view, the *Kommunist* article points out, the duty of the examining magistrate is not to consider all the facts, both those in favour of and those telling against the accused, so as to try to discover the truth, but to extort and "confirm" a confession from the accused. Moreover, Vasiliev, going even further than Vyshinsky or Stalin's 1934 decree, wanted to apply this procedure to all criminal cases and not only to crimes of counter-revolution.

Soviet law, the author recalls, forbids extorting confessions or an admission of guilt by the accused through force, or threats, or similar measures. Any kind of compulsion to extract confessions renders the interrogator liable to imprisonment for anything up to five years. But during the "cult of personality" period this rule too became a dead letter.

Those who take the Stalinist view, it is pointed out (although the term 'Stalinist' is not used), also, of course, dislike the presumption of innocence—that is, the principle that an accused must be held innocent unless and until he is proved guilty. Although this principle is basic in Soviet law, it has been extensively ignored in practice and has been contested in theory by Vyshinsky and other Soviet jurists.

Vyshinsky, in his *Theory of Evidence Admissible in Court under Soviet Law*, says another writer, argued that the defendant must prove his own innocence in the same way as it was up to the prosecution to prove him guilty. According to other Soviet jurists, the defendant, by the mere fact of being brought to Court on a criminal charge, became guilty unless he could prove himself innocent. In their view, too, an accused person who was acquitted because what he had done was considered not to constitute an infraction of the law was considered fully

* Writing, of course, during the 'personality cult' era.

rehabilitated, whereas someone acquitted because the prosecution had failed to prove its case was regarded as still under a cloud.

A particularly blunt expression of the view of this school, continues the article, was contained in an article by V. S. Tadevosian* on 'Establishing Evidence in Soviet Legal Procedure': "Anyone who transfers the burden of proof to the shoulders of the State, of Society and of all those suffering from the crime that has been committed, and frees the accused from every obligation, offers to give him the benefit of every doubt and refuses to condemn anybody so long as his crime has not been proved as conclusively as 2 and 2 equals 4, may perhaps very splendidly and beautifully defend the freedom of the individual; but he will not make the interests of the State and of Society the corner-stone of his teaching." But Soviet law, counters the *Kommunist* article, is quite clear on the point that the rights of the individual must be defended, and insists that an accused must be presumed innocent so long as he has not been proved guilty.

The nature of what constitutes proof is also being hotly discussed. Here too the late Public Prosecutor, Vyshinsky, comes under heavy fire for his views. A discussion on this subject, it is recalled, went on from 1950-2, but Soviet jurists were prevented from pursuing the matter to conclusions by pressure from Stalin and his Secret Police, who feared that the result might be condemnation of their wholesale disregard of Soviet legality. Vyshinsky is accused of having imported into jurisprudence ideas from the philosophy of dialectical materialism, about relative truth and the balance of probabilities, which he said was enough for judges to render a verdict on, as contrasted with "absolute" truth in the shape of conclusive evidence, which he said was not a thing a Court could reasonably expect to obtain. He and his followers also argued that a man's class background, personal history and general attitude should all play a part in deciding whether or not he was guilty. Finally, he put forward the theory that a "causal nexus" between

* This too, like Vasiliev's article quoted earlier, was written before the repudiation of Stalin and most of his works at the 20th Congress of the C.P.S.U.

an individual and a crime was sufficient to condemn the individual as being guilty of the crime. But although there can be no criminal without a causal nexus between himself and a crime, there may be a causal nexus between a person and a crime without the person being criminally responsible. The connection between an individual and a crime may be purely fortuitous, may be due to ignorance, or may in some other way have arisen without any criminal intent.

Here again Soviet law and the majority of Soviet jurists, say these articles, sharply oppose the 'Stalinist' views and insist that the only matters that a Court is entitled to take into consideration are the facts about what the accused is charged with having done and the relation of those facts to the law, as formulated in the charge ['*sostav prestuplenia*']. Guilt by association and all extraneous considerations, such as a man's class background, family history, general frame of mind, etc., should be treated as irrelevant and inadmissible. On the point of "guilt by association" Vyshinsky again took a line sharply in conflict with post-Stalinist views. He claimed that 'association' meant any kind of connection between the accused and the crime, or those who had committed the crime. By this definition a man might be held criminally responsible for a crime committed by other people with whom he was known to associate, although he himself might not have taken part in that crime and even have known nothing about it. This view is strongly condemned as being contrary to Soviet law, common sense and justice.

Apart from reforming the law or restoring it to its pristine purity, there is the matter of seeing that it is observed: there are still careerists and bureaucrats in Government employ, say these articles, who consider that the laws were not written for them and that they can ignore them whenever that seems the most convenient way to achieve their purpose. But officials should not be allowed to observe the law only when it suits them. The law must bind everyone at all times.

There is an enormous amount to be done in educating Party, social and official organisations to understand and respect socialist legality, is the conclusion of this discussion. This is particularly true of Government and Party officials. The raising of the standards of education in the people has greatly facilitated the task of enlisting their support for this cause, which concerns their rights and freedom.

Such are the views expressed in Soviet periodicals, by jurists and others who are discussing ways of implementing the decisions of the 20th Congress and the Central Committee of the Party. As they themselves remark, what matters is not so much individual measures as the general attitude of the Government and the people, that is, the political climate. Since the death of Stalin that climate has become increasingly favourable to the effective functioning of the Courts without political interference, so as to ensure the rule of law and the rights of the individual. But there is a great deal of leeway to make up. And the judiciary cannot be regarded as independent of the executive and legislative branches of the Government in anything like the Western sense in the structure of the Soviet political system. The real question, therefore, is, how far the latter can evolve into something that will give Soviet citizens the substance (although in forms different from the West) of democracy, that is, allow them effectively to exercise the rights of free speech and association and the supreme right to choose their rulers, as well as protecting the rights of individuals and minorities against majorities and the State.

CHAPTER THREE

Peasants, Workers and Social Security

THE READINESS—indeed, eagerness—of people in all strata of society to talk with foreigners was a great help in gathering impressions about how far the wave of post-Stalinist reforms was affecting what in Soviet jargon would be called the 'toiling masses', or in other words, the main bodies of the Soviet people, the workers and the peasants. I put it this way because the best I could do during my limited stay was to learn a few solid facts and a good deal about plans and the new atmosphere from the sources available in Moscow and current literature on the subject. But I was able to get some useful sidelights from the people I came across, such as Vasily Grigorievich Solodolnikov, of the Institute of World Economy and International Relations. He met me on arrival at one o'clock in the morning. He is one of those broad, warm, immensely likeable Russian characters, with a sense of humour too, so that we soon became friends and he told me a good deal about his life.

He started as a peasant from a collective farm on the Volga, became a mechanic on a tractor station (all the collective farms in an area are served by a common Government tractor station), studied and took degrees through the "Rabfak" (*Rabochii Fakultet*, or Workers' University, a sort of glorified University Extension lecture system for workers), fought in the war, and now here he was, a young research worker at the Institute of World Economy and International Relations, with his roots in the soil but free of the academic world. To him and the millions like him, the revolution is history and the Soviet régime has meant the chance to rise from the condition of the illiterate *muzhik*, keeping body and soul together on a miserable plot of land with a wooden plough, to the altogether different existence and social status of a collective farmer, with the sense of being a full citizen and every opportunity to rise through free education, as he had done.

In the Soviet Union, as in the People's Democracies, the peasantry are not so much a class as the primeval foundation and raw material out of which all classes have been formed and on which the whole of society rests. But before the revolution the peasants of the Soviet Union, unlike those of the People's Democracies, were not politically organised nor even conscious (unless one counts the peasant rebellions with which Russian, like European, history is studded).

Again, unlike the People's Democracies, where the peasants' sense of private ownership of land was highly developed before their revolutions, the Russian peasants under the Czar were still for the most part economically so primitive that they were organised in village communes tilling the land on the medieval strip system. Only a small enterprising minority had taken advantage of Stolypin's land reform to buy themselves out of the commune.

After the Revolution the peasants, having divided the land of the landowners and of the Church among themselves, were left for some years in undisturbed possession. This was long enough for two things to begin happening: on the one hand the more pushful peasants began to acquire the lands of the weaker brethren, lend them money at exorbitant interest, hire labour, etc., and on the other, peasant holdings were being divided and sub-divided more and more to accommodate all the members of the family. If this process had gone on unchecked, new estates at one end, landless and almost landless peasants at the other, would have begun to emerge. Meanwhile, production was falling.

Something drastic had to be done, to get more food from the land and to prevent capitalism rising again from its ashes. Co-operative farming looked like the only way out.

To begin with, there was a certain amount of voluntary collectivisation among ex-partisan peasants and others who had acquired socialist political views during the Revolution. But the actual collectivisation when it was made compulsory was carried through with a ferocity and brutality that led to the expropriation and deportation to Siberia or forced labour of some two million *kulaks* (literally, "fists", meaning the rich peasants, a somewhat elastic term). A million or so peasants actually died of starvation, after burning their crops, eating their seed-corn, slaughtering millions of livestock, and destroying farm implements, in a sort of desperate agrarian Luddite rebellion against collectivisation.

But finally the thing was done, and a new type of social organisation emerged in the countryside embodying a compromise: peasants had their homes, a small plot of land and a limited amount of livestock (unlimited poultry) for themselves. For the rest, they worked their combined farms collectively and after the State had been paid its dues in kind, shared the products among themselves according to the value of the work each had done during the year.

All this happened a generation ago. To-day the Russian peasant is on the way to becoming something different—a collective farmer with a new political consciousness, a different social condition and higher technical and educational levels than his father or grandfather before the Revolution.

During the last war the Nazis attempted to de-collectivise the farms and restore private ownership. The results of that experiment showed that there is no longer what might be called a politically effective demand among the collective farmers for going back to the old backward individualist peasant economy. Indeed, the simple economic fact is that if they did, food-production would drop by half and there would be an industrial breakdown and famine. That is one tremendous difference between the Soviet Union and the People's Democracies.

Nevertheless, the condition of the peasantry has always been the sensitive spot in the Soviet economy, and their attitude to the powers that be is the political acid test of the Soviet régime. The perennial problem is how to increase the production of food and industrial crops so as to keep pace with the rising standard of living, the increasing population and the growing needs of Soviet industry.

A great deal of attention has been devoted to that subject

since the death of Stalin. It was one of the major topics at
the 20th Congress. It became the centre of a whole morning's
conversation I had with the heads of the Economic Institute
of the Academy of Science, the Institute that specialises in the
economics of the Soviet Union and the other Socialist States.

The long discussion followed a pattern that was to become
familiar in my talks with various groups of scientists, trade
unionists, journalists, economists, etc. The form on these occasions was that we would all sit around a table strewn with
boxes of cigarettes and plates of fruit and biscuits, drinking
innumerable cups of tea with lemon, smoking and talking *à
bâtons rompus*. I generally had to answer a hail of questions as
well as putting my own, then discuss the answers with this
person or that, or listen to them arguing the point among
themselves. This kind of 'polylogue' was fascinating and fun,
and out of it would emerge some specific points and broad
conclusions, as well as that indefinable something known as
the 'feel' or 'atmosphere' of the meeting. But it was the very
devil to get down on paper afterwards. The notes I scribbled
down while we talked and conned over and entered in my
diary every night were reminders rather than a record.

This time the chief speaker was Mr. Dolgov, the Deputy
Head of the Economic Institute. But as usual there was a
good deal of cross-talk and argument, not to mention cross-
questioning, by the six or seven others who were present.
Occasionally he would call on one of his assistants who was
a specialist in the particular subject under discussion to put
his view—or the specialist, without being called, would join
in to put it himself in the form of dissent from or confirmation
or elucidation of what had been said.

A slight, greying man in early middle age, Mr. Dolgov had
an air of quiet authority, and carried an impressive store of
knowledge in a matter-of-fact way, with none of the pomp
and circumstance of erudition. His replies to questions were
little masterpieces of analysis with here and there a glint of
humour. An able man with a clear mind and plenty of drive,
I should say, *primus inter pares*, but not a little tin god to his
staff.

I began by asking my stock question: how the work of the

Institute had been affected by the ending of the 'personality cult'. Mr. Dolgov said Stalin had permitted them to do their research work, but had never taken any notice of the results. Once he convened a conference of 300 economists and let them discuss freely for four months—and then took his own line. On the whole of course their work had been strait-jacketed and they had been made to feel futile under Stalin, whereas they were free now and Government authorities took reasonable notice of their findings and recommendations.

Stalin, said Mr. Dolgov, was a great Marxist, and did much to develop Marxism-Leninism practically and theoretically. He met new issues boldly and worked out many of the answers to the questions raised by the working of economic laws in the building of Socialism. In particular he had made a positive contribution in his insistence on the objective character of economic laws and the role of the State in shaping economic policy. He had pointed out that the State cannot arbitrarily change or override economic laws, and this was a valuable contribution.

But some of his theoretical positions were wrong and had had the gravest practical consequences when embodied in the policies of the State. He considered for instance that the exchange of goods [i.e. an economy based on cost and effecting exchanges through the medium of money] contradicted his contention that Soviet Socialism had now reached the stage where it was beginning to turn into Communism, and therefore should give place to the direct exchange of products [i.e. barter based on mutual need].

It was true that under Communism, commented Mr. Dolgov, where each was to contribute according to his capacity and receive according to his needs, there would be direct exchange of products and no exchange of goods through buying and selling based on cost. But that state of affairs was remote. [That is, although he did not say it, Stalin was wrong to believe Soviet socialism had begun the transition to Communism, or at least in trying to translate this idea from the realm of theory to practice.] The exchange of goods based on the law of costs would continue to be necessary for as far ahead as anyone could see. That meant that a planned economy must pay attention to the law of costs and that State or collective enterprises must pay their way.

Stalin attempted to ignore all this, both as regards the capital goods produced by heavy industry and in agriculture. He arbitrarily fixed prices for deliveries to the State of, e.g., meat, milk, wool, vegetables, potatoes, corn, etc., that took no account of production costs and were so low that only the best of the collective farms could make ends meet at all. Agriculture suffered severely as a result.

Mr. Dolgov was in effect conveying to me, not without dead-pan humour, that Stalin, after portentously announcing the somewhat trite discovery that even the State cannot override economic laws, had tried to prove himself a liar by behaving as though the Communist millennium had arrived and economic laws, like the State, had withered away. The only thing left was the will of Stalin, the super-man and infallible genius. But the vitality and resilience of Soviet society are as remarkable as the things that have been done to it by the Stalin régime, and no less remarkable is the scope and vigour of the present movement for reform.

In the case of the collective farms, Mr. Dolgov told me, the price paid by the State for taxes in kind had been raised progressively over the last three years. At the same time the collective farms were no longer subjected to compulsion and direction but left free within very wide limits to decide what and how much they wanted to grow (with what the State wants to buy and for how much as their chief economic incentive and guide), and to run their own internal affairs, including the election of their managements.

As a result of these measures, there had been a considerable increase in production, and the income of the collective farms rose by 20 milliard roubles during 1954 and 1955 (at the official rate of exchange this would be nearly £190 million, but if the purchasing power of the rouble is reckoned at sixpence, which is what Western diplomats regard as a fair figure, it would be only £50 million). At the same time the State had pumped into collective farming, for those two years, nearly 34½ milliard roubles, which was one-third more than the capital expenditure on agriculture for the whole of the Fourth Five-year

Plan. The number of engineers, mechanics, technicians, agricultural specialists and equipment "ploughed back" into the collective farms, the State farms, and the tractor stations for this period had also risen sharply. So did the area under cultivation.

Lastly came Khrushchev's bold policy of ploughing up the virgin lands in Asiatic Russia. All this had resulted in the biggest crop in the history of the Soviet Union. The new target of a 70% increase in food production during the Sixth Five-year Plan would, in the light of these achievements, actually be attained, in Mr. Dolgov's opinion.

The collective farmers had used their new freedom to devise a system, he also told me, which had now become almost universal, of paying advances in cash to their members, based on an estimate of what their share of the total product of the farm would be at the end of the year. Hitherto the collective farmer had had to work for his keep until the end of the year before receiving his share. Now he got what, for all practical purposes, was a weekly wage in addition to whatever he could make out of his private plot of land. This measure, and the greater prosperity of the farming community in general, had attracted back to the land a certain number of former collective farmers who had previously left for work in industry. That, said Mr. Dolgov, was not exactly what the authorities had wanted, as industry was chronically short of labour. But as workers were now free to leave their jobs there was nothing they could do about it—except to make conditions in industry more attractive. "We rely on persuasion and money inducements now, not on compulsion."

In reply to my question as to how far collective farming made agricultural labour redundant and how such labour was channelled into industry, Mr. Dolgov explained that the result of mechanising agriculture and large-scale production was of course to release a good deal of man power for industry. But the whole social structure of collective farming was co-operative, and therefore there would always be more people on the land than in the highly mechanised capitalist agriculture of, for instance, the United States and Canada. The children of collective farmers were all going through primary and secondary school, and the brightest were going on to universities and technical colleges. Some would be trained as agronomes or other specialists who would go back to work in the farms or the tractor stations, but others would find their way into industry. There was a regular system for advertising the jobs available in industry, the rates of pay, where to apply, etc., so as to recruit labour from the young people on the collective farms.

Stalin's ideas had also borne heavily on industry in his last few years. For instance, he thought that capital goods escaped the law of costs (!), and that taking scarce goods off the ration for privileged minorities was a step to that direct exchange of products under Communism that he imagined was just round the corner. Nor in his time were wages connected closely enough with productivity and the qualifications of workers.

Since then there had been a raising of the lowest wages and wages were more closely adjusted to the different trades, the amount of output, professional qualifications, etc. The highest pay was given for the most onerous or dangerous work or for the best technical qualifications. There had been pretty far-reaching decentralisation in the planning of industry. In 1954 and 1955 11,000 big enterprises were turned over entirely to the direction of the constituent republics. After the 20th Congress this process was going on apace.*

I came away from the morning with Mr. Dolgov and his colleagues with the feeling that the reforms in industry and agriculture were as sweeping, and were being pushed as energetically, as those in the political and judicial systems. But how long would the impetus of the reformers last and how much could it accomplish unless they could somehow join forces with the energy and aspirations of the 'reformees', that is, the peasants and workers themselves? And could the peasants and workers make their will felt effectively under the existing political system?

These questions were in my mind when I took up the subject of the workers in the new dispensation with the members of the General Council of the All-Union Soviet T.U.C., around

* Since then, of course, there have been sensational developments in this field, which are described later.

the customary table and cups of tea, at the Transport House of the Soviet Union. Mr. Soloviev, the Deputy Chairman, confirmed Mr. Dolgov's information about the new wage policy. He insisted on the great part the trade unions were called upon to play in administering social legislation and determining conditions of work, as well as in shaping the national and local economic plans to determine wage-scales, negotiating the contracts with factory directors and seeing that their terms were observed. He also mentioned the abrogation of the Draconian laws and administrative rules that used to punish workers for coming late or being slack on the job, and the impending seven-hour day.

I knew, of course, that constitutionally—that is, on paper— the all-Union Soviet T.U. General Council, elected (again on paper) by the constituent unions whose leaders are elected (on paper) by their rank and file, does have very important functions that include taking part in the drafting of the national economic plan and working out and submitting to the Government draft legislation on wages, labour protection, social insurance, welfare and cultural services, etc. The trades unions also run the working men's clubs, of which there are 200 in Moscow alone, including eleven big ones. I visited one of these —it had everything. But workers cannot live by social clubs alone. And I also knew that so long as the trades unions were run by the Communist Party and the Communist Party was run by Stalin, they did not in fact enjoy their constitutional rights nor carry out the duties assigned to them on paper, and could not defend the interests of their members as understood by the rank and file.

Now, however, there had been two fundamental changes, Mr. Soloviev explained. The first was that any worker might leave his job and take another. As there was an overall shortage of labour that had made an enormous difference to the attitude of the workers and of the factory managers. The second change, which fitted in with this one, was that there was now a genuine effort to find out what the workers wanted and to try to meet their demands. The principle that responsibility for management should be concentrated in the hands of the "director" of the factory, was still upheld. But factory directors now felt it necessary to reach agreement with their works councils (factory T.U. committees), and in case the two could not settle their difficulties, the trade union would take up the matter. All this, which used to exist only on paper, was now becoming a reality. So was the work of the trade unions in the field of social insurance.

The new law of social insurance had been passed in July, and came into force on October 1st, just before my arrival in Moscow. There was no doubt of its popularity and the fond pride with which it is regarded by the Government and the Party. I learnt all I could about it first from reading and stray talks, and then spent a morning with the Deputy Minister of Social Security of the Russian Soviet Federal Socialist Republic, Mr. Laptiev.

Each Republic has its own Ministry of Social Security. But they simply apply the law adopted for the whole Union by the Supreme Soviet, on the initiative of the Party. As the R.S.F.S.R. comprises three-quarters of the whole Union, its Ministry of Social Security is incomparably the most important.

Mr. Laptiev described how his Ministry works, in close contact with the Ministries of Health, Housing, and Finance (particularly Finance, he said ruefully), and also the trade unions. The Unions have their representatives in the Committees for allocating pensions. They also supervise the work of these bodies to make sure pensions are being properly and promptly paid and resources are being wisely spent, as well as acting as intermediaries between the official bodies and their own members who are qualifying for pensions.

Mr. Laptiev was very proud of the new law, which represents a great advance on anything attempted previously in this field in the Soviet Union. In 1940, 8,600 million roubles were spent on social security; in 1955 the amount had risen to 26,500 million; in 1956 the total budget was 38,200 million. At the same time the whole system was recast from top to bottom, so as to cover a far larger number of people and raise the scales, as well as introducing new principles of allocation.

All who serve in industry or in Government employ, or in the Police, or armed forces, or in education, become eligible for pensions. This covers more than half the population, primarily the urban and industrial half. The total amount of pensions is contributed by the State, and none of it comes from the wages of the workers, Mr. Laptiev pointed out.

The amount of pension is directly related to the wages previously earned by the pensioner, to the nature of his work, and to the amount of time he has worked. But there is a minimum and a maximum.

For instance, up to a maximum wage of 350 roubles a month, the pension is 100%, but with a minimum of 300 roubles, so that if you earn less than that your pension will be higher than was your wage. From 350 to 500 roubles a month the pension is 85% of the wage. In the case of workers and employees working underground, doing dangerous work, or work deleterious to health, the pension is 90%, with a minimum of 350 roubles. From 500 to 600 roubles the pension is 75% of the wage, with a minimum of 425 roubles (80% and a 450 roubles minimum for the underground, etc., workers), and so on to 1,000 roubles a month and over where the pension is 50% (in the case of the underground, etc., workers, 55%), with a minimum of 550 roubles (underground, etc., workers, 600 roubles). The maximum pension is 1,200 roubles, but this is paid only to a few of the highest-paid workers and employees.

Men become entitled to their pensions on attaining the age of sixty, provided they have completed twenty-five years of work, and may·get this pension on reaching sixty, even if they completed the required twenty-five years and stopped working some years before. For women, the age is fifty-five, and the number of working years, twenty.

But for those who have done work underground (e.g. miners) or in conditions that are dangerous or adverse to health, the pensionable age for men is fifty, with twenty years' service; for women, forty-five, with fifteen years' service.

There is an intermediate category of fifty-five years of age and twenty-five years' service for men; of fifty years with twenty years' service for women, in employment that involves physically exhausting labour (there are less and less women performing such tasks, explained Mr. Laptiev, and they hoped soon to do without female heavy labour altogether).

Women workers and employees who have borne not less than five children, and brought them up to at least the age of eight, get their pensions on attaining the age of fifty, with fifteen years' service. Blind workers and employees qualify for pension for men at the age of fifty, with fifteen years' service, for women at the age of forty, with ten years' service. Those not qualifying for full pensions will get a pension proportionate to the amount and nature of the work done and wages earned.

In addition there are pensions for those who are industrially incapacitated either wholly or partially (the blind come into the latter category), and for families deprived of the bread-winner.

The figures given above are the minimum figures, without the supplementaries that are granted under various conditions.

It is difficult to estimate just what these scales mean in terms of standards of living. Accepting the Western Embassies' estimate of 40 roubles to the £1 (official exchange rate is 11) as representing the real value of the rouble, the minimum pension works out at about £1 17s. 6d. a week. But the Russians contest the accuracy of this computation, claiming that the real value of the rouble is substantially higher. They also point to the supplementaries, to the fact that rents are nominal (on the other hand, prices of food are high, and of clothes, very high) and to pensioners being able to go on working at full pay.

My Parliamentary colleague, Mr. Douglas Jay, who is a competent economist, was in Moscow at the same time as I, and made a special study of the Soviet standards of living. He came to the conclusion that they were still about one-third lower than ours. Considering what they were before the revolution and all that the Soviet Union has gone through since, especially the fearful damage wrought by the Second World War and the amount it spends on defence, that figure represents a great advance. But my Soviet friends were a little put out when I told them that British standards of living, social services and pension rates (the latter admittedly largely based on the insurance principle) were still substantially higher and the whole population was covered by social security.

In the Soviet Union the collective farms establish their own pension schemes for their members, although, said Mr. Laptiev, he hoped that in due course there would be State contributions. The only collective farm for which I obtained figures had a scheme ranging from a minimum of 50 roubles to a maximum of 350 roubles a month. But two years' experience had been enough to show that the figures could be substantially increased, which it was the intention of these collective farmers to do. And of course, in a collective farm the pensioners have their own homes and raise their own food. Moreover, they, like all Soviet pensioners, are at liberty to do whatever (usually light) work they can and receive the rate for the job—the pensions are not retiring pensions in the same sense as British pensions.

These things that I saw and heard during a crowded ten days were but glimpses and impressions. But they do give an idea of the matters that are filling the minds of the Soviet people and their leaders, and show what they are doing and want to do, what is the stuff of their lives. What is difficult to convey on paper is the sense of great energies released, of liberation from a monstrous, looming figure, a vast tyranny that had darkened men's lives for a generation.

CHAPTER FOUR

The "Personality Cult" through Soviet Eyes

THOSE I TALKED WITH in Moscow were generally agreed on indignantly rejecting the view, so widely held in the world outside, that the evils of Stalinism (always referred to by the polite circumlocution of "the personality cult") were the outcome of a bad system. This, to Soviet ears, sounds like a condemnation of the structure of Soviet society itself. The very term 'Stalinism' is considered objectionable. For those whose terms of reference are derived solely from Soviet experience find it impossible to distinguish between the foundations of Socialism, that is, the structure of Soviet society, and the present organisation and monopoly of power of the Communist Party. They cannot see the former existing without the latter. Any such idea indeed is denounced as smacking of the slogan of the Kronstadt rebels in 1921: "the Soviets without Communists". What Party democracy was like in Lenin's day or the fact that he originally thought of Soviet rule as a democracy in which all the parties represented in the Soviets—the Social Revolutionaries, Mensheviks and Bolsheviks—would exist legally, the Bolsheviks acting as a constitutional opposition to the other two or *vice versa*, all this has either been forgotten or is dismissed as irrelevant to present conditions.

But although there was agreement in repudiating any criticism of the system, I found a wide range of opinions about the meaning of the consecrated phrase "the personality cult". At one extreme were the sea-green incorruptibles, the Simonpure, strait-laced and earnest Party men. They held that

Stalin was a great man who had done a tremendous job for which they had nothing but awe and admiration. But, as he grew older, he became more and more isolated from the people. He had not, for instance, visited a collective farm for twenty years.* In his last years Stalin had implicitly trusted the bandit, Beria, who was a foreign agent and had taken advantage of the old man by supplying him with false information, from which Stalin could not help drawing wrong conclusions and acting mistakenly.

It was no coincidence that one of those who, in all good faith, gave me this beautifully simple explanation, also urged me to visit the Lenin Mausoleum. I said I was not a tourist and saw no point in gaping at corpses, however illustrious. He was a little shocked, and made a most illuminating reply: "It isn't a matter of being a tourist at all. I often visit the Mausoleum, and each time I do I experience feelings of reverence for those two great men."

That started me on a little investigation. I discovered that for Soviet people the Lenin Mausoleum has become a sort of cross between Madame Tussaud's and Westminister Abbey. It is a "must" for visitors from all over the Soviet Union, because anyone who returned to his or her native town or village and confessed to not having visited the Mausoleum would cut a very poor figure indeed. At the same time those who do visit the Mausoleum experience somewhat the same feelings as the pilgrims who used to wander all over Holy Russia to visit some monastery where there was a famous ikon or the shrine and relics of some great saint.

At the other extreme were those whose views of the "personality cult" of Stalin, its consequences and what should be done about it, were not much different from those I encountered later in Yugoslavia and Poland. But even these bold spirits were unwilling, or unable, to see that there was anything wrong with the system. They claimed that the 'personality cult' was a case of an individual who had distorted the system by abusing his power, and that all that had to be done to restore the system to its original excellence was to free it of these distortions

* This remark was made to me several times. In the light of Mr. Dolgov's observations at the Economic Institute (see p. 41), I knew what it meant.

and abuses. They could not see or would not admit that it was bureaucratic centralism in the party that had bred Stalinism, and that bureaucracy and the concentration of power were evils with their roots deep in the Communist Party and the so-called 'dictatorship of the proletariat'. Nor did they appreciate my remark that reformers had often invoked a return to a mythical golden age in the past as the pattern and motive for their innovations, and that this might be the case with the fervently proclaimed return to Leninism. Nevertheless, though they do not admit nor perhaps even realise it, the changes wanted by those who take this view amount to a pretty drastic reform of the whole system.

In between these two extremes is the official view, as expounded by Khrushchev and others at the 20th Congress, and later by the Central Committee's pronouncement on how to overcome the consequences of the 'personality cult', and also in the discussions that have gone on ever since in the Party organ, *Kommunist*. It was this view that was most frequently expressed in the innumerable talks I had with all kinds of people during those crowded days in Moscow.

The most striking and fullest official account of the meaning and consequences of the 'personality cult' was that given by Khrushchev in his famous secret report to the 20th Congress on February 25th, 1956, of which a translation (allegedly from a copy obtained in Poland) was later published by the U.S. State Department. All that the official verbatim report of the 20th Congress has to say on the subject on February 25th is: "The Congress in private session heard a report of the First Secretary of the Central Committee of the C.P.S.U., Comrade N. S. Khrushchev, on 'the personality cult and its consequences' and adopted a resolution on this subject. After an interval the Congress resumed its public session."

The resolution, adopted unanimously, instructs the Central Committee "to take all the measures necessary to dispose finally of the personality cult, which is alien to Marxism-Leninism, to remove all traces of it in every field of Party, State and ideological activity, and strictly to apply the rules of Party conduct and the principles of collective leadership that were framed by the great Lenin."

The secret report was read and discussed, after the Congress, all up and down the country, at meetings of Party members and candidates, so that it may be taken for granted that all 7 million of them have heard and talked over its contents. That means a great many active 'non-Party' workers must know about it too. Indeed, a general awareness of what Khrushchev said seems to be well-nigh universal among all politically conscious people—helped no doubt by Western broadcasts. The report was also communicated to the Roumanian, Bulgarian, Hungarian, Czechoslovak and Polish parties and similarly discussed by them. The impression on the rank and file of those parties was very great indeed, and on the Western Parties, who read it in the Press, devastating.

The declaration on how to *Put an End to the Personality Cult and Its Consequences*, published by the Central Committee on June 30th, was little more than a bowdlerised summary of Khrushchev's secret report. It was apparently put out to 'steady' Communist opinion in the West, particularly in France, and non-Communist opinion in the Soviet world. By implication the discussions on the various aspects of the subject that have gone on ever since in the Soviet Press and reviews assume knowledge of one or both these documents.

"The principle of collective leadership is elementary for a proletarian party, for a Leninist party," Mikoyan told the 20th Congress, "but we have to emphasise this ancient truth because for about twenty years we have in fact not had collective leadership. Instead, the 'personality cult', condemned not only by Lenin but even by Marx, has flourished, with the most disastrous consequences to the Party and its work."

Again and again in discussions on the subject it is stressed that the Party has, for over three years, been wrestling with the problem of making good the damage inflicted by the 'personality cult', and is still bending every energy to that task.

These comments give an idea of the magnitude of the problem and of the spirit in which the Soviet leaders are tackling it.

Khrushchev and the Central Committee's June 30 declaration both quoted Lenin's letter on December 22nd, 1922, about the way Stalin, as Secretary of the Party, had "accumulated in his hands immeasurable power", and Lenin's doubts as to

whether he would use it with the required caution and consideration for the views of others. This concentration of power,
explained Khrushchev in his secret report, and the methods
of mass terror at that time, were the inevitable result of the
class struggle aggravated by allied intervention. He quoted
Lenin's report of February 2nd, 1920, to the Central Executive
Committee: "We were forced to use terror because of the
terror practised by the Entente, when strong world powers
sent their forces against us and stopped at nothing. We would
not have lasted two days had we not answered these attacks
by foreign forces and white guards in a merciless fashion. This
meant the use of terror. But it was forced upon us by the terrorist methods of the Entente."*

As soon as the war had been won against intervention and
the class enemy at home, Lenin had insisted, terror would
cease. After Lenin's death there had, however, been a long
and tough struggle against the Trotskyites, Bukharinites and
bourgeois nationalists. What had been done to them Khrushchev regarded as necessary and right, although he stressed
that "even during the progress of the furious ideological
fight . . . extreme repressive measures were not used". It was
several years later, after the fight had been won, he pointed
out, that Stalin began overtly and on a vast scale to abuse
his limitless power to liquidate his opponents, justifying it by
the false proposition that the class war became more acute
with progress in the building of Socialism.

Khrushchev pin-pointed the turning point as beginning with
the assassination of S. M. Kirov, the Secretary of the Leningrad Party and member of the Politbureau, in December 1934.

* Sir Robert Bruce Lockhart, in his book, *Memoirs of a British Agent*,
pointed out that in the beginning the Bolshevik régime was comparatively
tolerant. "The cruelties which followed later were the result of the intensification of the civil war. For the intensification of that bloody struggle,
allied intervention, with the false hopes it raised, was largely responsible.
I do not say that a policy of abstention from interference in the internal
affairs of Russia would have altered the course of the Bolshevik revolution. I do suggest that our intervention intensified and increased the
bloodshed and . . . was indirectly responsible for the terror. Its direct
effect was . . . to galvanise the Bolsheviks into a strong and ruthless
organisation."

He gave a horrifying picture of the wholesale violence and terror, swelling into the great purges of the middle '30's under Yagoda and his even more ruthless and repulsive successor, Yezhov, and Stalin's direct responsibility for the torture and assassination of thousands of wholly innocent Party members, including some of his closest friends and associates and men with distinguished revolutionary records stretching back to the early days of the Party.*

Another part of the indictment was that Stalin had decided everything himself and mostly did not bother even to go through the formality of consulting his colleagues. A Party Congress was not called for thirteen years. The Central Committee did not meet for years either, and even the Politbureau was seldom called and when it did meet merely rubber-stamped decisions already taken. In his last years Stalin became so morbidly suspicious that he saw "enemies" and "spies" even in eminent Party workers whom he had known for many years. As Bulganin once remarked to Khrushchev: "When Stalin invites you to see him you never know whether you are going to end up by going home again or appearing before a firing squad." In these circumstances, as Soviet commentators are fond of remarking, the 'personality cult' was a bad influence on collective leadership and inner-party democracy (surely one of the most remarkable instances of meiosis on record).

The Central Committee's public declaration of June 30th, 1956, stressed the responsibility of capitalist hostility and pressure for the 'personality cult'. For more than a quarter of a century, ran the argument, the Soviet Union was isolated and like a besieged fortress in the capitalist world. After the failure of intervention to crush the revolution this hostility was manifested in other ways until, with the rise to power of Fascism in

* What Khrushchev told the Congress in his secret report about the assassination of Kirov and all that followed from it goes a long way to confirm the account in *Letter of an Old Bolshevik*, first printed in 1938 in the *émigré* Menshevik paper, *Sotsialisticheski Viestnik*, published in Paris, then translated and circulated by the Second International and finally issued as a pamphlet by Allen and Unwin. The author was a member of the Central Committee of the C.P.S.U. at the time. Weissberg's *A Conspiracy of Silence* also tallies with Khrushchev's awful revelations about the great purges.

Germany in 1933 and the formation of the anti-Comintern axis, a new and greater intervention was openly prepared with the connivance of the Western powers.

Capitalist hostility and war preparations were accompanied by an embittered class struggle within the Soviet Union and activities of hostile factions—Trotskyites, the Right Opportunists and bourgeois Nationalists—against whom the Party had to wage a merciless fight because their policies would have led to the restoration of capitalism.

"This complex international and domestic situation required iron discipline, a constant increase in vigilance, the strictest centralisation of leadership. All this inevitably damaged the development of some forms of democracy in the Party. In the course of a desperate contest with the whole world of imperialism, our country had to accept some limitations on democracy, justified by the struggle of our people for Socialism at a time when it was surrounded by capitalist countries. But even then those restrictions were looked upon by the Party and the people as temporary and due to be removed as the Soviet State grew stronger and the forces of democracy and socialism developed in the world. The people consciously accepted these temporary sacrifices, seeing the day-to-day successes of Soviet society."

In these accounts, it will be noticed, the origins of the evil are dated back only to 1934. The concentration of power in Stalin's hands up to that date, partly as a result of how he defeated Trotsky, Zinoviev, Kameniev and Bukharin, is regarded as inevitable and unexceptionable, and mostly due to the hostility of the capitalist world. But Lenin warned against the evils of 'Stalinism' in 1922, and even Khrushchev, in his secret report, contrasted Stalin's liquidation of his opponents with Lenin's leniency in much more critical times. The causes of 'Stalinism' lie deeper, the evil is greater, and the process started earlier than the present leaders are ready to admit.

I equipped myself as best I could for talks on the sixty-four dollar question, the democratisation of the régime, by reading Soviet literature—chiefly *Kommunist*—on the 'liquidation of the personality cult and its consequences' and kindred topics.

What follows is a summary of what is being said by Soviet writers on this subject.

The Soviet discussions on these matters all start with the point that Stalin had been credited with omniscience and infallibility in every field of human thought and endeavour. His words had become dogmas and holy writ, on which others might comment and embroider, but which it would be sacrilegious (and fatally dangerous) to question. He was increasingly disinclined to consult or even listen to anyone, and no one dared to say what they really thought—they would tell him not what they believed but what he wanted to hear. This attitude spread throughout the Party, for at every level there were some who received instructions from their superiors, deriving their authority ultimately from Stalin, and therefore brooked no criticism. The democracy had dropped out of democratic centralism.

The avowed object of the reformers in this field is now to restore the democracy that existed within the Party in the days of Lenin, which have become the "golden age" to which they want the Party to return. After three years they admit there is still a great deal to be done. But progress, they say, has been encouraging: at the top there is now real collective leadership in the Presidium (formerly Politbureau) of the Central Committee, and the latter meets regularly, discusses all the great issues and exercises a controlling influence on the leadership. In the country there are still places where Party organisations do not meet, and the job is left to the Party officials. But they are exceptional.

They also give instances of officials who still try to run Party meetings, impose candidates on them, decide beforehand who is to speak and even censor or write the speeches. But, they claim, there is now growing opposition to this kind of thing by Party members, who are beginning to stand on their rights and to treat the officials as their own elected servants and not their masters. *Kommunist* of June 1956 cites as indications of growing inner-party democracy the fact that in the meetings of the 'base' Party organisations of the Russian Federal Soviet Republic, discussing reports on their activities and electing officials, 40·5% of those present (who for all the 'base' organisations together totalled 1,150,000 Communists) took part in the discussion. At the regional and city level 10% of the delegates made speeches at the various conferences. In the Ukraine the corresponding over-all figures for the local, regional, municipal and county organisations were 425,000 members out of a total of just under 900,000, speaking at the various meetings.

However, as another commentator remarks, very often the speeches, instead of contributing to a discussion of issues, are mere reports of conditions in the speaker's own area, or echoes of the report.* This, he says, is a way of avoiding political responsibility. Again, he points out, speeches may be vague, general and not to the point. Or local Party leaders may have written out their speeches beforehand and treat the whole occasion as one for obtaining formal approval for their reports, threatening to complain to higher authorities if members express views of their own or dare to criticise the local boss.

Great stress is laid on the increasing number of collective farmers and workers who have become Party 'activists' and begun to give reality and freshness to Party discussions. But the prevailing complaint is still about the evils of bureaucracy and red tape, of officials being little tin gods and Party members taking an attitude expressed in such phrases as "The boss [khoziain] told me" or "He gave orders that".

Khrushchev himself, in his Central Committee report to the 20th Congress, described the opposite extreme in the Party. "We still have Party workers in leading positions," he remarked, "who might be described as belonging to the category of 'busy do-nothings'. At first glance they seem very busy. Indeed, they are most active. But their activities run in neutral. They hold meetings until cock-crow and then scurry from one collective farm to another, blasting the backward ones, calling meetings and making speeches, generally written beforehand and couched in general terms, in which they urge everyone to 'pass the test', 'overcome all difficulties', 'break through', 'justify confidence', and so forth. But however much this kind of Party leader fusses, it turns out in the end that

* A lot of the speeches at the 20th Congress of the C.P.S.U. were of this character.

nothing gets done, and that the man has been very busy
getting nowhere." (Khrushchev's actual expression was a
comic one, that rhymes in Russian, of a man jumping out of
his skin while marking time.)

Again and again Soviet commentators stress that what is
necessary is for the rank and file in the Party to be active, to
know and exercise their rights, and through the Soviets, trade
unions and collective farms to bring to bear public opinion
and the "pressure of the masses".

Trade union members are being encouraged in every way
to exercise their rights, both in electing the representatives
they want and seeing that they do their jobs properly. And
the trade unions, it is pointed out, have 45 million members,
of whom between 2 and 3 million are active in posts of responsibility in the factories and workshops, in social security organisations, or in connection with economic planning.

As for the Soviets, their total membership is about $1\frac{1}{2}$ million deputies (soviet, literally 'council', now means any elected
Government body, from town and county councils up through
the Republican Supreme Soviets to the All-Union Supreme
Soviet with its two chambers, the Chamber of Nationalities
and the Chamber of People's Representatives). Up to now
the higher Soviets have met rarely, only once or twice a year
for a few days, and have confined themselves to approving the
budgets and plans put forward by the Executive on the initiative of the Party. But under the new dispensation they are
meeting more regularly and for longer periods and taking a
much more active part in controlling and criticising the work
of the Government, going through and amending its proposals and so forth. The change is particularly marked at the
lower levels, where the soviets dealing with local affairs are
becoming quite lively bodies. The intention is that this shall
also be the case in the Supreme Soviet of the U.S.S.R.

But the gap between even the reformed state of affairs and
what we understand by democracy in the West is still wide
and deep.

Then there was the question of how elections are conducted.
I discussed this most of one morning with the five members
of the Editorial Board of *Kommunist* (all, of course, high-powered

Party members, and some of them members of the Central Committee), over the customary tea and cigarettes.

Candidates to any Soviet are nominated by the groups authorised to do so (Communist Party, youth and women's organisations, factories, collective farms, if in the country, trade unions, professional bodies, and so forth). Non-party candidates as well as Communist Party members are eligible, and the soviets contain a large number of them. There may be as many as a dozen nominees for one ward or constituency.

Thereafter each of the nominating bodies elects a representative, and the representatives of all these bodies meet to go through the list of candidates nominated, discussing the merits and demerits of each, until they reach agreement, if necessary by majority vote, on the one they select. That is the one for whom the electorate is then asked to vote.

If the candidate receives less than 50% of the votes of the registered electorate, either through absenteeism or spoiled ballot papers, or both, the election is invalid and there must be a new election. There is, in addition, the power of recall through an appeal by any group of electors in the constituency to the Soviet of which their representative is a member. That is, the actual decision to recall or not to recall is made by a majority of the elected person's colleagues. All this, I was told, was really more democratic than the practice in our benighted capitalist democracy.

I objected that the groups nominating candidates taken together would hardly exceed, say, 3,000 out of a total of 300,000 electors (which is the size of a Soviet Parliamentary constituency). But this 1% decide for whom the remaining 99% must vote if they did not want simply to spoil their ballot papers or stay at home. The Communist Party was the highest common factor in all the various nominating groups, and in fact decided who was to be the sole nominee selected for election. The power of recall was illusory (apart from being very rarely used), for it was not exercised by the electorate, but by the man's colleagues in the elected body of which he was a member. In practice, again, that meant that the Communist Party could organise a petition in a constituency and then command a majority of votes in the legislature for simply expelling anyone who became awkward or too fond of speaking his mind.

But on the main issue we had a really interesting discussion. The Editors of *Kommunist* admitted that there was nothing in the Soviet constitution that prevented more than one candidate being put forward for the voters to choose between. "And it may come to that some day." But, they argued, there did not seem to be any need for this procedure since it was merely a matter of choosing the individual best qualified to put forward a policy on which all agreed. "What would be the sense in my standing against you," said Soboliev, a thin, grey, earnest chap, turning to his neighbour, Roumiantsev, a large, ruddy (in harmony with his name), bouncy sort of man, "when we see eye to eye?" "If you did, I'd stand down in your favour," replied Roumiantsev promptly, not to be outdone in courtesy and comradely feeling. They evidently felt they had made a point. So they had, but not quite the one they meant.

For what they had succeeded in demonstrating was that the idea that the real issue was not whether either of them should stand down in favour of the other, but whether electors should be free, if they liked, to reject them both and put up some other candidate of their own choosing, simply was not in their terms of mental reference. It was outside their universe of discourse, beyond their ken.

Parties, they went on to explain, represented class interests, and there were no longer contending class interests in the Socialist society of the Soviet Union. Suppose the Labour Party had socialised our economy, would it consider it necessary to put up two Labour candidates in constituencies?

At this point I got a word in edgeways and explained that the process of socialising our economy would go on through the combined action, reaction and interaction of the Government and Opposition, that our system of government and conception of democracy made it necessary for both to exist and for neither nor even both together—for above them stood the law and behind them the people—to have a monopoly of power, and that in the end we should have Conservative Socialists and Radical Socialists or something of that sort (in fact, we already had something like that in the Labour Party, let alone what the Tories might develop into!). But the two-party system would go on even on the basis of a largely soci-alised economy, though by then there would probably be far more common ground and co-operation between parties, as there is, for example, in the Swedish and Finnish Parlia-ments.

My hosts regarded those observations as interesting but irre-levant, and went on with their discourse: the Soviets were going to be more active, sit longer and do a bigger job. But they, like the trade unions and collective farms, would con-tinue to be guided by the Communist Party, which was the educating, organising and leading political force in Soviet society. Anyone could become a member of the Communist Party who took the trouble to qualify. It might be that the ways in which the people of the Soviet Union could be repre-sented in and influence the governing bodies through the Party, the trade unions, the collective farms, as well as the Soviets, were making the classic techniques of capitalist demo-cracy out of date.

I, for my part, found their point of view interesting rather than convincing. But it did cast light on what Soviet Com-munists are thinking to-day. They are honestly incapable of grasping the idea that democracy means the people deciding issues through their elected representatives. To them, policy decisions must be taken in the Communist Party and the job of Soviet M.Ps. or Councillors is merely to keep the executors of those policies up to the mark by supplying information and 'constructive' criticism on how they are working and the people are feeling, perhaps even by suggesting amendments within acceptable limits. But no major policy initiative from outside the Party, nor indeed from below within the Party, would be in order. Indeed, it is difficult to see how it could come into existence at all, or be tolerated if it did.

To Soviet Communists the monopoly of political power in the hands of the Communist Party and the monopoly of policy initiatives in the leadership, are part of the Socialist State, which is the dictatorship of the proletariat and will last until it has effected the gradual transition to Communism. This seems to them the natural order of things, without which there can be neither Socialism nor democracy.

On the other hand, no one who reads *Kommunist*, which after all is the house organ of the Party, in which its members discuss with each other how to apply the Party's policies and try to draw appropriate lessons from the results of experience, can doubt that a real and serious effort is being made, as part of the great clean-up after Stalin, to democratise the internal life of the C.P.S.U. and to open it as widely as possible to the influence of the 'masses' through the trade unions, collective farms, soviets, etc. This the reformers regard as going back to the golden age of Communist inner-Party democracy under Lenin, and as constituting 'Socialist democracy' under the dictatorship of the proletariat, as represented by its vanguard, the C.P.S.U., pending the transition from the Socialist State to a Stateless Communist society.

By relegating the latter to the Greek calends and being dim and misty about how the process of transition and the concomitant withering away of the State are to take place, the C.P.S.U. reformers as well as leaders are in fact preserving and perpetuating the dictatorship of the Party over the proletariat and the people. They specifically and indignantly reject the notion that any lessening of the monopoly of power of the Party, or, to put it the other way around, any admission to a share of power of non-members of the Party in any organised or collective fashion, would be a step toward more Socialist democracy. They regard that on the contrary as a step backward toward bourgeois democracy, which in their view is only camouflage for the dictatorship of the capitalist class.

This view involves Soviet Communists in intellectual difficulties: for Khrushchev himself admitted in his Central Committee report that in some countries it might be possible to effect the transition from capitalism to Socialism by constitutional and Parliamentary means. But if so, political democracy as understood in the West must be something more than camouflage for a capitalist class dictatorship. And if it is capable of being used to effect a social revolution in societies with capitalist economic foundations, why could not democracy and political freedom in something like the Western sense, serve in communities with Socialist economic foundations to introduce more Socialist democracy and promote the progressive change-over from Socialism to Communism in the Marxist-Leninist sense?

The origin of the difficulty is the old trouble: the capitalist world has neither destroyed the Soviet Union nor itself gone Socialist. The trouble has been accentuated by the fact that the H-bomb rules out major wars and so the revolutionary upheavals that follow war. The paramount need to preserve peace carries with it the necessity to circumscribe and discourage revolutionary upheavals and to favour social change by peaceful rather than violent means. Soviet society, now forty years old, and for over a decade part of a Communist-ruled group of Socialist States totalling nearly two-fifths of humanity, must continue indefinitely to coexist peacefully with the non-Communist-ruled three-fifths of the human race, as the only alternative to mutual destruction.

In this situation the problem of the Soviet leaders is how to explain to their people why they still have not got as much intellectual and political freedom as the peoples living under 'bourgeois democracy', and when they may expect to get it. Hitherto they have tried to solve the problem partly by falsely representing to the Soviet people that their 'Socialist democracy' gives them more freedom and power to order their own affairs than the peoples of the 'bourgeois democracies' enjoy, but above all by making the most of the war-talk of Western cold warriors and the nuclear war preparations, intransigence and policies of 'anti-Communist liberation' (which, seen from Moscow, look like policies of intervention and aggression) of Western governments. Time, however, is not on their side.

For the society in which the Soviet régime is functioning is no longer a primitive, backward society. The Soviet Union already has a large number of professional men and women, scientists, technicians, skilled workers, mechanics, etc., and is turning out tens of thousands more every year. They must have mental freedom to do their jobs. Below that the people are now literate and many millions have a secondary school education.

A politically effective demand for greater freedom and for a more active part in deciding the matters that concern them is being engendered by this new, more complex and relatively educated society. And, of course, it can be doctrinally justified in terms of either the transition to Communism or the return to Leninism, besides corresponding to practical necessities.

But how far is this demand to go? Who is to draw the line, and where and how? No one I talked with in Moscow seemed very clear on these points.

But neither did anyone deny that they were logical and pertinent questions. After all, the April (No. 5) and June (No. 9) 1956 numbers of *Kommunist* both express their disapproval of the lengths to which some Communists are taking this business of speaking one's mind: "The Party wholeheartedly supports and encourages bold and basic criticism inspired by concern for the cause of Communism and the interests of the people, and directed against those who have not yet got rid of bureaucracy and red tape in their conceptions of leadership, are hostile to everything new and progressive, and who are careless about their responsibility for the matters entrusted to them, about their duty to the people. But in some Party organisations there have been politically misguided and even anti-Party utterances. Under the guise of condemning the 'personality cult' some rotten elements have tried to cast doubts on Party policy and its Leninist foundations—a policy which is unanimously supported and approved by the Soviet people. [How does he know? K. Z.] Such states of mind, even if they are only individual instances, are intolerable in our Party. The constitution of the C.P.S.U. gives every Communist freedom to discuss all questions of Party policy within the framework of Party loyalty. But to use this freedom to propagate views that are alien to Marxism-Leninism, to vilify Party policy, means to violate the Leninist rules for Party life that are incorporated in the constitution of the C.P.S.U. . . .

"A party which is a fighting alliance of like-thinking Communists cannot tolerate among its members anti-Party laxity and utterances. It is necessary also by means of criticism and explanation to deal with such incorrect views as that the rejection of the 'personality cult' means the rejection of the role of leadership by Party workers, the rejection of the principle of the unity of management in production, and of discipline and organisation" (*Kommunist*, No. 5). No. 9 of *Kommunist* adds to this indictment the complaint that "In some Party organisations an incorrect liberal attitude has been shown to these anti-Party utterances. Some Communists, even Party leaders, out of fear of demagogic accusations of suppressing criticism, have taken no action against declarations alien to Marxism-Leninism. In this way the interests of the Party have sometimes been sacrificed to demagogues and rotten elements."

All this merely raises the question—who is to decide when a criticism is legitimate and at what point it starts to become incorrect, anti-Party, rotten, liberal, etc.? Where does reason end and authority begin, by whom is the line drawn, and how is respect for it to be imposed? And supposing those of the 210 million or so Soviet citizens who are not members of the 7 million strong Communist Party, but are trade unionists, collective farmers, electors to or members of the soviets, begin to push insistence on their rights and views to the point where the Communist Party will either have to surrender its monopoly of power or go back on its professions of democracy? Freedom is an almost impossible thing to ration—you can either deny it altogether or you must concede it. Halfway houses are apt to prove temporary and precarious halting-places.

CHAPTER FIVE

Peaceful Co-existence after Stalin

'PEACEFUL CO-EXISTENCE' in some form has been the avowed object of Soviet foreign policy ever since the Russian Revolution and the civil war, fomented and prolonged by Allied intervention, when Lenin proposed an armistice, leaving the Bolsheviks on the one hand and the Whites and their Western backers on the other in possession of their respective areas of Russian territory. He first applied that conception to the boundaries and arrangements imposed by the Germans in the Peace Treaty of Brest Litovsk, later to the Allies during intervention, and later still to the annexationist peace insisted on by Marshal Pilsudsky of Poland. But Lenin to the end thought essentially in terms of a breathing-space or armistice, after which either the social revolution would spread to the capitalist countries or they would renew their attack on Soviet Russia. He did not believe in any lasting peace between the capitalist world and the country of the social revolution, and thought the issue between them would ultimately be settled by internal or international violence, or both.

Stalin, too, from the beginning proclaimed the slogan of 'peaceful co-existence'. But he was not haunted, like Lenin, by the idea of world revolution round one corner and armed intervention round the other. To him, peaceful co-existence meant the armistice becoming a stalemate of indefinite duration and uncertain outcome. During it the Soviet Union would develop 'Socialism in one country' at home, while it acted abroad as a great power protecting and promoting its national interests in the hostile capitalist world by the methods of power politics, i.e. by taking advantage of capitalist divisions, being strong in armaments, tough, cunning, and opportunist in its foreign policy.

Stalin did what he could to head off the Second World War by diplomatic means. His policy was as unscrupulous and short-sighted as those of the British and French Governments, but even tougher—and in the end no more successful.

When the war came he fought it, not as a clash between revolution and counter-revolution, but as a national patriotic war, in which the Soviet Union was the ally of some capitalist powers against others. Before he was attacked he ordered the Communist Parties in Allied countries to oppose the war in the interests of his deal with Hitler. After he had been attacked, he tried to reconcile Tito with the King and Mihailovich in Yugoslavia and the Chinese Communists with Chiang Kai-shek, in the interests of his dealings with his Western Allies.

Throughout the war and after Stalin was concerned with the national economic and security interests of his country, as he saw them, first, last and all the time. He took back Bessarabia and the Baltic States, torn from Russia at Brest Litovsk and later by Allied intervention, and the White Russian and Ukrainian parts of Poland, split away from Austria-Hungary and Russia after the First World War by Pilsudski. He 'rounded out' these frontiers at the expense of East Prussia.

This was straight, old-fashioned power politics, in which ideological motives played no part. So was Stalin's recovery of Dairen, Port Arthur and a half-share in the Chinese Eastern Railway. So was his reluctance to leave Persian Azerbaidjan without guarantees against the Soviet protégés, the Tu-Deh or Progressive Party, being slaughtered (as they subsequently were) by the reactionary protégés of Britain and the United States in South Persia, his objection to the Americans establishing bases and taking over oil resources in the North, and his desire to gain recognition of the Soviet Union's equal right with Britain and the United States to a share in settling Middle Eastern affairs. His claim to the Turkish Armenian provinces of Kars and Ardahan, adjacent to Soviet Armenia, and to a share with Turkey in controlling the outlet to the Mediterranean in the Dardanelles, was all traditional national policy and far less than the Allies had conceded Tsarist Russia in the secret treaties of the First World War.

Stalin's insistence on friendly governments in Russia's small neighbours which Soviet forces had liberated was accepted as reasonable by the Western Powers, and was also in the classic tradition of power politics. The imposition of heavy indemnities on the ex-enemy States Bulgaria, Roumania, Hungary and East Germany, in spite of their Communist governments, was another instance of a purely national, self-regarding, Russian policy, which paid lip-service to but was not appreciably influenced by, ideological considerations.

Since the death of Stalin Soviet policy has restored the Chinese Eastern Railway, Dairen and Port Arthur to China and the Porkkala Peninsula to Finland; the indemnities were long ago halved and substantial aid given (on pretty generous terms) to the countries concerned, and more or less successful attempts made to adjust Soviet relations with the other 'Socialist States' on a basis involving less coercion and more freedom. But all this still comes under the definition of a policy of more enlightened Soviet national self-interest.

Soviet foreign policy has never been governed by the interests of 'international Communism' since the defeat of Trotsky by Stalin on the issue of 'Socialism in one country' *versus* 'permanent revolution'. That is, it is not, and never, since the 1920's, has been, an 'ideological' foreign policy which thinks in terms of imposing Communism on other countries by force of arms. This fact may sometimes be obscured by the habit of the Soviet leaders of rationalising their pursuit of national self-interest in ideological terms. And of course the national interests they are defending are those of a society that has issued from a social revolution. But it is nevertheless the basic reality about the Soviet Union in world affairs, and should never be forgotten.

Stalin indeed never fully adjusted his thinking to the new post-war situation resulting from the spread of the social revolution to Eastern Europe, China, and parts of Korea and Indochina (a process for which Soviet policy bore only an indirect and involuntary responsibility), as an 'incident' of the 'great patriotic war'. He paid lip-service to, and for a short time actually respected, the right of the People's Democracies to national independence and equal status. That was while there still seemed hope that the powers who were allies during the war would continue to be partners in the peace, or at least would not fall apart to the point where they began to prepare for war against each other. But this hope soon faded and gave way to a policy of ruthlessly subjecting the Communist-ruled States to his own will and making sure that their régimes were obedient and reliable, in order to weld together the Socialist bloc under Soviet leadership in the East-West cold war. In this the Russian security motive was predominant, although ideology was grotesquely twisted to serve its purpose.

Stalin was as convinced as Lenin that Communism would in the end inherit the earth. But the end seemed to him indefinitely remote, and in his international policy he was concerned above all else with the national interests of the Soviet Union, which he considered it the duty of Communist parties everywhere to put first—with the corollary, of course, that they must accept Stalin's word for it as to what those national interests were. As a major national interest in Stalin's eyes was to avoid trouble with the capitalist great powers and their clients, provided they left him alone, Soviet influence on Communist parties in other countries on the whole opposed their becoming so radical and obstreperous as to make trouble for the Soviet Union. Contrariwise, of course, if Soviet relations worsened with any particular country, the Communist Party in that country was apt to become militant and aggressive. Ultimately, Stalin thought, but he was hazy about when and how, the capitalist economies would break down or the capitalist world would break up in internecine wars and Communism would take over bit by bit throughout the world, through the action of the working class in one country after another. The Soviet Union, he believed, had grown too strong after the Second World War to be attacked successfully, although she must, of course, remain armed and watchful.

Khrushchev, like Stalin and Lenin before him, has proclaimed peaceful co-existence as the aim of Soviet foreign policy, and believes passionately that the future belongs to Communism. But he also realises that, as he told the 20th

Congress, "The main feature of our age is the fact that Socialism has grown out of the limits of one country and turned
into a world system. Capitalism has proved powerless to prevent this world-wide historic process." In the words of the
Party review, *Kommunist* (No. 5, 1956): "Up to the Second
World War the Socialist system covered 17% of the earth's
surface and about 9% of its population. To-day the countries
of the Socialist camp occupy more than 25% of the territory
of the earth and include more than 35% of its population.
The Socialist camp already accounts for about 30% of the
total industrial production of the world, and the economies of
the Socialist countries are developing systematically and successfully."

The whole thinking of the present Socialist leaders is conditioned by this new fact. In particular, they stress the great
importance of China. I was struck, while in Moscow, by the
amount of literature about China I saw in the bookshops and
the great attention paid to Chinese affairs in the Press. *Pravda*
gave a practically verbatim account of the Chinese Communist
Party's Congress, publishing page after page of speeches in
successive issues. I was repeatedly urged by Soviet acquaint-
ances to read these proceedings, because the Chinese were
producing some highly interesting and important new ideas
about the building of Socialism. To the Russians, China is a
companion great power, to be treated in all respects as an
equal and in a different class from the small States. However,
the new leadership has learnt something about the small
People's Democracies too from Stalin's experience with Yugoslavia, as their reconciliation with that country has shown
(and also the tone of their subsequent controversy with it over
Hungary—indeed, the very fact that there is a controversy).

The second basic fact that underlies the international thinking of the present Soviet leadership is the hydrogen bomb and
the literally life-and-death necessity for the great powers to
avoid getting embroiled with each other, since a nuclear war
would mean the extermination of humanity. For public con-
sumption, this is usually put as meaning the end of capitalism.
But no one I talked with in Moscow had any illusions about
the fact that it would equally mean the end of the Soviet

Union. These two facts have compelled the new leaders to think differently from Lenin, and not only differently from but much more clearly than Stalin, about their relations with the capitalist world and the meaning of peaceful co-existence.

Khrushchev put the gist of the new approach into his Central Committee report to the 20th Congress: the world situation had changed fundamentally, he said, since the 19th Congress nearly four years ago. The existence of the powerful Socialist bloc and the 'resolute and consistent peace policy' of the Soviet Government had greatly strengthened the forces for peace even in the West and improved the international atmosphere. Moreover, "The forces of peace in the world have been greatly strengthened by the appearance on the scene of a group of peace-loving States in Europe and Asia, who have proclaimed that their foreign policy is founded on the principle of non-participation in the rival blocs. . . . As a result there is now a wide 'peace zone' in the world, including both Socialist and non-Socialist peace-loving States in Europe and Asia. . . .

"The Leninist principle of the peaceful co-existence of States with different social structures remains, as it always has been, the general line of Soviet foreign policy. This is not a matter of tactics but a fundamental principle of Soviet policy. It means that no threat to peaceful co-existence will ever come from the Soviet Union or the Socialist camp. Could a Socialist State ever have a single reason for starting an aggressive war? Have we got any classes or groups that would be interested in war as a means of getting richer? No. They have long ago been liquidated in our country. Maybe we have too little territory and natural resources; or do we perhaps lack raw materials or markets for our goods? No, we have all that we need in abundance. Why then should we want a war? We don't need a war."

Those charges were made from the West simply to confuse people's minds and to excuse the plans and preparations of those who wanted to conduct a 'crusade' against the Socialist countries.

"To this day the enemies of peace try to make everyone believe that the Soviet Union allegedly has the intention of overthrowing capitalism in other countries by 'exporting' revolution. Of course, there are no supporters of capitalism among us Communists. But that doesn't mean that we have interfered or are preparing to interfere in the internal affairs of countries that have a capitalist social order. Romain Rolland was right when he said that 'you cannot import freedom from abroad, like the Bourbons, in the train of an army'. It is silly to think that revolutions are made to order. Not infrequently one may hear representatives of bourgeois countries reasoning in this fashion: 'The Soviet leaders claim that they are in favour of the peaceful co-existence of two systems. But at the same time they declare that they are fighting for Communism and assert that Communism will triumph in all countries. Well, how then can we have peaceful co-existence with the Soviet Union if it is fighting for Communism?' This kind of reasoning is the result of bourgeois propaganda. Bourgeois ideologists, distorting the facts, deliberately confuse the question of an ideological struggle with that of the relations between States, in order to present the Communists of the Soviet Union as people with aggressive intentions.

"When we say that in the competition between two systems —the capitalist and the Socialist—the Socialist system will win, we do not mean that victory will be achieved by the armed intervention of Socialist countries in the internal affairs of capitalist countries. Our confidence in the victory of Communism rests on the fact that the Socialist method of production has decisive advantages over the capitalist. That is why the ideas of Marxism-Leninism are more and more capturing the minds of the broad masses of the workers of capitalist countries, as they already possess the minds of millions of people in our country and in the countries of people's democracy. We believe that the working people of the whole world, as they become convinced of the advantages of Communism, will sooner or later begin to try to get Socialism for themselves."

The Soviet Communist Party and people were creating a society in which there could be abundance and freedom for all. Their aim was the greatest and noblest in history, and they were pursuing it with titanic energy, unlimited devotion and self-sacrifice and prodigious success.

"That is why the ideas of Communism have such tremendous attractive force and are winning more and more people over to their side. There is nothing more ridiculous than the tales about people becoming converts to Communism under compulsion and pressure from outside. We are convinced that the ideas of Communism will conquer and that no 'iron curtains' and barriers interposed by bourgeois reactionaries will be able to stop its spread among more and more millions of people."

There is no reason to doubt the sincerity of Khrushchev's belief that their system is so superior that it will inevitably attract and win over the masses in the non-Communist world. On the contrary, that is precisely what Soviet leaders really do believe. But it would be surprising if subsequent events in Poland and Hungary and their repercussions throughout the Communist world had not sicklied o'er the native hue of self-satisfaction with the pale cast of thought. For they suggest that the future belongs to democratic Socialism in a much fuller and more Western sense than anything regarded as compatible with Marxism-Communism by the present leaders in Moscow.

At any rate, holding the views they do, they are perfectly sincere in their desire for peace, which they believe will favour the spread of Communism. As Khrushchev put it: "Building Communism in our own country, we resolutely oppose any idea of resorting to war. We have always insisted, and continue to insist, that the establishing of a new social order in any country is the internal affair of the people of that country. That is our position, grounded in the great teachings of Marx and Lenin. . . .

"The choice lies between only two courses: either peaceful co-existence or the most destructive war in history. There is no third way.

"We consider that countries with different social systems cannot merely exist side by side. They must go further, improve their relations, strengthen confidence between each other, co-operate. The historic importance of the famous five Principles proposed by the Chinese People's Republic and the Republic of India and supported by the Bandung Conference and a large number of nations, is precisely that they formulate the best kind of relationship in the circumstances of to-day between States with different social structures. Why shouldn't these Principles become the basis for peaceful relations between all countries in every part of the world? The adherence of all States to the five Principles would satisfy the desires and serve the vital interests of their peoples."*

The danger of war would subsist, Khrushchev explained, so long as capitalism existed anywhere. But there was no reason to be fatalistic or feel that war was inevitable, for the social and political forces opposed to war were now so strong that they could prevent it and preserve peace indefinitely.

The Soviet leaders of course realise, as well as the rest of us—I had confirmation of that in my talks in Moscow—that the two waves of social revolution in the world came as a result of the more or less far-reaching breakdown of many capitalist societies in the First and Second World Wars. Consequently, if war with each other has become so destructive that the great powers must avoid it at any price, and if the forces for peace are so powerful that they will prevent the outbreak of war, it follows that revolutionary social change by violence becomes increasingly improbable. And so the present Soviet leaders have been logically impelled to proclaim the possibility of the transition from capitalism to Socialism by peaceful and Parliamentary means.

Lenin insisted that the roads to Socialism would be different for different countries, Khrushchev pointed out in his report to the 20th Congress. In Lenin's day there had been no possibility of using constitutional means for revolutionary social

---

* The five Principles, included in Sino-Indian, Sino-Soviet and Indian-Soviet agreements, as well as in the resolutions of the Bandung Conference, have increasingly become one of the cardinal points—or at least propaganda points—in the foreign policies of the Soviet and Afro-Asian groups. They call for (1) Mutual respect for each other's territorial integrity and sovereignty, (2) Non-aggression, (3) Non-interference in each other's internal affairs, (4) Equality and mutual benefit, (5) Peaceful co-existence.

These principles, it will be observed, are a rather vague, tautologous and negative formulation of some of the purposes, principles and obligations of the United Nations Charter. They would not appear to contain anything not already in the Charter. But they are none the worse for that.

change. Now the situation was radically different, thanks to the existence and success of the Socialist countries and their prestige in the eyes of the workers everywhere. The European People's Democracies, the Chinese People's Republic and the Federal People's Republic of Yugoslavia were all advancing to Socialism by different paths.

"It is highly likely that the forms of transition to Socialism will vary ever more widely. Nor is it necessarily true that these different ways to Socialism must always pass through civil war. Our enemies like to portray us Leninists as advocates of violence everywhere and in all circumstances. It is true that we recognise the necessity for a revolutionary transformation of a capitalist society into a Socialist society, and that it is this that distinguishes us revolutionary Marxists from the reformists and opportunists. . . . But there are many different kinds of social revolution. And it is not true that we regard violence and civil war as the only way to change society. . . ."

Khrushchev then pointed out that Lenin had twice during the Kerensky period tried to induce the Mensheviks and Social Revolutionaries to join in making a bloodless Soviet revolution while they had the chance. He went on to discuss whether it was possible to effect the transition to Socialism by Parliamentary means. That had been impossible for the Bolsheviks at the time of the Russian Revolution. But in the conditions of to-day "the working class, drawing together the peasantry, the intelligentsia, all patriotic forces, and decisively rejecting the opportunists that are incapable of giving up the policy of appeasing capitalists and landowners, can defeat reactionary, anti-national forces, gain a solid majority in Parliament, and change it from an organ of bourgeois democracy into a genuine instrument of the will of the people. In that case this institution, which is traditional in many highly developed capitalist States, can become the instrument of a genuine democracy, a democracy of the workers. The winning of a solid Parliamentary majority resting on a mass revolutionary movement of the proletariat and of all who toil, would create conditions for the working class in a number of capitalist and former colonial countries that would guarantee the carrying out of radical social changes. . . .

"In all forms of transition to Socialism the necessary and decisive condition must be the political leadership of the working class headed by its most advanced elements. Without this the transition to Socialism is impossible."

The idea of Communist-led revolutionary movements winning solid Parliamentary majorities by constitutional means is a classic case of trying to have it both ways. But what is more important than this confusion is the fact that the two great new realities—the existence of Communist governments in 35% of the human race and the invention of the H-bomb— have driven the Soviet leaders to enlarge their conception of peaceful co-existence and of the variety of ways to Socialism. This has quite logically led to the next step: though claiming that the Communist parties were the most consistent and intrepid fighters for peace, Khrushchev acknowledged that there were also other forces in society that were fighting the danger of war. "Of course the effectiveness of their action would be still greater if all the various forces that support the cause of peace were less scattered. In this connection, the problem of the unity of the working class becomes particularly important —i.e. trade union unity and unity in action of the political parties—Communist, Socialist, and other working-class parties.

"The origins of not a few of the misfortunes of the world of to-day may be found in the fact that for many years the working class in a number of countries has remained divided and its different sections have not acted unitedly, thereby benefiting only the forces of reaction. In our opinion, however, the present situation gives an opportunity for changing this state of things. Life has raised a number of issues which not only require the drawing together and co-operation of all working-class parties, but great opportunities for this co-operation. The chief of these issues is the prevention of another war. If the working class were to act as a single organised force that knew what it wanted and had the courage of its convictions, there would be no war.

"All this lays a historic responsibility on active members of the working-class movement. The interests of peace require them to drop mutual recrimination and to seek points of contact, and on this basis to find common ground on which they can co-operate. In this connection it is not only possible but necessary to co-operate also with those sections of the Socialist movement that differ with us on the question of how to effect the transition to Socialism. Among them are a considerable number who, in all good faith, hold mistaken views on the subject. But this should be no obstacle to co-operation. To-day many Social Democrats are actively engaged in fighting the dangers of war and militarism and are campaigning for a *rapprochement* with the Socialist countries and the unity of the working-class movement. We sincerely greet these Social Democrats and are ready to do everything necessary to join forces with them in the noble cause of defending peace and the interests of the working classes."

The various proposals and declarations of the Soviet Government for the unification of Germany, organisation of European security and agreements on disarmament, give an idea of how the present Soviet leaders want to apply their 'peaceful co-existence' line in Europe and the Middle East.

The striking feature of the Bulganin-Tito declaration concluded in Moscow on June 20th, 1956, which was of particular interest to me as my next visit was going to be to Yugoslavia, was the extent to which it pledged the two Governments to making the United Nations the instrument for their peace policy. The declaration begins by referring to the improved international atmosphere and ascribing it in large part to the 'summit' Four-power Conference in Geneva in July 1955. "In this new atmosphere the power of the United Nations has increased, as has its capacity for dealing with and solving problems by the organised participation of all countries on the basis of equality. The success of the Conference for the Peaceful Uses of Atomic Energy, convened by the United Nations in Geneva in August 1955, and the good beginning made in setting up an International Atomic Energy Agency, is closely connected with this new atmosphere. The growing part being played by the United Nations and its increasing efficacy have also been shown by the progress made towards making it a universal organisation through the admission of new members." In this connection the failure to recognise the right of the People's Republic of China to take its place as a permanent member of the Security Council is deplored and the urgent need for action in this sense is insisted upon. Atomic energy for peaceful purposes must be developed by international co-operation and atomic weapons must be prohibited.

The two Governments, says the declaration, "believe that a wider agreement for all-European collective security, economic co-operation, and the strengthening of cultural ties would make it easier to put an end to the division of Europe into military blocs, and to solve the basic issues that are an obstacle to all-round co-operation between the nations of Europe."

The United Nations should be used, continues the declaration, to deal with all cases of local conflicts and friction between States that cannot be settled by direct negotiation. It should play a part of the first importance in the emancipation of dependent territories. Broadly conceived international action was the way to deal with the major problem of the gulf between the developed and the underdeveloped countries. In this connection the two Governments would "do all in their power to see that wider and more effective measures are taken through the United Nations to give economic and technical assistance to insufficiently developed territories. Both Governments consider that such help and co-operation should be given to undeveloped countries for modernising their economic systems, without any military or political conditions."

No less important was the declaration on inter-party relations signed on the same occasion by Khrushchev and Tito, this time as the Secretary of the Central Committee of the Yugoslav League of Communists (whereas he had signed his treaty with Bulganin on inter-State relations as President and Prime Minister of the Federal People's Republic of Yugoslavia). In this case it took three days of close, and sometimes hot, argument, and a good deal of stubbornness by the Yugoslavs, before a text was agreed upon—based on the Yugoslav draft. The first two paragraphs celebrate the renewal of relations of friendship and trust between the two parties, which share the common aim of building a Socialist society in their respective countries, as well as a common desire for strengthening peace and contributing to the progress of mankind, and says that the development of co-operation between them will promote good relations between their two States and peoples. The part about which there was an argument begins with paragraph 3:

"3. Both sides, being of the opinion that Socialist development will proceed on different lines in different countries and conditions, that the rich variety of forms in which Socialism can develop contributes to its strength, and taking into consideration the fact that neither side has any intention of trying to impose its views on the correct road to Socialism and the forms Socialist development should take, are agreed that the co-operation between them referred to above should be based on entire freedom and equality, friendly criticism and exchanges of views on controversial questions between the two parties in a comradely spirit.

"4. Co-operation between the C.P.S.U. and the Y.L.C. [Yugoslav League of Communists], based on these principles, will take the form primarily of both sides fully informing themselves of the way in which Socialism is being built in their two countries. They will also learn from each other's experience and exchange views freely and in a spirit of comradeship on matters of common concern about the development of Socialist thought and practice, and on questions concerning peace, co-operation between nations, and the progress of mankind in general."

Para. 5 says that the two parties will also discuss questions of Marxist-Leninist social science.

"6. The C.P.S.U. and Y.L.C. delegations also agreed that they would co-operate through personal contacts and written and verbal reports and exchanges of views, through exchange visits of delegations and of material and literature, and also through meetings of representatives of the two parties, whenever necessary, in order to discuss current problems of common concern. In general there should be every form of constructive and comradely discussion.

"7. The representatives of the C.S.P.U. and Y.L.C. further consider their mutual co-operation to be an integral part of their contacts with other Communist and workers' parties and also with the Socialist and other progressive movements in the world.

"8. The C.P.S.U. and Y.L.C. consider that in the interests of the campaign for a lasting peace, for the security of all nations and for social progress, the widest possible co-operation between all progressive and peace-loving forces is necessary, in the most varied forms and on a world-wide scale. Such co-operation is one of the inescapable necessities of contemporary social development. Contacts should be frank, democratic, based on equal rights and open to the public opinion of the world. They should serve the purpose of mutual consultation and information on various problems of common concern and should make it easier to achieve mutual understanding on the basis of patient explanation of the various positions and views involved. It will be understood that every participant in these forms of co-operation would be free to act according to his circumstances and in ways corresponding to the progressive aims held in common by all."

The twin topics of relations with Social-Democratic Parties and the possibility of effecting the transition from capitalism to Socialism by Parliamentary means were being hotly discussed while I was in Moscow. Among the Social Democratic parties the Labour Party was of course recognised as by far the most important, and great interest was shown in its attitude. The Labour Party's stock had gone up sharply in all the countries I visited, I found, because of its campaign in August and September against the Government's policy over Suez and its firm stand on the Charter when the House met in extraordinary session in the middle of September. The proceedings of the Blackpool Conference early in October, and particularly its resolutions for substantial reduction in arms expenditure and the size of our forces, against further H-bomb tests and in favour of working for the abolition of nuclear weapons, and for the unification of Germany within an all-European treaty based on the Charter but outside the rival alliances, had been widely publicised in the Soviet Press. One of the first articles I read on reaching Moscow was an article in *Novoe Vremia* (New Time) entitled (in Cyrillic characters, but in English), "Keep Left." The Labour Party came into most of my conversations in Moscow.

There was general disappointment at the way the French

Socialist Party National Executive delegation, after a highly successful visit as the guests of the Central Committee of the C.P.S.U., went home and took a very different line from what they had done in Moscow. There was considerable feeling about the way Bulganin and Khrushchev were treated at that famous dinner party when they were the guests of Labour's National Executive and Parliamentary Committee. But, for instance, *Kommunist* of April 1956 (No. 6), after complaining of all this and of the negative attitude of the Bureau of the Second Internationale, quoted with approval Khrushchev's remark, in his comments on the dinner party fiasco, that: "The Central Committee of our Party will continue its endeavours to carry out the decisions of the 20th Congress of the C.P.S.U. on establishing contacts with Socialist and working-class parties. We are convinced that the Labour Party will understand us and will take the steps necessary for this purpose. We are prepared to rise above personal insults and the provocative attacks which some Labour leaders have seen fit to make on the Communist Party of the Soviet Union, and in spite of them we are ready to get into touch with the British Labour Party if, on their part, they show the necessary understanding and desire to do so. For obviously such contacts are very important in the interests of the working people of both Britain and the Soviet Union."

After quoting this passage, the *Kommunist* leader goes on: "Different opinions and conflicts of opinion are inevitable within the working-class movement. Communists do not refuse to declare and to defend their views. But ideological differences on this or that question can and should be solved in an atmosphere of friendship and co-operation. In any case, these differences cannot, and should not, prevent the unity of action of the working class in the fight for peace and Socialism. There is no doubt that co-operation and common action by the parties of the working class will lead to the disappearance of some of the differences, since many of them are the result of a mutual lack of understanding, of unnecessary charges and unfounded suspicions."

To the Soviet mind, the question of their relations with Social Democratic Parties is closely connected with the new

F

light in which they are now seeing the idea of Parliamentary
roads to Socialism. But just as most Soviet commentators make
no distinction, in discussing the former topic, between Socialist-
Communist contacts on the international level and promoting
Popular Fronts within the countries concerned, so they seem
to imagine that the parliamentary road to Socialism means
Communist Parties leading a 'revolutionary movement' of
oppressed but militant workers and 'peasants' to electoral
victory. *Kommunist* for September 1946 (No. 14) and *Miezhduna-
rodnaia Zhisn* ('International life') of September 1946 (No. 10),
both had articles on the subject that took this line. But I had
to agree with the Soviet Communist Party intellectual who
drew my attention to them, that they were 'not much good'
and 'rather unreal'.

What I had to say on these matters is described in the next
chapter. I want to close this one by bearing witness to the
eager desire of Soviet folk, even influential Party members, to
hear and weigh strange and often unpalatable Western points
of view, and their readiness to admit that there was much
they did not know and needed to learn about these matters.
There was no arrogance or hostility, nor did I come across
any hermetically sealed minds. Of course, even within the
limits the Party now allows its members to let their minds
rip, the C.P.S.U. mental terms of reference resulting from the
Soviet experience of forty years and the Russian national
traditions underlying and informing that experience are so
vastly different from ours that the effort to understand each
other must be very great—and that applies to the West as
much as to the Soviet Union. But that these human contacts
are a good thing I have no doubt, and that if we, in the West,
will make the effort, the people of the Soviet Union and their
leaders at every level will respond, I am equally certain. For
the time being Soviet justifications of their action in Hungary
and Western exploitation of the situation to revive the cold war
have made such contacts almost impossibly difficult. But the
sooner they are renewed and the more they are developed,
the better, for a new birth of freedom and the peace of the
world.

CHAPTER SIX

Soviet Interest in the Labour Party

THOUGH I HAD GONE to Moscow to learn what I could of the current political atmosphere and of developments since the death of Stalin, I soon found that learning was a two-way process. Such was the interest in Britain and, in particular, the Labour Party that I usually found myself answering as many questions about my own country as I was asking about the Soviet Union. I lectured to the Institute of World Economy and International Relations on "Peaceful Co-existence" and was invited by the President of the University to give a lecture on "The Transition to Socialism by Parliamentary Means." But this lecture was cancelled when it conflicted with an invitation from the Academy of Social Sciences attached to the Central Committee of the C.P.S.U., to give a lecture on the Labour Party. Most of the students who were to have heard my University lecture and some of their professors attended the latter lecture instead.

The lecture to the Institute of World Economy turned out to be little more than a rehearsal for the one I gave to the Academy of Social Sciences, in spite of the different titles. For the points I made about peaceful co-existence were that:

(*a*) It should mean *active* co-existence, i.e. economic and political co-operation, disarmament agreements, etc., as once defined by Tito, and that to act on this policy meant basing our relations on the Charter of the United Nations and not on rival blocs and alliances.

(*b*) Democracy and political freedom facilitated that kind of co-operation and mutual understanding, and were a necessary political instrument for successful 'active co-existence'.

(*c*) Democracy and political freedom were also important as an end in themselves, as part of our conception of the good life and of the sort of society we wanted to build, where the State existed for the individual and not the other way around. Ultimately, active co-existence postulated that we agreed on this common aim, however much we differed about the means for attaining it.

In elaborating these points I found I was in fact making the case for parliamentary democracy and the kind of world in which the Labour Party believes. The questions asked were almost all directed to these last two points and were covered by what I had to say at the lecture to the Academy.

Linguistically, too, the Institute lecture was a rehearsal: I have spoken and read a good deal of Russian since I learnt it in Siberia in the First World War. But this was the first time I had ever attempted to make a speech in that language, and so for the Institute I had had my lecture translated, with the idea of reading it. But I found I needed to refer to the script only to read quotations. So for the Academy speech I simply made notes as I would for a lecture in English (or Swedish, French or German, since I have lectured in all three).

When the invitation came through it was conveyed to me that this was something rather out of the ordinary. "You realise, I hope," said a member of the Institute, "that you are going to address the cream of our youth." I asked what he meant, and was told that my audience would consist of young people from the middle twenties to the early thirties, who were already doing key jobs in the Party as local Party secretaries, or officials responsible for propaganda and education, or secretaries of trade union branches. Of these the best were picked from all over the Soviet Union and sent to the Party Academy of Social Sciences to take a post-graduate course of higher studies. They were, in fact, picked young people, the best and most promising of the future cadres of the Party, undergoing higher training.

To let me loose on this audience was a sporting and generous offer and a bit of a challenge and responsibility. I decided I would do my best to be intellectually honest and to give a fair picture of the Labour Party, couched in terms appropriate to the background, experience and outlook of my audience. I would respond to the spirit of friendliness and good faith that prompted the invitation—but I would pull no punches and would try to tell a few home truths where they might do the most good.* The lecture hall was a big one supplied with microphones and seating about 500 people. There must have been at least 600 present, for they were lining the walls and standing in the aisles.

Anyone who does public speaking learns to sense whether his audience is with him or not. I have seldom addressed a keener or friendlier audience than this one. They could not possibly have agreed with a great deal of what I said, but undoubtedly accepted me as someone who was speaking to them in good faith and in what they would describe as a friendly and comradely spirit. Also I know from what I was told afterwards that a great deal of what I had to tell them in the way of facts and inferences was new to them. They were deeply interested, they took all the points and jokes, their questions were all 'on the ball' and they gave me a warm welcome before I started and a tremendous one when I had finished. I spoke for just over an hour and answered questions for nearly an hour and a half. After that I had to go to another engagement—so far as the audience was concerned, apparently, they would have liked to go on asking questions for another hour or so.

What I had to say about the Labour Party was of course not new for a Western audience. But I tried to put it in such a way as to be within the mental terms of reference of the young Soviet folk I was addressing, to whom it certainly came as strange and startling food for thought. So I began with Marx and Engels, explaining why the latter considered that Britain was a unique society from the working-class point of view, where the obtaining by the workers of the vote would

* I was very glad that I had thought of taking with me the Blackpool Conference resolutions of the Labour Party as well as some of the latest N.E.C. policy documents and G. D. H. Cole's *A Short History of the British Working Class Movement*. I became quite a dab-hand at translating the Blackpool Conference resolutions on Germany, disarmament, the H-bomb and Suez into Russian (and later into Polish and Serbo-Croat!).

itself be a great step toward Socialism, and why Marx had considered that Britain was one of the capitalist countries where it was possible to effect the transition from capitalism to Socialism by constitutional and Parliamentary means.

Lenin had denied this, but his judgement was influenced by the fact that he believed the semi-autocracy of the Germany of William II was a more advanced form of bourgeois democracy than what we had in Britain. I quoted the passage from Lenin's *The State and Revolution* in which he says this, and suggested that history had indubitably proved him wrong on this point, and that he had made the mistake because he exaggerated the importance of the German Social Democratic Party, which at that time enjoyed great prestige, whereas the infant Labour Party was little known on the Continent and was directing its energies almost wholly to issues of social legislation, trade union rights and local government. But now in Khrushchev's Central Committee report to the 20th Congress it had been once more conceded by the Soviet leaders that the parliamentary road to Socialism was a possibility in at least some capitalist countries.

Labour was a reformist party, and reformism had its laws, just like revolution. It meant that we and the Conservatives, although we represented broadly those who live by their labour and those who live by rent interest and profit respectively overlapped at some points both in our following and our programmes, that neither party was monolithic and that the great majority of both considered that it was a lesser evil to accept defeat at the polls than to try to combat the verdict of the electorate by unconstitutional means. Our system of government, in fact, was a kind of co-operation in competition between H.M. Government and H.M. Opposition, and the idea that we differ on methods but agree on the ultimate aim of the good of the whole nation was more than a formality. We were political opponents belonging to different sections of the same nation, not enemies.

The fact that we were an old democracy and a practical, empirical people who distrusted theory and ideology and rather favoured rule of thumb and muddling through cut both ways: Labour was cautious, slow, and short on ideology. But we would not submit to being pushed around and having our democracy taken from us by radicalism of the right (i.e. Fascism), rather than forsake the paths of constitutionalism, if necessary to defend it, as in the classic case of the German Social Democrats and their ignominious collapse before Hitler. Nor were most of the Conservatives likely to produce or put up with anything like Hitler!

That was why we believed that our democratic Parliamentary system, with its elastic unwritten constitution, which had seen us through so many and such great changes and weathered such terrific shocks, could serve as the instrument for effecting a peaceful and progressive social revolution.

Finally, I stressed the unique character of the Labour Party as a sort of popular front under Social-democratic leadership, rooted in the wholly working-class Trade Union and mostly working-class Co-operative Movement (not forgetting that wage-earners are more than two-thirds of the total population of Britain and that only 5% of the population are engaged in agriculture, and they are divided into farmers and agricultural labourers; the peasant is an extinct species).

One question picked up the point I had made, quoting from G. D. H. Cole's data, that the Marxist 'law of absolute impoverishment of the proletariat under capitalism' had not worked, as the real wages of the British working class had risen by 80% between 1850 and 1900. I was asked whether the real wages of British workers had continued to rise since 1900 and answered, yes, but the advance was slowing up, and to-day we were marking time and finding it difficult to keep up with the rising cost of living, although on a pretty high standard of life, about one-third higher than in the Soviet Union.

There were questions about Labour's attitude to the Government's policy on China; Malaya and Cyprus; Anglo-American relations; what I thought of the Soviet proposal for an all-European treaty with a system of collective security for Europe. On the last out came the Labour Party Blackpool Conference resolution on Germany again, as well as Alfred Robens' speech in the House on February 27th, 1956. It was a great relief to have Labour international policies to expound that made sense!

That was true too on colonial issues, where the Blackpool Conference adopted a progressive colonial policy report of the National Executive. It was a good policy. The only question was whether we would have the guts to carry it out when we came into power. That depended partly on how well these matters were understood in our Party and supported by popular opinion.

As for Anglo-American relations, I explained why our two peoples were so mixed up in the world and had so much in common that we were never likely to part company, although I hoped and believed that it would ultimately be the policy of the Labour Party (it was not so yet) to convert the Anglo-American alliance into a partnership for peace inside the United Nations and taking its stand on the obligations of the Charter, and not on a military alliance.

I was asked such questions as "What is Labour's attitude to Adenauer and the present situation in Western Germany? Have the Labour Party any definite foreign political programme and if so what is its aim? What is the position of the Labour Party on the question of further improving British-Soviet relations, and what practical steps should be taken to this end? How do you explain the swing to the left that became apparent at the last Conference of the Labour Party? How deep and permanent is it? What, in this connection, are the chances, in your opinion, of a *rapprochement* between the Labour and Communist parties?"

But the $64 question was, from the point of view of my audience, the relations between the Labour Party and the British Communist Party. I think they were rather taken aback by my treating it as a matter of minor importance. My whole speech and the questions were, I believe, taken down by tape-recorder, because early in 1957 I ran into Harry Pollitt at a Czechoslovakian Embassy reception in London, and he told me he had seen the report of my speech in Moscow. He seemed rather grieved at my observations on the British Communist Party.

Here are the questions (they were written, and I kept them) and my answers on the subject of the relations between the Labour Party and the British Communist Party:

1. *Q.:* What, in your opinion, is the reason why the British C.P. has not been able to become the mass party of the British working-class movement?

2. *Q.:* What is the attitude of the leadership and rank and file of your party to establishing unity of action with other workers' parties—in particular with the Communist?

3. *Q.:* What is the position of the Labour Party with regard to international co-operation in the working class? What are the relations of the Labour Party to the Communist Party of Britain?

4. *Q.:* What is the position of the Labour Party on the cardinal question of our day—the unity of the international working-class movement?

5. *Q.:* What is your own attitude and that of the Labour Party to the British Communist Party and its foreign policy?

6. *Q.:* Are the Labour Party thinking of entering into an alliance with the Communists of Britain in the fight for the interests of the working class?

7. *Q.:* What is the explanation of the fact that the leaders of the British Trades Union Congress do not want to have any contacts with the Soviet trade unions?

In reply to all these questions, I gave an analysis of the position, as follows:

In the trade unions, Communists were members on the same footing as members of the Labour Party, who were the overwhelming majority (although there were a few trade unionists who were Liberals and even Conservatives, and a considerable number who were politically uninterested). In general, Communists in trade unions, because they were a closely organised and energetic minority, played a part out of proportion to their numbers. Where they obtained commanding positions they naturally influenced the policy of their unions. But there were limits to this process. For when Communists became important trade union officials it was generally because they were such good trade unionists that they overcame the prejudice attaching to their membership of the Communist Party, and they often had to put their loyalty to

the policy of the trade union before the policy of their Party.
For instance, Arthur Horner, as Secretary of the N.U.M., had
had on occasions to take a line with his Union members, in
response to the orders of his Executive, that was clean contrary
to the policy of the British Communist Party.

In the political field, on the other hand, there was only a
handful of people in the Labour Party who wanted any kind
of association with the Communists whatsoever. On the Left
we were opposed to the idea on realistic political grounds, and
without importing any animus into the discussion.* But in
most of the Labour Party there was a pretty strong dislike of
the Communists, based on their record as transplanted Russian nationalists, i.e. as thick and thin supporters of Stalin's
political line and apologists for everything he ever did in the
worst days of the 'personality cult'.

The political objection to any association with the Communists was that our job as a Labour Party was to win power
by obtaining a majority of votes for our candidates. The Communists not only could not win a single seat in Parliament for
themselves, nor attract more than a handful of votes in any
constituency, but they would lose us a great many votes if we
had any truck with them. There had never been more than
two Communist M.P.s in a House of 630, and since 1950 there
had been none. The Communists did not venture to contest
more than a handful of seats—about twenty—and even in
those seats, picked as being the most favourable to their cause,
they scored an average of less than 1,000 votes each in elec-
torates of 50,000, with 80% participation in the poll. To believe that the Communists could lead the British workers to
victory for Socialism by Parliamentary means was like expecting
a spastic to win gold medals in the Olympic Games.

An electoral alliance between 30,000 Communists and the
7 million strong Labour Party would be the union of the
chicken with the elephant. Nor was the Communist proposal
that they should affiliate to the Labour Party acceptable, for
we did not want two parties within our party.

It was no accident that the British Communist Party had

* After the way our pocket Stalinists have behaved over Hungary, the
Left in the Labour Party dislikes them as heartily as the Right.

been so politically ineffective throughout its forty years of existence, for it had all the way through mechanically copied Soviet models that had no application to British conditions. The Bolshevik Party was Lenin's original and brilliantly successful solution of the problem of how to organise a party that could function as an underground conspiracy and ultimately carry out a revolution and take power in Czarist Russia. His use of the soviets, a spontaneous creation of the 1905 Revolution, to found the revolutionary régime was equally brilliant. But to take all this as the model for winning power in our twentieth-century British Parliamentary democracy was merely silly.

Again, having taken a very good line for some years about the need for fighting Fascism, the British Communists discovered after the Stalin-Hitler friendship and non-aggression pact that the war was an imperialist war which should be opposed·by the British workers, and tried to run some kind of people's front for this purpose. I could understand how Stalin had been pushed into that position by the British Tories' policy of appeasement of Hitler in order to give him a free hand to expand eastwards and why, through the Comintern, Stalin had wanted to keep Communist parties from supporting Hitler's enemies, in order not to provoke that gentleman. But Britain was alone and fighting for her life against Hitler. And the British Communist line, as I had pointed out at the time in various articles, was a half-baked and dishonest imitation of Lenin's line of revolutionary defeatism, turning the imperialist war into a civil war, etc., in the First World War. Did our Communists, I had asked them, believe that our British democracy was more backward and oppressive than Hitler's Fascism, as Lenin had argued that Czarist Russia was the worst of the belligerents from a Socialist point of view? And did they think that with mechanised warfare and the air arm, when Hitler had over-run France in a few days, it was possible to overthrow our Government and afterwards organise a revolutionary defence against Hitler? The whole thing merely illustrated the truth of the old saying that everything in history happened twice, first as a tragedy and the second time as a farce.

Again, the British Communists at the end of the war had
caricatured Stalin's line of a national front of all patriotic and
anti-Fascist elements, by arguing that the Labour Party should
not attempt to win the post-war election alone, but should
enter a coalition with the Liberals and with the patriotic and
anti-appeasement Conservatives led by Churchill and Eden!
But we won a tremendous majority in 1945 single-handed.

Some years ago, with a flourish of trumpets, the British
Communists had brought out a pamphlet on *The British Road
to Socialism*, which turned out to be an attempt to transfer to
Britain the form of social revolution carried out in the People's
Democracies, after Fascism, Hitler occupation and the total
breakdown of the old order following the expulsion of Hitler's
armies.

It was this sort of nonsense that disqualified the British Communists from being taken seriously even by the Left in the
Labour Party and made them pretty unpopular all round. On
top of that the publication by the U.S. State Department of
what the Communist parties, like everyone else in the West,
believed was the authentic text of the report on "the consequences of the personality cult" made by Khrushchev to a
closed session of the 20th Congress on February 25th, had
plunged the British Communist Party into a major crisis and
faced it with an insoluble dilemma. Their dilemma was whether
to go on being Stalinists, i.e. to preserve their old monolithic
organisation as a conspiratorial revolutionary party, and their
old Soviet or 'People's Democracy' attitude to British Parlia-
mentarism, or, as a minority in the party were urging, to become in effect a left-wing Marxist Social Democratic Party.

In the former case the process of decay and discredit would
proceed in the already tiny and futile British C.P. In the latter
case the Communist Party would lose even its formal *raison
d'être*. For we did not have proportional representation, and
the Labour Party had an organic link with the trade unions
through their affiliated membership. Therefore, there was no
room in British politics nor lodgement in the working class for
two Social Democratic parties. Whereas there was plenty of
room in the British Labour Party for left-wing Marxist Social
Democrats. But they would have to come in on the Labour

Party's terms and not their own, i.e. as individuals with no other political ties and accepting the constitution, programme and principles of the Labour Party. That was the only way to achieve complete working-class unity in Britain.

On the international plane there was, however, a great deal to be said for contacts between the Labour Party and the Communist and working-class parties of the People's Democracies and the Soviet Union, provided the latter recognised the Labour Party as the authentic and official representative of the British working class and forebore to interfere in our internal affairs by advocating a popular front with the British Communist Party, which had no relevance to our circumstances. The Labour Party was, of course, a member of the Second International and in touch with the Asian Socialist parties. But there were many of us in the Labour Party who thought that we should go further and take a more active part through wider contacts in preparing the ground for the next Labour Government to make peace.

As for the trade unions, their position, as I understood it, was not that they refused contacts with Soviet trade unions. In fact, so far as I knew, every important British trade union had already paid visits to their opposite numbers in the Soviet Union or accepted invitations to do so, and *vice versa*. It was the next step that they were boggling at, viz. any kind of organised relationship or co-operation, in view of the difference in structure and functions of Soviet and British trade unions, as well as the background of conflict between the W.F.T.U. and the so-called free trade union organisation. I hoped that with patience and goodwill on both sides there would be progress in this field too.

The last question of all was on what the Labour Party means by Socialism. Here it is, with my answer

Q.: Tell us, please, what kind of Socialism do you Labour-ites want to build in Britain? Socialism in the spirit of Marx or something different?

A.: It was Marx who said that under Socialism the State would wither away and be replaced by a community in which freedom for the individual to develop all his faculties was the condition for the welfare of society as a whole. If that is what you mean by Socialism in the spirit of Marx, it is not far from Labour's conception of Socialism. For what we want is a society in which the vast forces of production, released by modern science, become, through public ownership and planning, the servants and not the masters of man, and are used by human beings to build a society in which all men are free, all men are equal, and all men are brothers. I believe that, however great are the differences between us Labour folk and our Soviet comrades on methods, and however tragic the history of our past differences, that too is the kind of society you want to build. I believe I speak the mind of my Party in saying that, if that is so, from the bottom of our hearts we wish you success in achieving that aim.

This lecture was on the afternoon of October 18th, five days before the beginning of the Hungarian revolt. If I had spoken a week later I would have put the point rather differently— if, in the circumstances, I had had an opportunity to put it at all. Be that as it may, I still think that what I told my Soviet audience that day about our sharing the aim of building a society where there is freedom and equality and democracy, on the basis of public ownership and planning in our economic life, remains true.

There is not much doubt that that really is the aim of very many in the coming generation in the C.P.S.U. and the country, that they care about these things and that they mean by them much what we do. Oddly enough, the reason for this last is that they have had to make such a thorough study of the Marxist-Leninist classics. For Marx and Lenin were in many respects the proletarian (and in the case of Lenin, Russi-fied) heirs of European revolutionary liberalism and of the British philosophical radicals. Stalin carried Russification to the point of eclipsing the European tradition of Communism and infusing elements of Asiatic despotism. But against the background of the modern, complex, literate Soviet society of to-day the European tradition is coming back into men's minds as they return to the Marxist-Leninist sources, or even, daringly, look beyond them into the history of Europe.

The longing for freedom and equality can never be wholly extinguished in human hearts, nor can men indefinitely be deceived into believing they already possess freedom when in fact they do not. That is as true of the absence of economic and social democracy under capitalism as it is of the lack of political democracy under Communism.

CHAPTER SEVEN

Talk with Khrushchev and Final Reflections

I HAD BEEN WARNED at the Soviet Embassy in London not to count on seeing Khrushchev, whom I had met on his and Bulganin's visit to England, but to write him on arrival in Moscow and hope for the best. This I did. The days passed. The end of my stay drew near and still no word came.

But that was according to form. It happened in 1947, when we (there were eight of us Labour M.Ps. that time) had asked to see Stalin. Then it was on the eve of our departure, at the end of a long talk with Molotov in the Kremlin, that he observed, just as we were saying goodbye, "I understand you have expressed a desire to see the head of our Government. Unfortunately, Comrade Stalin is not in Moscow and you are leaving to-morrow [pause—long faces]. But if you could stay on twenty-four hours longer we could take you down by 'plane to see him at Sochi on the Black Sea and fly you from there direct to Warsaw" (our next port of call).

This time I had had hints the morning before and a definite intimation the same evening. Professor Arzumanian, the Acting President of the Institute of World Economy and International Relations, said I might find something cropping up that interfered with the programme I was arranging for the next day. That evening at dinner my host told me he thought that next morning I might get the interview with N. S. Khrushchev for which I had asked. The next morning it was a matter not of taking a special 'plane for the Crimea, but of being picked up by a ZIS (a step up in the world—I had been going about in ZIM's up to then) at the Leningrad Hotel and whisked off to the Central Committee Headquarters dead on time for a ten o'clock interview (in Russia when stress is laid on punctuality it means you are dealing with someone really important —or with an eccentric).

A big barrack-like building on a main street, not in the Kremlin; long carpeted corridors; sentries and uniformed men at strategic points; smiles, heel-clicking, saluting. And then, after passing through various anterooms, a vast office with a long table for committee meetings, and beside it Nikita Sergeievich Khrushchev, First Secretary of the Central Committee of the C.P.S.U.

What sort of man is he? Milovan Djilas, the former Yugoslav Communist Leader, once described him as "a genial bandit without principles". Although not wholly·unrecognisable as a lightning sketch, that description springs from a jaundiced view and is unfair to Khrushchev. Sir William Hayter, then British Ambassador in Moscow, was nearer the mark: he had told me at luncheon two days before that when the Foreign Office had asked him to describe Khrushchev he had replied that Mr. Khrushchev reminded him of Ernest Bevin. As I had been saying ever since meeting Khrushchev in London that he was a Russian Ernest Bevin, I was delighted: both earthy, forthright characters, colourful personalities, with plenty of confidence and drive and a habit of command. But the Ukrainian ex-miner Khrushchev has the lively temperament of the South, the wide knowledge of a trained Marxist, and the rich and often harrowing experience of the Russian Revolution, of the wars against counter-revolution and intervention, of the tremendous effort to lay the economic foundations of Socialism and of twenty years in Stalin's Secretariat, including the years of the Terror.

Short, chunky, full of bounce and *bonhomie*, highly intelligent, with a face that would go like a breeze on TV*—a homely, humorous face with irregular features, small eyes snapping with life, a wart on each side of a very Russian potato nose. The whole marked with the lines of effort, experience and suffering, but alight with vitality—which does not necessarily mean saintliness. Rather far from it in this case. Instead, warmth and wit, a salty character with a kind of ferocious geniality, even charm. Behind it all, a faith for which the man would

* Since then it has!

die—or kill others. A formidable personality, but withal, as an American journalist put it, "He's so damn' human you can't help liking the guy."

Khrushchev received me with great cordiality. He said he had heard much about my doings and sayings on international affairs over the years and considered that "your line towards us has all along been correct and consistent". To which I was tempted to make the obvious retort: "Well, it's been consistent, anyway. I didn't know you had always thought it correct." But I bit off that crack on the tip of my tongue. The years of Stalin's Terror were such a nightmare, and those mixed up in it feel so sick and sensitive about the whole ghastly business, that a jocose allusion to it, even with the best of intentions, might have been misunderstood.

So I made amiable noises and we sat down—this time to vodka and cigarettes for a change, with tea as a chaser. The conversation lasted two hours and was desultory, friendly and wandering. A good deal of it was confidential. But since our talk on October 18th so much has happened that the substance of what Khrushchev told me then has since come out, in the controversy with the Yugoslavs over Hungary and in connection with other international developments. So that I do not feel I am violating a confidence by telling of these matters now. Here is the substance of what Khrushchev told me:

The Soviet Union wanted peaceful active co-existence with the rest of the world and an end to the arms race and the cold war, for the plain reason that to end them was very much to her interest. War would be suicidal for all concerned because of the destructive power of nuclear weapons. The cold war was a nuisance that got nobody anywhere, and the arms race was diverting precious labour and raw materials from the great constructive projects to which the Soviet people wanted to harness their energies.* On the other hand, given peace and

* Cf. Defence Minister Duncan Sandys in the House on April 16th, 1957. "During my visit to Russia last summer I saw something of the vast programme of social and industrial work upon which the Soviet Government are engaged. With those immense schemes of domestic reconstruction on hand, it is hard to see how the Russians, any more than we, can have any interest in war, or any desire to go on spending so much of their substance upon military preparations."

trade, the Socialist economic system would show itself so over-whelmingly superior to the waste, disorder, social injustice and exploitation of capitalism, that it would, in time, win over the rest of humanity, although in each country the build-ing of Socialism would be the job of the workers and their political allies, according to their own conditions and tradi-tions. Peace was fatal to capitalism because then Socialism would inherit the earth.

He hoped that the capitalist governments had been cured at last of the folly of believing that they could build up posi-tions of strength from which they could intimidate the Soviet Union into yielding to their demands. If not, they would have to learn the hard way that they were attempting the impos-sible. To-day the people of the Soviet Union felt secure from aggression and threats because they knew their country pos-sessed all the latest weapons and had China as an ally, with its enormous hinterland and inexhaustible man-power.

The Soviet Union was rejoicing in a bumper crop, the biggest in the history of the country. It was a triumph for the policy of putting the virgin lands in Asiatic Russia and Western Siberia under the plough. There was now an abund-ance of vegetables and dairy produce* as well as corn. The peasants had produced so much butter that they did not know what to do with it. It had been suggested that it should be exported. But he had said no, better lower the price and let our people eat it themselves. Next year they would have all the meat they wanted and for the first time the Soviet people would have an abundance of every kind of food. It was part of the Sixth Five Year Plan to raise the national standard of living by thirty per cent. not later than 1960. He was confident they would achieve that aim.

The cause of peaceful co-existence seemed to be making head-way among working-class parties everywhere. The C.P.S.U. would like contacts and discussions with Social-Democratic parties on the best ways of ending the cold war, achieving

* Ralph Parker, former Moscow correspondent of *The Times*, then of the *Daily Worker* and at present of several American and Continental papers, told me he was now getting milk delivered regularly at his flat and could order as much as he liked, the same as in London.

agreements on disarmament and negotiating settlements based
on the five principles of the Bandung Conference. The visit
of the delegation from the Executive of the French Socialist
Party on the invitation of the Central Committee of the
C.P.S.U. had, on the whole, been a success, and certainly the
atmosphere during their stay in the Soviet Union had been
excellent and the discussions frank and cordial in tone. But on
their return, he complained, some members of that delegation
had taken a line which hardly seemed consistent with what
they had been saying while in the Soviet Union. As for the
Labour Party, it looked, said Mr. Khrushchev, as though
some of its leaders were unwilling to contemplate any kind
of contacts, even in the interests of peace, with the Soviet
Communist Party.

At this point I put in the suggestion that policy was more
important than procedure, and that the decisions on defence
and foreign policy taken by the Labour Party at Blackpool
were of more significance than the fact that the Conference
had rejected my own motion on talks between the Labour
Party and the parties ruling the U.S.S.R. and the People's
Democracies. The policy resolutions adopted by the Conference were, I thought, within negotiable distance of the Soviet
position on these questions. As for Gorton's 'procedural' resolution, which I had moved, calling for talks between the Labour
Party and the East European and Soviet Communist Parties,
it had been rejected by Conference partly because it had been
confused with the question of a popular front with Communists at home, which almost no one in the Labour Party
wanted, but mostly because the majority of delegates considered that it was too early to judge the extent and meaning
of the changes that had occurred in the Soviet Union, and to
know whether the parties in the People's Democracies were
really functioning as independent parties, or were still under
the orders of the C.P.S.U. leadership, as they had been in
Stalin's day.

What it seemed to me justified the belief that common
ground existed between us were the international policy resolutions that the Conference had passed. I translated the
resolutions on disarmament, on the hydrogen bomb and on

Germany, and asked him what he thought of the latter. Was it not near enough to the Soviet position to provide an acceptable basis of negotiation?

Mr. Khrushchev was cagey at first, saying that he had not really followed these matters. But on my insisting, he admitted, cautiously, that yes, it did denote a considerable step forward. But it did not go far enough. It still treated the unification of Germany in a mechanical manner, whereas the real point was the existence of two different societies in the two halves of Germany and the necessity for the Germans in east and west to agree with each other on the procedure for uniting their country and what to do about the new Soviet order in Eastern Germany. However, if not a basis, Labour's proposals could at least be a starting point for negotiations.

No disagreement, he said, with the H-bomb resolution, so far as it went. In the disarmament resolution the Labour Party were proposing the kind of unilateral action for Britain that the Soviet Government had in fact taken already.

But what I most wanted to hear from Mr. Khrushchev's own lips was what he had to say of the changes resulting from the end of the 'personality cult', and I was now able to bring the conversation round to this topic. Accordingly, I said I had been much interested by the reference in the Central Committee's declaration of June 30th on "overcoming the personality cult and its consequences", to collective leadership, internal party democracy and Soviet democracy. The meaning of collective leadership was plain enough. But what did internal party democracy and Soviet democracy mean? Did inner-Party democracy mean what it meant in the days of Lenin? In those days big issues were raised and thrashed out by the rank and file during discussions in which not only individuals, but groups, supported contending points of view and discussed them hotly, until a Congress or at least the Central Committee plenum, took a decision—after which, under the rules of "democratic centralism", minorities had to accept and help to carry out the decisions of the majority.

"No," said Khrushchev, "the revolution was then still in the formative stage and there were some issues on which the Central Committee could not reach agreement, so that the matter was referred to the whole Party membership. To-day we are no longer in that situation. Democracy in the Party means that when the Central Committee adopts a policy, it will be referred as a draft to the rank and file for fullest discussion, in the light of which the Central Committee will modify and improve its draft, before being submitted through the Government to the Supreme Soviet. As for Soviet democracy, it means that the elected soviets will sit longer, have more work to do and generally play a bigger part in public life. They will supervise the working of the machinery of Government, and, in the republics and their soviets, discuss and amend the draft laws submitted to them. But the guiding and organising force in them, as well as in the trade unions and the collective farms, will be the C.P.S.U."

He stressed how much had been done in the way of cutting down the numbers and powers of the political police and letting out those serving sentences on charges of "counter-revolutionary activities". "We have let an awful lot out and not put anyone in," was his summing up on that score.

He told the story of how, on his recent visit to a Black Sea watering resort with Marshal Tito, he found himself sitting beside an old gentleman, lightly clad, as they were, in a pair of bathing trunks and also taking his ease in the sea air and sunshine in a deck chair on the beach.

"Suddenly, he leaned over to me," said Khrushchev, "and whispered, 'Comrade Khrushchev, I was in for eighteen years. But all that is finished now, isn't it? Those are my wife and children over there. Now we are all together again.'"

"You know," said Khrushchev, "he might have shouted all that at me and denounced the Government for having done these things to him, but, no, he saw I was with foreigners and so he whispered, because he didn't want them to hear. He knew it was all right now and all that was over and he was not bitter or despairing. That is the spirit of our people."

That gave me the opportunity I wanted for asking just what took place between him and Tito during their talks in South Russia, about which, as I explained to him, there had been feverish interest in the West. "The Yugoslav Press Bureau," I commented, "says there were disagreements between you, but did not say what they were. What was it all about? Then, too, what was this business about the letter you are supposed to have sent out, not only to the members of the C.P.S.U., but even to some other Communist parties, telling them that Yugoslav Communism was not quite the thing and should not be copied?"

In reply, he began with generalities, true no doubt, but hardly new, about the renewal of Soviet-Yugoslav friendship, and how solid and unshakable it was, how the old quarrels had been ended for good and so forth. But finally he got down to it. "Yes," he said, "there were disagreements. I will tell you what they were, but this is for you: We do consider that Yugoslav Communism is not 100% Marxist-Leninist. It has been a bit adulterated with Social-Democracy, and it has become a little distorted during the years when Yugoslavia was dependent on the capitalist States. It is true Soviet policy under Stalin was responsible for creating a situation in which they had no alternative. But that has nevertheless had certain consequences affecting Yugoslav Communism. Their peasants are still a primitive and anarchic element and the régime will probably have trouble with them one day. Then, too, they have carried the idea of workers' management in factories to the pitch of inefficiency and fragmentation of planning. But these things are the internal affair of the Yugoslavs and not our concern. It is for them to arrange matters in their own country as they see fit.

"On the other hand, when it came to international relations, I could not quite understand Comrade Tito's attitude to the socialist camp. I said to him, 'You are a socialist State too, so why don't you join our camp?' But Comrade Tito kept saying no, he did not want to join. When I asked him, 'Well, all right, you don't want to join the socialist camp, so where do you belong—surely not in the capitalist camp?' Comrade Tito said no, he did not, but he did not want to belong to the socialist camp either. He did not want to be in any camp. But how can he say that—he must belong somewhere."

My comment on this was: "Look here, after all, you said in your report to the Central Committee that there was a group of States, both socialist and non-socialist in their internal structures, that made it a cardinal principle of their foreign policy not to belong to either camp, and that they constituted a major factor for peace. Why cannot Yugoslavia make her contribution to peace through being a member of this 'uncommitted' group?"

"That group," said Khrushchev, "consists of countries that have only just freed themselves from the yoke of colonialism and are taking their first steps as independent States. Yugoslavia does not belong to that category—after all, she is a fully developed socialist State, so her natural place is with us."

"But cannot Yugoslavia in her present position act as a bridge between East and West?" I asked.

"*Shatki most*" ("A shaky bridge"), was Khrushchev's comment, accompanied by a dubious shake of the head.

It was plain that in Khrushchev's view the "uncommitted" group of States was a sort of infant class or prep. school through which ex-colonial countries pass before graduating as socialist States and joining the Socialist camp (or alternatively, as he would see it, succumbing once more to the yoke of colonialism in the capitalist camp). But he ended his analysis of Soviet-Yugoslav differences as he had begun, by stressing that they were unimportant as compared with the wide area on which the two parties and governments saw eye to eye. "The main thing is that we now discuss our respective views freely, as comrades. Patience and time is all we need to clear up our differences and show where the truth lies."

This led naturally to the second topic on which I particularly wanted to hear Khrushchev's views—the relations between Russia and her East European allies. I did not then know the tragic urgency that this question was to acquire in the next few days, nor did Khrushchev mention that he was leaving for Poland next day. Indeed, it is far from certain that he even knew it himself at that time, for, according to Polish accounts I heard later, it was a last-minute decision carried in the Party Praesidium against strong opposition.

I asked him whether the declarations on inter-State and inter-party relations adopted in Moscow on June 20th by Bulganin and Tito and himself and Tito applied only to Soviet-Yugoslav relations, or were to be taken as the model for future relations between the Soviet Union and all the People's Democracies?

"They apply to our relations with all the People's Democracies," said Khrushchev firmly.

"Does that mean that the parties and governments of the People's Democracies can discuss matters and reach agreements with each other without having to secure the approval of Moscow, as they had to under Stalin?"

"Certainly it does," said Khrushchev. "But sometimes a Party comes to us and asks for help in solving some problem, and then we do not want just to send them away, for that would be discourteous and unhelpful. I have just had a case of that sort, when a Party from a People's Democracy asked me about a problem that they really ought to have been able to settle for themselves. In such cases we say, 'Well, Comrades, since you ask us, we would suggest that perhaps the matter could be dealt with on such and such lines. But of course it is your affair and you may well think some other solution preferable.'"

That was interesting, but not really to the point. What Khrushchev had said, in effect, was that some Parties were still asking Moscow to help them solve their own internal affairs. Whereas what I had asked was whether the Parties and Governments in the People's Democracies could discuss their mutual relations without benefit of Moscow. The answer here, too, would appear to be that they could if they wanted to, but would presumably bear in mind the feelings and interests of their great ally.

Khrushchev went on to say that the very fact that the bonds had been loosened between the Communist Parties, that the Cominform had been dissolved, and that each was now free to go its own way, had made it necessary to try to work out some up-to-date forms for contact and discussion between them. "Of course, we must be careful to avoid the imputation that we are trying to revive the Cominform. The contacts must be on more elastic and different lines. But they must be effective. I can tell you now that these matters are being studied, and one of the first things we will do is to bring out some kind of common discussion journal, in which all Communist and workers' parties can air their views and benefit by each other's experience. Remember, I told you that this journal is going to be launched in the next few months.''

The final point I asked may seem rather theoretical, but it drew an illuminating answer: "I have just been re-reading Lenin's *The State and Revolution*," I said, "and was struck by how strongly he emphasises that the State is the outcome of the irreconcilable nature of the clash between rival class interests, and is the organ by which the dominant class upholds its interests against those of the oppressed classes. Now, as early as in your Constitution of 1936 you proclaimed that there were no longer irreconcilable class interests in the Soviet Union, because you had a socialist society. Well, why is the State so powerful and showing no signs of withering away? And how can you have a State Plan without a State?"

"We must have a strong State," replied Khrushchev, "because of the danger of attack from the capitalist world. How can we relax or diminish the powers of the State or the strength of its armed forces so long as we are constantly menaced? In so far as the State is now organising economic life, it is no longer the coercive State in Lenin's sense, but simply the community taking care of its common concerns by systematic joint action. That is a permanent function."

In Stalin's heyday the State was glorified and the increase of its powers of coercion identified with building socialism. Khrushchev's reply showed a considerable change in what might be called the ideological and practical attitude of the régime on this crucial point, but also the virtual abandonment of the 'withering away of the State' in any but a Pickwickian sense.

Khrushchev was as frank as he was cordial—but he was adroit. There were obviously clear limits in his mind to the processes of inner-Party and Soviet democracy, and freedom and equality between the Soviet Union and the small People's Democracies were bounded by the concept of the Socialist camp and the need for unity in face of a still hostile capitalist world. I wrote in my diary that evening that I thought he had learned the negative lesson that coercion tends to disintegrate the Socialist camp, but did not understand that freedom could act as a cement. Twenty-four hours after that came the Soviet visit to Warsaw, and a few days later the rising in Hungary and its savage repression. But I believe Khrushchev had to rally to majority decisions on those matters.

After the morning with Khrushchev, I still had a day and a half in hand before taking off for Belgrade. They were as crowded as the rest with talks and farewell visits.

Among others, I met the veteran economist Varga, the Hungarian Communist who fled to the Soviet Union after the downfall of the Bela Kun Government in 1919 and the installation with the help of the Allies of the white dictatorship and terror of Admiral Horthy. He is one of the old teachers who have been brought out of retirement and are lecturing to students at the university. Now seventy-five, he is mentally as alert as ever and was busy writing a book. But his eyes, he explained, were now too bad to write except in full daylight, so that his working hours were short. This frail, gentle little old man with a green eyeshade lives in a roomy flat over-flowing with books in the remote quarter of Moscow containing the numerous buildings of the University and the Academy of Science. He was very proud of the wonderful view of the city from his balcony.

Like other Communists of Jewish origin that I met in Moscow and Warsaw, he went out of his way to rub in his anti-Zionist and anti-Israeli sentiments and to take a 100% "assimilationist" line. My reply was that even in our "unenlightened" capitalist society, I had many Jewish friends who managed to be good Zionists and good British patriots too, including Members of Parliament, and that it seemed to me, speaking as a Gentile myself, that there was room for tolerance and elasticity in these matters.

There is, of course, in the anti-Zionism in these régimes a substratum of the old anti-Semitism, coupled with the un-willingness of a totalitarian régime to allow any of its citizens, whether Catholics, Jews or Boy Scouts, to feel any kind of loyalty to some body or authority beyond the frontier. And, of course, the strident anti-Israeli and anti-Zionist assimila-tionist sentiments of citizens of these countries of Jewish origin is a certificate of orthodoxy in their Communist opinions and a sort of political insurance policy.

During the last thirty-six hours, and in the long 'plane journey (from 7 a.m. to 4.15 p.m.) from Moscow to Belgrade, I reflected on all I had seen and heard in those ten days. One thing as plain as a pikestaff was that Soviet society had outgrown the semi-Asiatic methods by which Stalin jerked a primitive, illiterate, mostly peasant community, with an infiltration of nomads and other half-civilised peoples, up to the position of the second industrial power in the world.

Stalin did in the twentieth century what Peter the Great did in the eighteenth and by much the same methods. This is a view generally taken by Soviet leaders themselves. Nor was there much dissent from the remark that, whereas Stalin had begun like Peter the Great, he ended like Ivan the Terrible.

The present conditions and the present mood are different. In British terms the difference is a little like the disappearance of the Victorian conception of leading statesmen as tremendous figures, almost demi-gods to their contemporary public. Stalin was all that and more. But Soviet society has now expanded and its leaders have shrunk to the point where the relations between them are devoid of the awful overtones of Stalin's chieftainship.

In Stalin's day, the political police had become a power, greater than the Party or the Government, which was at his private disposal. After his death, Beria tried to use his position as Head of the Secret Police in order to gather supreme power into his own hands. That was why he was treated to his own medicine, i.e. branded as a traitor and foreign agent, secretly tried and shot.

Of the present leaders, Molotov and Kaganovich go back all the way to the Revolution, as does Khrushchev. But none of them played a big enough part in those heroic days to be able to boast of any revolutionary glamour. That is even more true of Bulganin, who is a 'civilian' Marshal with no martial record to speak of. Malenkov belongs to the post-revolutionary generation.

Of them all, Molotov, at one time, looked the most likely successor to Stalin. Tito told me once how, on his visits to

Stalin, he always found him sharing an office with Molotov. In those days the two were very close, and Stalin consulted Molotov more than anyone else. But for that very reason, and because of his age (he is now sixty-eight), Molotov was outstripped by events. The changes that occurred were so big and so rapid that he smacked too much of the past to have a future in post-Stalin Russia.

His stone-walling line in foreign policy, although dictated to him by Stalin, made him unsuitable for the more elastic and conciliatory policies pursued since the death of Stalin. It was he, who, with Stalin, signed the offensive letters that started the historic row with Tito. It was therefore logical that he should disappear from the front of the stage when the Government's policy was to end that quarrel.

Kaganovich is an organiser of genius, but has never been a political figure in the same class as the front-rank leaders. His role is essentially that of an outsize glorified backroom boy. He too belongs to the older generation that has been left behind by the march of time.

Marshal Bulganin is smooth and polished—an admirable foil to that very rough diamond, Mr. Khrushchev, but without his dynamism. "He looks so like a stage Southern colonel that you expect him to offer a mint julep," said an American journalist.

All these men, of course, are vastly experienced, extremely able and tough. The ablest of them all perhaps is the youngest, Georgi Maximilianovich Malenkov.

Malenkov's tour of Britain was an astonishing performance: here was a Soviet leader who had never been abroad in his life. He was only seventeen at the time of the Revolution, so that his whole experience as an adult has been in Soviet Russia. He knew no foreign language. He came over as the head of a technical mission after his demotion from the post of Prime Minister and a few weeks before the State visit of Bulganin and Khrushchev.

In that difficult and complex situation he seemed to sense the atmosphere, never put a foot wrong, charmed everyone he met and was genial and at ease with everyone, high or low, of any political opinion or none. With it all he gave the

impression not only of subtle intelligence, but of goodwill and
humanity.

Bulganin and Khruschev handled their 'off-the-cuff' answers
at a big Press conference to British and foreign journalists
admirably. They showed that the new leaders are not afraid of
meeting and arguing with representatives of the capitalist
world at any level. But Bulganin lacked the common touch
and in Khrushchev it was too common—he was crude and
opinionated on several occasions. Malenkov combined the
qualities of both and seemed to be free of the defects of
either.

But the whole attitude of these men and their relation to
their own public and to the representatives of foreign countries
in Moscow (the mass invitations to diplomats and foreign
journalists to attend State receptions, etc.) are so different
from Stalin's that the way back would seem to be closed. Nor
is any of them likely to forget the fact, pointed out in Khrushchev's secret report, that in the last few months of his life
Stalin had reached the point, with or without Beria's prompting, when he was getting ready to massacre most of the Politbureau, including the present leaders. "We must hang together
lest we hang separately" is one excellent reason why the
present leadership is determined to remain collective.

But how far all the good intentions about inner-Party and
Soviet democracy will develop is another matter. Here too the
changes have been so big and the public attitude so different
that the country could never go back to the conditions under
Stalin. But they still have a long way to go before catching up
with Western ideas of democracy and political freedom. The
only thing clear is that to-day, as always in the history of the
Soviet Union, internal developments will continue to be
conditioned by the international situation.

By the time I left Moscow very early in the morning of
October 21st it was already known that Khrushchev had left
precipitately for Warsaw at the head of a high-power delegation from the Praesidium of the Party. It was also known that
they had been told on arrival that the plenum of the Polish
Central Committee was a private affair to which they could not
be admitted. It was obvious that they must have gone to protest

against the appointment of Gomulka and all that that meant, and had been more or less snubbed by the Polish leaders.

Beyond that, at that date, I knew nothing. But even that was difficult to reconcile with what Khrushchev had told me about the two agreements with Tito on June 20th being the model for the relations between the Soviet Union and the other People's Democracies, and between the C.P.S.U. and their governing parties.

I remembered how, on Stalin's seventieth birthday, during the height of the quarrel with Tito, Khrushchev, as Editor of *Pravda*, the C.P.S.U.'s official newspaper, on December 21st, 1949, wrote a leader, which, after the usual panegyrics about the great man, contained the following passage: "Loyalty to the great cause of Lenin-Stalin, to the cause of internationalism, is determined and tested by the attitude towards the Soviet Union, which stands at the head of all the forces of democracy and Socialism. Betrayal of the Soviet Union, betrayal of proletarian internationalism, inevitably leads to the camp of nationalism, or Fascism, the camp of Imperialist reaction. An example of this is the Tito-Rankovich gang of murderers and spies which has completed the transition from nationalism to Fascism, which has turned into a direct agent of Imperialism and become its tool in the fight against Socialism and democracy.

"The freedom-loving peoples of the world, all progressive mankind, brand these traitors with the mark of shame and rally still closer around the great and invincible banner of Lenin-Stalin for a resolute struggle against the enemies of the Soviet Union, against the enemies of proletarian internationalism."

Of course, all that had been repudiated and condemned with bell, book and candle. But that outlook had been the official one for twenty years and the present generation of Soviet leaders had been brought up in and conditioned by it for most of their adult lives. Moreover, it was the ideological rationalisation of something much older: the view that the national interests, particularly the security interests of a great power over-ride any interests of smaller and weaker neighbours. The latter had had to draw close to the Soviet Union and accept its leadership because their régimes felt themselves threatened from the West and by sections of their own people, and depended for their survival on Soviet economic and military support.

Stalin had abused this one-sided relationship so monstrously as to drive first the Yugoslavs and now—since the evil that men do lives after them—in different and milder form the Poles, to revolt (I did not know that two days later the same would be true of Hungary, which would go beyond both Yugoslavia and Poland). The present leaders were doing their best to rectify Stalin's mistakes—but how far could they go without the contradiction emerging between their security interests as a great power and the pattern for relations of equality, freedom and friendship between Socialist States, that they had accepted on paper in their agreements with Yugoslavia?

In this connection I thought too of what Khrushchev had told me about his idea of a new international review or journal, for discussion and exchanges of information and views between the parties of the 'Socialist Commonwealth' (a phrase beginning to creep into Soviet usage even then, but that has become current since), backed by some kind of permanent contacts between these parties.

The Cominform journal until the break with Yugoslavia was published in Belgrade, the headquarters of the Cominform. It was edited by a Soviet Communist, Mr. Judin, who imported his own staff, worked behind locked doors and had at his disposal a special plane to rush the proofs of each edition to Moscow for censorship before publication. Even signed articles by leading Communists of other countries were slashed, rewritten or 'spiked'. Once, after 200 or 300 copies had already been printed, a whole issue was condemned and scrapped on orders from Moscow. The Cominform journal bore not the faintest resemblance to the picture of a 'discussion organ' between the different national parties that it was supposed to be, and was, of course, appallingly dull and badly written.

Presumably the present leadership do not intend to go back to anything like that. But how far will they go forward to the kind of genuine freedom of inter-Party discussion desired by the Yugoslavs and the Poles?

The ten days in Moscow had posed more questions than they had answered. But three things at any rate were clear: the widespread and intense desire for peace and friendly relations with the rest of the world. The very real determination to clean up and have done with the evils and horrors of the Stalin era. Great national pride in the achievements of Soviet society and boundless faith in the future.

CHAPTER EIGHT

The New Mecca

I FOUND BELGRADE inundated by a stream of delegations. There were trade union, Parliamentary and Party delegations from the Socialist States, and from Asian and other 'uncommitted' countries, and delegations from European Socialist parties and from the Italian Communist Party. The stream had been flowing for months and was still running strongly, with no end in sight. My old Yugoslav friends were distracted and overworked from coping with the hordes of distinguished visitors—but felt that it was all almost as flattering as it was overwhelming. "If you will set up in business as a new Mecca, what else can you expect?" I asked. They laughed and replied that they felt like the man who prayed for rain and got a cloudburst.

My first visit to post-war Yugoslavia had been in November 1945. Tito had given a general invitation to British M.Ps. to come over and see for themselves how the Yugoslavs understood democracy. I was one of the eleven who went (Tito sent his own plane for us) and was deeply interested by all I saw. There was much that reminded me of Russia in the early days of the Revolution.

After that I visited the country annually, learnt Serbo-Croat and followed Yugoslav affairs as closely as I could. Then came the thunder-clap of the Cominform denunciation of Tito and the Yugoslav Communists in June 1948. As soon as the House rose, I went there to find out what it was all about. I was the first Westerner to see Marshal Tito after the break, and he spoke very frankly and, as it proved, prophetically: the issue, he said, was a new one that was bound to be raised sooner or later, for it involved a principle of vital importance—namely, what should be the relations between Socialist States. Not Parties, Tito emphasised, but States. These relations must be close and fraternal, not those of exploiter and exploited or potential enemies, as in the case of capitalist States. They must be based on the equal rights and common interests of all, great or small, and not on a big fellow keeping the little ones in order with a club.

"I'm glad it has fallen to us to settle this issue once for all," said Tito. "Any other Communist Party would have broken before Stalin. But we shan't. We're going to stand up to him."*

He thought there was an element of misunderstanding in the whole business and that when the Soviet leaders found they had been mistaken in believing that Yugoslavia would enter the Western camp and start restoring capitalism, and that, on the contrary, the Yugoslavs maintained their independence and went on building Socialism, they would come round and put an end to the quarrel.

All through 1948 Stalin expected the collapse of the Yugoslav Communist Party that had dared to defy him, while the Yugoslavs went on hoping that Stalin would see reason and agree to some face-saving compromise. But just before I went out to Yugoslavia again in September 1949, a friend in the Czechoslovak Embassy warned me that "All hope of a compromise has now disappeared. Stalin has made up his mind to liquidate the Tito régime." "Oh!" I said. "He has, has he? Well, how does he propose to do the job—by war?" "Oh! no," said my Czech friend. "By peaceful means." "And how long does he reckon that is going to take him? I think he may find Tito a tougher nut to crack than he thinks." "Oh, Stalin knows what he is doing. He is thinking in terms of three or four years." Long before that Stalin had lost the game, and at the end of four years it was he and the Cominform who had disappeared, not Tito.

But that autumn—1949—I found my Yugoslav friends strained and worried. Stalin had tried everything—first to

* Cf. Khrushchev's remark in his secret report on Stalin's boast that he would shake his little finger and Tito would disappear: "In the end he shook everything he could shake, but Tito didn't budge."

split the leadership (the secret Cominform letters); then to turn the rank and file against the leaders (the public Cominform resolution); then to goad the people into revolt against the régime (the boycott measures applied under Soviet orders by all the Cominform States that nearly wrecked the Yugoslav economy and created great distress); then military threats (the troop movements and preparations on Yugoslavia's Cominform frontiers, accompanied by floods of terror propaganda on the air, by leaflets, agents, etc.).

As that had not worked either, the only thing left seemed to be to go to war, and this, the Yugoslavs reckoned, might be Stalin's next move. They were by no means certain whether they would get Western support if that happened, for at this stage the West, although it had given up hoping that Tito might be overthrown by a counter-revolution in Yugoslavia—which was what I found the wiseacres in the Western embassies in Belgrade gleefully predicting in 1948—was still far from seeing the importance of supporting Tito's stand for independence.

The only man I talked with then who seemed completely relaxed and unconcerned was Marshal Tito himself. But even he admitted that he did not like the latest development: "So long as they were moving troops about by day that was only part of their nerve war and did not bother me. But I now have information of troop concentrations and military build-ups near our frontiers that are going on by night and very secretly. I do not like that." However, he said, if attacked the Yugoslavs would fight and go on fighting, even if they had to take to the mountains, as they did against Hitler, until their country was free again. But he did not think it would come to that after all.

I spent one evening with a group of Yugoslav leaders at the home of one of them. Nobody put it into words directly, but a sense of strain and apprehension hung over the talk on the general position. Finally they turned to me and said: "Look here. When are some of you Socialists in the West going to speak out about this business? You know we are standing for a principle that concerns you as much as it does us."

I explained that the reason why the Left in the West had

been keeping quiet so far was partly because we had clung to the hope of the whole thing ending in a compromise and did not want to add fuel to the fires of the cold war. The Left wanted an accommodation with the Soviet Union through negotiation and compromise, and did not want to give a handle to those who thought in terms of preparing for or threatening war as an instrument of their policy towards the Soviet Union. And we wanted our country to be independent of the United States, as much as the Yugoslavs wanted to be independent of the Soviet Union. But beyond a certain point a political question ceased to be merely political and became a moral issue, where it was one's duty to speak out and tell the truth, regardless of consequences. I believed that point had been reached now in the Soviet-Yugoslav conflict, and when I returned home I would say exactly what I thought.

So I did, and there was quite an uproar in the Cominform countries and the U.S.S.R. From then on I was regarded by the Yugoslavs as a friend, which indeed I was, and also a bit of a hero, which I was not: I never could get them to understand that there was nothing heroic in denouncing Soviet policies in Britain.

Once the break with the Soviet Union was complete, the Yugoslavs, in the usual Communist way, rationalised the whole business ideologically. They began a root-and-branch critique of Stalinism that anticipated in many ways what is now being said in the Soviet Union. But they went a good deal further.

The trouble, they concluded, was that Stalin had failed to take the necessary next step after the Revolution, which was to begin the withering away of the Socialist State. The first stage, wrote Milovan Djilas, then one of the four secretaries of the Central Committee (the others were Tito, First Secretary; Kardelj; and Rankovich) and the top authority on matters of ideology, in a pamphlet, *Reflections on Problems of Our Time*, was that the Socialist State, which was the dictatorship of the proletariat, representing those who had won the social revolution, took over the means of production. This stage was really State capitalism. It must give way as quickly as possible to far-reaching measures of democratisation and workers' management, or it would harden into a bureaucracy, that in time would become a totalitarian tyranny, as had happened under Stalin.

One of the most striking analyses of Soviet Communism from this point of view appeared in the Yugoslav Party review, *Komunist*, of January 1st, 1951. The author was a young member of the Central Committee, Najdan Pasic, who specialised in Soviet affairs. Much of what he wrote then anticipated what is being said now, just as the Yugoslav reforms after the break with the Cominform countries in many ways foreshadowed the processes of de-Stalinisation since the 20th Congress of the C.P.S.U.

Mr. Pasic's article, entitled "The Distortion of Marxist Teachings about the State", analysed what he calls the "fetishisation of the Soviet State" by the Soviet (Party) bureaucracy, who thereby enhanced their own authority. His central argument is that the Socialist State must be melted down into the people through economic and political democracy, or it will harden into a tyranny that is above the people and oppresses the people. Either the Socialist State withers away or it swells into a totalitarian State.

"The strengthening of the bureaucratic apparatus of the State to the point where it becomes omnipotent and the mass of the people are deprived of all rights," he further points out, "has since time immemorial been accompanied by one characteristic phenomenon—the creation of a personality cult of the head of the State administrative machine, as the personification of the State itself. In the eyes of the millions from whom submission and absolute obedience is required, the personality of him in whom the omnipotent power of the State becomes flesh must appear in an aura of supernatural, god-like qualities. That, incidentally, is entirely in line with the spirit of bureaucratic hierarchy, in which at every degree a man's merits are determined by the position he occupies; he who occupies the peak position automatically and as a matter of course possesses all the highest qualities, human and superhuman. The present position of the personality of Stalin in the U.S.S.R. is a typical example of this bureaucratic idolatry. . . . He is a God-sent military leader, a statesman and administrator of genius, an infallible diplomat, the summit of philosophical thought, the supreme and omniscient authority in every field of science and art."

Mr. Pasic traces the whole process, step by step, through the proceedings of the 1933 and 1934 Congresses, the pronouncements of Stalin, and the writings of Soviet jurists, of the elevation and apotheosis of the leader, and of the development of the doctrine that the strengthening of the State, and particularly of its police and security organs, was necessary in face of the external enemy and also in order to build Socialism and even to effect the transition from Socialism to Communism.

Their criticisms of Soviet Communism were also the ideological justification for the changes which the Yugoslav Communists began to work out in their own social and political organisation, that had been based on Soviet models. But in fact what they were doing was partly to adapt themselves to national traditions, partly to react emotionally against their uncritically pro-Soviet past, and partly to yield to practical necessities. They had over-industrialised and over-centralised and the need for relief in both directions had become imperative.

And so the autonomy of the different Republics in the Yugoslav Federation was made a reality. There was greater decentralisation in industry and planning. The criminal code was revised. Whereas hitherto its main concern had been the protection of the State against the individual, now something had to be done, said Yugoslav jurists, to safeguard the rights of the individual against the State. The numbers and powers of the political police were reduced and the force was put under strict Party and Governmental control. The Courts were freed from Party interference and their importance and independence was stressed. The Federal and Republican Parliaments were given a greater share in controlling the activities of the Government, and their functions of initiating, approving and amending legislation, which had previously been a mere formality, was taken more seriously. The electoral law was interpreted so as to encourage the putting forward of more than one candidate in every constituency.*

* For a full-length account of the Yugoslav revolution, the break with Stalin and subsequent developments in Yugoslavia, see my book, *Tito of Yugoslavia* (Michael Joseph).

The boldest experiment in Yugoslav social planning has been the system of workers' (including all staff) management in factories and public enterprises. At first they went into this with more zeal than discretion and applied to economic life Macaulay's dictum that self-government is better than good government. There was so much local initiative and going it alone that the economy of the country got into grave difficulties.

With experience the system has improved steadily, and a compromise has now been reached between local self-government and the needs of a planned economy, although to this day the Russians and the Czechs look upon the whole thing as amateurish and inefficient. It probably is, like a good deal else in Yugoslavia—the Yugoslavs are better at heroic improvisation than at systematic organisation. During the height of the row with the Cominform a wisecrack circulating in Belgrade was: "God preserve us from three things: American aviation, Cominform agitation and Yugoslav reorganisation." It may be, too, that it is affected by the political stagnation mentioned below. Or, to put it in another way, that the workers' management system has reached the limit of development possible within the existing political framework.

But workers' management in Yugoslavia has the dynamism and drive, resilience and capacity for correcting errors and learning from experience that is inherent in democracy. It is now a central feature of Yugoslav Socialism, having a good deal in common with producers' co-operatives and the ideas of guild Socialism in Britain. The Yugoslavs have every right to be proud of it and to regard it as a success.

The Yugoslav economy still suffers from too much capital investment out of national income. This is aggravated by the very heavy defence expenditure, which in 1955 amounted to nearly 11% of the national income, and in 1956 was still almost 10%. This compares with 9% in Britain, an average of 5% for the European members of N.A.T.O. and 4% for West Germany. This expenditure was no doubt justified during the toughest period of the struggle with Stalin, but there does not seem much reason for it now.

The weakest point in the economy, and one that is much discussed in Yugoslavia, is the peasantry. In Britain 5% of the population produce half the food for the whole country, and in the United States 15% not only feed the whole population, but produce a good deal for export. In Yugoslavia the peasants are nearly two-thirds of the whole population. But they cannot quite manage to feed themselves and the remaining one-third in the towns. The problem is how to double production while halving the number of people on the land, in order to man Yugoslavia's industries and raise the standard of living.

After the break with the Soviet Union the Government abandoned the attempt to keep peasants in collective farms against their will. The peasants for their part mostly turned a deaf ear to the arguments for going in for various forms of voluntary producers' co-operatives, although they took somewhat greater interest in consumers' co-operatives. For the most part they simply went back to their old primitive tilling of their own scraps of land. Yugoslav legislation prevents the buying up of land so as to form large farms, or the hiring of labour. So the countryside stagnates, as the peasants have only limited private enterprise inducements or possibilities, and are unwilling to try the techniques of co-operation.

Yugoslav Communists believe that education, environment and economic inducements will persuade increasing numbers to 'better themselves' by going in for co-operation in one way or another, so as to take advantage of modern techniques of production, State credit facilities, etc. But meanwhile production remains below its pre-war level, and in 1956 even dropped 12% in comparison with the previous year (partly because of devastating floods, whereas the year before Yugoslavia had been visited by drought).

This was the social and economic background to the boldest political experiment of all: the attempt to reform the Communist Party and its relation to the people. The Yugoslav Communist Party was, to start with, something rather different from the Communist Party of the Soviet Union. Something like nine-tenths of it had been recruited during the war. The rule was that if a man had been a good partisan and

fought bravely for eight months, he was fit for admission into
the Party, and could do his homework on Marxism-Leninism
in his spare time. That was a rough and ready application of
Tito's dictum that "Marxism is 90% practice and 10%
theory"; or perhaps the dictum was the rationalisation of
this way of recruiting Party members.

Such a Party was strong in revolutionary spirit and national
pride, but in the nature of things could not be as rigid, hierarchical and subservient to orders from higher-ups as the Soviet
Party during Stalin's supremacy. And, of course, Tito is no
Stalin, and has no use for this kind of thing, anyway.

The result was, as Vladimir Dedijer, one of the Yugoslav
leaders, pointed out to me some years ago: "In our Party
there really is a Party opinion among the rank and file and at
the level of local and regional leaders, with which the national
leaders must reckon. That was not the case with the Soviet
Party after Stalin had finished manhandling it."

For some years after the war the Party kept on the high
moral plane and maintained the solidarity and discipline of
partisan days. There was a revival of this during the struggle
against Stalin. But as time went on the Party leadership showed
signs of hardening into a bureaucracy and the same evils began
to creep in as in other Communist-ruled countries; Party members were preferred for all jobs, enjoyed special privileges and
generally developed into a ruling caste. The revolt against this
was led by Milovan Djilas.

Djilas was Minister without Portfolio in the Cabinet, and
apart from being the supreme authority on questions of ideology, propaganda and education in the Party, was also Chairman of the International Affairs Commission of the Central
Committee of the Party. The Secretary of that Commission was
Dedijer, who was also a member of the Central Committee,
and who ever since his student days had been a close friend and
something of a disciple of Djilas.

Djilas is a proud and fiery Montenegrin and became
a Communist while still almost a boy.

The fervour of his faith was equalled by the violence of his
reaction. His strong emotional urge to do everything the
opposite way to the Stalinist methods came out both in his

ideological critique of Stalinism and in his plans for the reorganisation of the Yugoslav Communist Party. He told me about those plans at the time, and in particular said something which afterwards turned out to be more important than I had then realised: "We have a good deal to learn from the old established democracies, even if they are still capitalist. In particular, we might look again at our one-party system."

The first thing he did was to enlarge the area of free discussion within the Party by getting through a decision that it was not only the right but the duty of Party members to comment fearlessly, even critically, upon any utterance of a national leader of the Party, however exalted his position, and that they should not hesitate to publish their views in newspapers or reviews or to put their points in public speeches. This right and duty to criticise was to cease only when some duly authorised body, such as the Party Congress, or the Central Committee, or its Politbureau, had taken a decision. After that the matter was closed and it became the duty of the minority to accept and help to carry out the policies decided upon by the majority. But the more free and vigorous the discussion preceding a decision, said Djilas, the greater the chance that the decision would be correct and fully understood by the Party.

In Djilas' mind this was only the first step. He wanted thoroughly to democratise the Party and came forward with proposals to reorganise it on a "territorial" basis instead of building it up from factory cells. He also proposed to water down the 'centralism' in democratic centralism to the point where the Party would practically have become a Social Democratic Party whose members shared the common aim of establishing a Socialist society and started with the Marxist analysis of capitalist society, but were free to differ on everything else, and even to argue about the exact meaning of their aim and analysis and how to apply either or both to current problems.

The 400,000 strong Communist Party of Yugoslavia was rechristened the Yugoslav Communist League and the Popular Front became the Socialist Alliance (comprising 8 million people, that is, practically the entire adult population of Yugoslavia). These changes in nomenclature were intended to denote the new policy. Hitherto the Yugoslav Communists had taken the decisions and used the other organisations of the 'Socialist alliance', such as the trade unions, women's and youth organisations, co-operatives, associations of collective farmers, professional bodies, etc., as conveyor belts through which the Party decisions turned the wheels of Yugoslav public life. Henceforward the Party was to confine itself to advising and guiding the other organisations and encouraging them to take their own decisions.

But Djilas did not stop even there. He has a logical mind and when he reached the final dilemma of Marxism-Leninism— how to reconcile the one-party system with democracy—said bluntly that it could not be done and it was necessary to allow freedom for the formation of a second party out of the Socialist Alliance. Djilas assumed that this Party would, like the Communists, accept the collectivist foundations of Yugoslav society and share the common aim of building Socialism, i.e. it would not question the achievements and purposes of the Revolution.

Tito and most of the Party, however, took a different view. I have often discussed this issue with Tito and would sum up his attitude as follows: "It is still too early to assume that the Revolution has been accepted by the majority of our people in the sense Djilas believes. And there is still a great deal of capitalist influence and interference from outside. A second party would inevitably become the refuge for all the counter-revolutionary elements that are still there, but that our present system deprives of any chance to try to stage a come-back. In these circumstances a second party could very easily, and almost certainly would, become a counter-revolutionary party inviting interference by the West in our internal affairs. We could not and will not take that risk. The degree to which we advance towards full democracy and political freedom depends on the growth of a Socialist consciousness in the people."

The differences on policy between Djilas and most of the rest of the Party leaders in the early '50s were envenomed by personal rivalries and questions of Party discipline. Djilas took the new freedoms which he had introduced into the

Communist Party very seriously, and published a number of articles in *Borba*, expounding his ideas, which he continued even after Tito had begged him to stop.

He attacked the privileges of leading members of the Party and the snobbery of their wives.

Finally he went to the Montenegrin General, Peko Dapčević, and complained that Tito was becoming a dictator and losing the common touch. The General was shocked and reported the incident to Tito, who was offended and angry.

As a Yugoslav friend explained to me, "Djilas should have gone to Tito and complained about the bureaucracy in the Party. One does not attack Tito. Tito is Tito. He is George Washington and Lenin rolled into one. Like George Washington, he is 'First in war, first in peace, and first in the hearts of his countrymen.' Like Lenin, he is the leader of our Revolution, or rather, of our two revolutions—the social revolution that was part of our war of liberation and our national revolution against the tyranny of Stalin. He has done Stalin's job too, of leading reconstruction after the war and laying the foundations of our Socialist society.

"In any case, it was not Tito who became dictator. It was the bureaucrats and little dictators in the Party who ganged up behind his back and took advantage of his frequent trips abroad and preoccupation with world affairs, to gather power at home into their own hands, bit by bit, and use it to stop all this freedom and democracy going too far. Djilas' articles were like the clangour of the geese on the Capitol that roused the sleeping senators—the Party bosses suddenly woke up to the fact of what he was up to. They realised it would end with their losing their power and privileges. And so they arraigned Djilas while Tito was in India. By the time Tito got back Djilas and his close friend and associate, Dedijer—who did not agree with his old friend's two-party proposals, but defended Djilas' right to speak his mind—had been tried, condemned and expelled from the Party. All Tito was in time to do, was to refuse twice to sign a sentence of twelve years that was proposed, so that the two finally got off with eighteen and six months' suspended sentence. Ever since the Party has been stagnating. The advance towards more democracy and freedom has slowed up and almost stopped. We badly need Tito's attention at home."*

I talked with many old friends, including Velko Vlahovic, Djilas' successor as the Chairman of the Foreign Affairs Commission of the Central Committee of the Party, and Mrs. Maria Wilfan, Dedijer's successor as its Secretary. What, I asked of everyone competent to answer, was the purpose of the foreign delegations arriving incessantly? What were they looking for in Yugoslavia? Was Yugoslavia becoming an additional or even rival centre of international Communism to Moscow?

No, said the Yugoslavs. They did not agree, I was told, with the Italian Communist leader Togliatti's idea of 'Polycentric' Communism. They disbelieved in the whole notion of Communist or working-class parties coagulating around any common centre, or even around three or four rather than one. They rather favoured bilateral contacts based on complete freedom and equality and with no attempt by the parties concerned to impose ideas on or bind each other in any way.

As for the delegations, they came for different reasons, and each was interested in something different. For instance, the Italians were interested in the Yugoslav experiments in decentralisation and workers' management in the factories. The latter, in particular, impressed them so much that they said they were going to include something like it in their own programme at home. The Poles had gone further and decided to apply this idea in their own country. They also liked the democratic, informal ways of the Yugoslav Party.

The Hungarian delegation that had only just left had had widely varying views and interests. They were an extreme example of something that had been noticeable in most of the delegations—the dying out of the monolithic mentality in Communist parties. Some of them had highly approved of what they saw in Yugoslavia and had been enthusiastic about developments in Poland (that is, developments between the Seventh Plenum, where the great change began, up to and during the Eighth, when Gomulka became Party Secretary

* Since then Djilas has been arrested and given three years' hard labour. See Chapter 16.

again). Others had been silent. None had wanted to speak
about the situation at home in Hungary; they seemed to have
something on their mind. (The Hungarians had gone home just
three days before the start of Hungary's national revolt on
October 23rd; I arrived in Yugoslavia on October 21st, and
the talks recorded in this chapter took place from the 22nd to
the 25th inclusive).

During that week in October the dramatic events in Poland
and Hungary figured largely in the Yugoslav Press and came
up in most of my conversations. Was this, at last, the Yugoslavs
asked themselves, that new phase in the social revolution, that
great movement of democratisation and liberation that had
begun to stir after the war and had then been snuffed out by
the cold war and Stalin?

For eight years the Yugoslavs had been hoping that their
stand for equality between Socialist States, with freedom for
each to work out its own path to Socialism and determine the
terms on which it wished to associate with the others, would be
accepted by the Soviet Union, and spread to the other People's
Democracies. Now it looked as though at last those things were
beginning to happen—and Tito was becoming a symbol, if not
the leader, of the 'new' Communism.

When Tito visited the Soviet Union in June, a Yugoslav
friend told me, it had been agreed between him and the Soviet
leaders that they would henceforward keep in close and constant touch. Mikoyan had already visited Yugoslavia in
pursuance of that agreement. More recent still had been the
visit of Khrushchev and Tito's return visit with him to south
Russia in September.

All this was very gratifying to the Yugoslavs. But already
they had begun to worry about the signs of opposition in
Moscow to the new tendencies. They knew about the letter
that had been sent out by the Politbureau to the members of
the C.P.S.U. warning them that Yugoslav Communism was
not as good as the Soviet brand and should not be used. What
irritated the Yugoslavs, however, was that the same or a similar
letter had been sent to the leaders of other Communist parties
without the Yugoslavs being informed.

This, said the Yugoslavs, was not only contrary to the June

agreement about inter-party relations, but had a nasty resemblance to Stalin's famous condemnation of the Yugoslav
Communists, sent to all the other Cominform parties, to prepare
the ground for their condemnation in the notorious Cominform
resolution of June 28th, 1948.

One story I heard in Moscow from a foreign diplomat was
that in his talks with Khrushchev Tito had complained about
this letter, particularly about its having been sent to other
Communist parties, and had taken the line: "I don't want to
see this letter or even ask you to confirm or deny its existence.
Nor do I want to question the right of anybody to send or
receive such letters. All I say is that if I were a Communist
leader in a People's Democracy I should not like to receive
such a letter from Moscow, denouncing a fraternal party
behind its back."

After three days of listening, reading and talking in Belgrade, I was ready to go to the fountain-head—President Tito
himself. He had very kindly invited me down to Brioni, the
island off Pola at the northern end of the Adriatic which is
his favourite retreat, although nowadays becoming rather a
crowded one.

I was there for two days, and Tito found time for a good
long talk between the departure of the Israeli Parliamentary
delegation and the arrival of a Rumanian Party Delegation.
Most of the top Yugoslav Party leaders, whom I had known
for years, had also congregated down there. The members of
Tito's Secretariat were also for the most part old friends whom
I had known in London and Belgrade. The whole place was
seething with activity and discussion. My time there was a
political crammer's course on Yugoslavia and Yugoslav views
on what was happening in the Communist world. The talk
with Tito was the grand climax.

CHAPTER NINE

Brioni

I FIRST SAW BRIONI in 1950, when I spent a three weeks' summer holiday with Marshal Tito on the island. It is an extraordinary place: before the First World War this low, sandy, scrub-covered isle that you can walk around in three hours was bought by a wealthy Austrian nobleman (it was then part of the Austro-Hungarian Empire), who built his summer residence on it, laid it out in walks and rides, imported trees and shrubs from all over the world and stocked it with hares, pheasants, three different species of deer, and ibex. After the First World War it became an Italian tourist centre, with luxury hotels, a polo ground, tennis courts (and, of course, wonderful sailing and bathing).

During the last war most of the hotels were smashed and the Germans shot all the ibex and decimated the rest of the game. Ceded to Yugoslavia after the war, it was used by Tito as his favourite retreat and summer home. In 1950 he still managed to keep the world at bay and get something like a holiday. True, he would work every morning from six o'clock to ten o'clock or even later. But after that we would take the launch to the small outer island and bathe, lie about in the sun, fish, play chess or just talk until evening.

There is a three-sided hut of roughly hewn stone slabs with a shingle roof on the outer or bathing island. The fourth side is open to the sea. It is furnished with plain wooden benches and a table. Always cool and shady it is used for picnic luncheons, drinks after bathing, conversation, chess, etc. In the evenings there was generally a film (the Marshal is a film fan and has his own projector and screen), or else we played

I

billiards. Sometimes at night when there was a *bonazza,* that is, a flat calm with the sea like glass, and no moon, we would go spear fishing by torchlight.

That was the time when I really got to know the Marshal. As a League of Nations official for nineteen years, I met a great many V.I.Ps., from Prime Ministers down. No man is a hero to his valet, and we Secretariat officials were political valets to the delegates, whom we would meet off duty at dinners and receptions as well as working with them. Usually one wondered how the man in question ever got his job or could keep it. But there were a few who bulked even larger in private life than they did in their official capacity.

Tito is one of the few. His private personality is even more remarkable than his public *persona.* He is a dedicated man who unashamedly enjoys the good things of life—sport, fishing, shooting, food and wine, nice clothes, books, films, plays, chess, music—he likes them all. A man with a mission who lives in the moment. A puritan, but a Mediterranean puritan, in the classic Greek, humanist tradition of "enjoy all things in moderation but always remain master of yourself". A clear mind, ripe with rich and varied experience, and lit with humour. And with all that, enormous strength and toughness, and, behind the humour and charm, something aloof and withdrawn.

I asked him once how it was he could enjoy himself and relax on the beach during the day and yet work every morning. "I learnt how to do that during the war," replied Tito. "At the very worst moments I used to make the best dispositions I could, give my orders and then switch off and go to sleep." He never forgets the load of responsibility and authority he carries with him wherever he goes—but wears it so lightly and 'naturally' that it becomes almost invisible.

Tito's strength lies in the fact that his life epitomises the history and the struggle for unity and freedom of the Yugoslav people.

To begin with, he comes from the peasantry, that social matrix from which all classes have evolved in Yugoslavia, for the most part recently. His father was a Croat peasant, desperately poor by Western standards and always in debt, but

in nineteenth-century Croatia reckoned as a 'middle' rather
than poor peasant. Tito's mother was a Slovene.

When he was thirteen Tito started his apprenticeship with
a locksmith and went on from there to become a skilled worker.
a trade unionist and a Social Democrat. He worked at a ship-
building yard on precision instruments, and in many different
engineering firms, in Croatia, Vienna, where he was a test
driver at Daimlers, in Bohemia, and in Western Germany.
He became familiar with the best industrial techniques and
equipment in Europe and with German and Austrian Marxism—and of course learnt German. At the same time he was
an ardent south Slav and as such had contacts with the trade
unionists and Social Democrats of Serbia.

He was an athlete and sportsman—one of the best fencers
and riders in the Austro-Hungarian Army—was taken prisoner
by the Russians in the First World War, learnt Russian, and
joined the Red Guard at Omsk (in Western Siberia) after the
Revolution.

He returned home after World War I just in time to take
part in the first (and last) legal election campaign of the new-
born Yugoslav Communist Party. The Communists won
sweeping victories in the municipal elections in all the big
towns, including Belgrade and Zagreb. But the Royalist Minister of the Interior bluntly told the victorious Communist
Councillors that he was not going to hand over power to
them, no matter how the votes went.

The Communist Party was banned, and the régime abandoned all but the thinnest pretence of democracy.

Tito became a whole-time revolutionary conspirator, while
at the same time an active trade unionist, earning his living
in one factory after another, interspersed by periods of imprisonment. For years he carried his life in his hand and
travelled illegally in and out of Yugoslavia under a variety of
false names and papers, doing more and more responsible jobs
for the Party, spending a couple of years in Moscow at the
headquarters of the Comintern, until finally he became Secretary of the Party.

Once he became Secretary he reorganised and rebuilt the
Party, which had been almost destroyed by faction fights and

the interventions of the Comintern. Even then he insisted upon remaining in Yugoslavia. He refused to stay in Moscow, as he was pressed to do, and stressed the need for the Party to be self-supporting rather than depend on subsidies from the Comintern.

It was his leadership in the partisan war that established him as the outstanding Yugoslav national leader. He was in the thick of the fighting all through, outwitted the best strategists and tacticians the Germans and Italians could pit against him, shared danger, hunger and cold with his men, and showed himself equal to the diplomatic and political problems involved in relations with the Russians and the Western allies. He never became callous. He said to Dedijer once: "A commander who begins to think of his men as numbers is lost. He must never forget that behind each number is a human being with an inner life of his own. When he knows every minute of the day and night, even in his sleep, that he has under his command so and so many human beings with their inner lives, only then can he do his job as a commander."

Nor has he lost the common touch. Once, when we were driving along the white roads under the hot sun of Istria in August, Tito leaned over and told the chauffeur: "Don't drive so fast through the villages. We don't want to cover people and their homes with dust." After that we crawled through the villages.

One evening, towards the end of a long talk about democracy, and Socialism, Tito broke out with passion: "If I didn't believe that Socialism also means humanism and freedom, I shouldn't think it worth working for Socialism." "But," he added, "revolution is a cruel thing (surova stvar). Those who have made a revolution cannot allow the beaten counter-revolution to try again under the guise of exercising democratic rights."

That, of course, is the dilemma of those who have made a social revolution and want to turn a revolutionary dictatorship into a democracy on the new social foundations. How far and how fast can they go without too much danger of political freedom being used to try to undo the achievements of the revolution? In practice this question is generally decided in terms of the monopoly of power of the Communist

Party, i.e. reforms are admissible up to the point where they might threaten that monopoly, but not further.

The internal situation in Yugoslavia seems to have reached that point. The general feeling among those I talked with was that the demands for more democracy could not be indefinitely checked and that there was great need for Tito to give his full attention to this issue. For he alone had such nation-wide prestige and popularity that he could prepare the transition from a dictatorship based on a more or less democratic Communist Party, more or less effectively consulting and paying heed to the wants of the people, to a true democracy.

But the impact of Yugoslav Communism and of Tito on what was happening in the other Communist-ruled countries was my chief concern. During the two days in Brioni, on October 25th and 26th, the one topic of conversation was what had just happened in Poland and was beginning to happen in Hungary. The Yugoslav Press was following these events very closely and, so far as I could see, objectively. In particular, Yugoslav correspondents in Hungary were constantly crossing the border into Yugoslavia to file their despatches, which gave clear and detailed pictures of the unfolding tragedy. At that time it was still at the early stage of the first phase: the peaceful demonstration of October 23rd had turned into a riot after Geroe's insults to the crowd, and the riot had turned into a rising after Geroe had called in the Soviet forces behind the back of Nagy. But it also looked just then as though Nagy's programme for de-Stalinisation and de-satellisation might win such support as to enable him to regain control and even reach agreement with the Russians.

Poland and Hungary came into almost every conversation with everyone I met on the island, interlarded with all the other subjects discussed. But in order to avoid confusion and overlapping I will begin with the earliest of these topics in point of time—Tito's visit to the Soviet Union in June—and give the Yugoslav views on Poland and Hungary as Tito put them to me himself.

Some of those who had been with Tito during his visit to the Soviet Union gave me a fascinating account of that extraordinary occasion: "We went by train," said one of Tito's secretaries. "It took fifty hours from Belgrade to Moscow. Several times we had to wake the old man up at night and make him put on his uniform and go out to greet the crowds. For at every station where we stopped, even for a few minutes, the place was jammed with people who had been waiting for anything up to two days to see him. They felt so strongly about it—some were in tears at the thought of missing him—that Tito felt he simply had to turn out. In Moscow the situation remained under control, although there were huge crowds. But in Leningrad the whole town came to a standstill and the factories emptied when Tito arrived. It is estimated that at least a couple of million people were milling about in the streets—most of the adult population of Leningrad. In Stalingrad it was the same—there the crowd nearly trampled him and Khrushchev to death in their excitement. Everywhere he had the most tremendous and fervent reception that can be imagined."

"At first we were stunned. It was wonderful, of course, and we were touched, almost awed, but at the same time puzzled," said another member of the party with Tito on that historic visit. "We could not understand what these fervent millions were trying to tell us. But after a time we understood: this was not just a tribute to Tito. It was a political demonstration. What the Soviet people were saying was, 'You were the first to stand up to Stalin and defeat him. This is our thanks. You are one of us and we are with you.' "

While in Moscow I had asked several Russians why there were these tremendous demonstrations for Tito. There was always a slight air of embarrassment and restraint, and then some such answer as: "Oh! We knew that what had been said about him was not true." The truth is that in the eyes of ordinary people in the Soviet Union Tito has a glamour and status at least equal to that of any of the existing Soviet leaders. Moreover, having once damned him with bell, book and candle, and then rehabilitated and raised him to the skies, it would be extremely difficult and might even be dangerous to repeat the operation in reverse.

Tito received me in his new residence, which is grander than the old and has a lovely view overlooking the sea. A bit stocky, but well-proportioned and light on his feet, Tito still looked fifteen years younger than his age—sixty-four—and was fit and bronzed, his blond hair only just greying, his eyes as blue and piercing as ever. Time seemed to have passed him by in the four years since I had seen him last.

Tito said he liked Khrushchev, who was open-minded, quick on the uptake, shrewd and frank, as well as having a sense of humour and plenty of drive. He thought that the Soviet leaders trusted the Yugoslavs because they knew exactly where they stood and were also aware that their régime was solid and strong, would not change its line and would remain genuinely Socialist, peace-loving and anxious for friendship and co-operation with the Soviet Union on the basis of equality and freedom.

Tito confirmed everything Khrushchev had told me about their talk in South Russia and added a good deal more: "Khrushchev tried hard to induce me to join the Socialist camp. But I told him the word '*lager*' [the German word for camp, which is also used in Russian] reminded me of our Serbian word '*logor*' [concentration camp]. It smells of barbed wire. How the hell can we sit in the same camp with a great power and remain free and on an equal footing with it?"

He confirmed that the text of the June 20th declaration on inter-Party relations was indeed based on the Yugoslav draft and that it took three days' tough argument before the Russians swallowed it. They were in fact finding it difficult to apply these principles of equality and freedom to their relations with the other People's Democracies. The Soviet leaders were still suffering from a hangover from Stalin's days and tended to think in terms of the hegemony of the Soviet Union over the small People's Democracies, and of the C.P.S.U. over the other Communist parties. But their attitude towards China was different. They treated that country as an equal.

"The truth is that the Soviet leaders are still thinking in terms of peaceful coexistence between two groups of States, divided into the Socialist and Capitalist camps, whereas our view is that the quicker these groups disintegrate and melt down into the United Nations the better for the world."

I asked whether this was what he had meant in his recent declaration, on the anniversary of the United Nations, that the principles and aims of Yugoslav foreign policy were those of the United Nations (I had heard that he had himself told his Secretariat that he wanted to make a declaration on this anniversary, and that what he had said was his own draft and very much the expression of his own ideas). "Yes," said Tito. "That is so—I want the obligations of the Charter to become binding, in fact and not only in word, in the relations of all States, and all other treaty obligations to take second place."

The same difference between the Soviet and Yugoslav views had come out, Tito went on, in the discussions with Khrushchev and other Soviet leaders about inter-party relations. "We Yugoslavs don't think that the Communist and workers' parties in the Socialist States have a monopoly of the performing rights of Socialism in the world. We believe that the whole world is in a state of social transition, that the old order based on private enterprise is being increasingly replaced by economic forms involving State intervention, planning and public ownership. The radical and progressive forces in all countries that are moving in this direction are doing so by very different paths and under different names. In England you have the Labour Party, in the United States New Dealers, on the Continent Social Democrats, and so on. . . .

"The most one can say," continued Tito, "is that the Marxist-Leninist parties in the Socialist States have gone further on the path towards Socialism and are working more scientifically and consciously to build a Socialist society.

"In the rest of the world the advance towards Socialism is largely due to the play of blind elemental forces without much political direction. But the Yugoslavs do not want to hive off into one camp: they want to have friendly relations with all the forces working for Socialism, on the basis of complete freedom and equality and scrupulous respect for the rule of non-interference in each other's internal affairs."

For this reason, Tito said, it was premature to talk about any form of multilateral grouping of Communist and workers' parties from different countries. They believed in bilateral contacts, not only with the parties of the so-called Socialist camp, but with Western Socialist, Labour and other progressive parties and movements. As these bilateral contracts multiplied and assumed various forms, some wider forms of contact and exchange of information and views would in due course evolve out of them. But this was music of the future and should be left to the operation of time and events.

From the general we passed to the particular—that is, to the two burning topics of Poland and Hungary. Tito was frankly delighted with the spirit and attitude of the Poles. What was happening in Poland, he said, was a really great event. The parallel with what had happened in Yugoslavia in 1948 was pretty close. What made it even more important was that this dramatic recovery of national independence had taken place with the assent—given reluctantly and under pressure, but nevertheless given—of the Russians. That was the measure of the changes that had occurred in the Kremlin too since the death of Stalin.

Gomulka he considered a good Communist and a strong man. He had been consistent and courageous all the way through, events had proved him right, and he was now reaping his reward. Tito believed he had a long and tough struggle ahead, but that he would succeed. He also looked forward to close and friendly relations between the Yugoslav and Polish Parties, which saw eye to eye on most things and were faced by much the same problems. He was particularly pleased that the Poles were going to experiment with some variant of the Yugoslav system of workers' management.

He thought the Soviet leaders had made a mistake in rushing to Warsaw, because all they had got by it was an advertisement that they still believed in interfering in the internal affairs of other Communist parties, followed by a resounding rebuff from the Poles. That mistake was due to Kaganovich and Molotov, who represented the old guard among the leaders, among whom Stalinism was still strong.

Whereas Molotov and Kaganovich represented the Stalinist rearguard, the advance guard were Khrushchev, Bulganin and Mikoyan; Malenkov and possibly Suslov were in the middle. He believed the retreat from Warsaw would redound to the credit of Khrushchev, who could now say, "I told you so," and that once the opposition of the old guard had been broken, the advance of the Soviet people to democracy and political freedom would go fast and far. Below the top level there would be little or no resistance.

The position in Hungary on the other hand Tito found profoundly disturbing. The worst part of this deplorable situation, he said, was the calling in of Soviet troops. The régime should have made the necessary concessions last summer and was greatly to blame for the present crisis. But that was largely the fault of the Russians. When Rakosi was dropped in July was the time to make Imre Nagy Premier and Secretary of the Party. Instead the Russians had insisted that Geroe, who was simply a carbon copy of Rakosi, should replace him. Tito had warned them against this during his talks in south Russia in September, but in vain.

Rakosi was an infamous ruffian, not only a Stalinist stooge, but a little Stalin in his own right, or rather, wrong. His régime had been a reign of terror and had also committed the grossest economic blunders and made life almost unbearably hard for the Hungarian people. However, making Nagy Prime Minister and Kadar the Party Secretary now might mean a new deal. Kadar, while with the Hungarian delegation in Yugoslavia, had been openly anti-Rakosi, and no wonder, because on the latter's orders he had been imprisoned for years and bestially tortured. (Later I heard it was Rakosi's son who had actually done the torturing.) He had been very violent about Rakosi in his talks with Tito.

It looked, said Tito, as though the new Hungarian Government were regaining command of the situation. If it also succeeded in its negotiations with the Soviet Government for the withdrawal of the Soviet forces, the harm done could still be undone. But the situation was very anxious and uncertain.

I asked why so many foreign delegations were coming to Yugoslavia. Mainly, said Tito, to study the internal Socialist development of the country. But foreign delegations were also impressed by Yugoslavia's stand for independence and equality in the mutual relations of Socialist States. The Yugoslav attitude, Tito emphasised, was to welcome visitors, but not to volunteer unasked advice or do anything that looked like interference in the internal affairs of other countries.

That evening I motored back to Ljubljana, caught the night train to Belgrade and took off early next morning by plane for Prague.

CHAPTER TEN

The Ghost of Slansky

MY VISIT TO PRAGUE brought me face to face with the striking paradox of Czechoslovakia, which is that, although it is the only Communist-ruled country that was a working democracy before the Communists took over, the move towards democratisation is markedly less now in Czechoslovakia than in the other principal People's Democracies.

The paradox was to me all the more noticeable in the light of my recollections of a visit to Prague in September 1946. For at that time it had seemed that Czechoslovakia might succeed in retaining democracy at the same time as rapidly socialising her economy. There were problems and difficulties enough, but there were also favourable factors and the experiment was by no means obviously doomed to failure.

There was freedom of speech, Press and association, except for ex-quislings, collaborators and Fascists, newspapers and reviews were co-operatively owned by political parties, trade unions, groups of journalists or writers, professional associations, etc.

The elections after the war had been reasonably democratic. The right-wing parties which had betrayed the country to Hitler or played a quisling role had been outlawed. The others had gone to the country as a coalition with a common reconstruction programme—but the electorate had had a choice of candidates and a choice of parties to vote for. The result of the election had been to give the Communist Party 38% of the total vote and the Social Democrats 13%, so that the two parties between them commanded a bare majority in Parliament This did not make much difference so long as the coalition held together. But it played a crucial part in the crisis that preceded the February *coup d'état*, as the account below of that event shows. The Communists, as the largest and also the most energetic Party, with the clearest idea of what it wanted, took the leading part in the Government and in working out the economic plan for reconstruction.

During my 1946 visit I met several of the leading men concerned in framing that plan, notably Frejka, who, in grey flannel trousers, soft shirt, Norfolk jacket and cardigan, smoking a big pipe, looked and spoke like a Cambridge don. He was proud of the fact that he had been working in Cambridge during the war and had studied our British wartime planning, as well as afterwards spending six months in the Soviet Union studying the Soviet system of planning. He said he had tried to borrow what was most appropriate for Czechoslovak conditions and traditions from both these plans, for his country must go its own way to Socialism. It would be a democratic, national way.

During the same visit I had a four-hour talk with Beneš, whom I had known during my years as a League of Nations official, when he was Czech Foreign Minister and a frequent visitor to Geneva. He took me home to his summer residence and we had tea on the lawn in true English style. He told the story of how he had negotiated with the Americans and Russians immediately after the war for the withdrawal of United States and Soviet troops from Czech territory, and how, soon after, he had taken the leaders of the Czechoslovak Communist Party—Gottwald and Slansky—with him to Moscow for a talk with the Soviet leaders. His conversation with Stalin ran somewhat as follows:

"I know you understand our position," Beneš had said, "but I am sometimes a bit doubtful about these boys here [pointing to Gottwald and Slansky]. I am afraid they might forget Czechoslovakia is not Russia and do something drastic."

Stalin, said Beneš, laughed and asked, "Well, what do you want me to do? Do you want me to talk to them?"

"No, no," said Beneš hastily. "That would be interference in our internal affairs. But I just thought you ought to know the position."

Then, Beneš told me, Stalin became serious, turned to the Czech Communist leaders and said to them: "Of course, I hope you will learn from our experience as well as from that of other countries. But do not forget that you have a different and happier heritage than we, who took over in a backward, primitive country that was ruined and exhausted. You have to work things out for yourselves and go forward to Socialism in your own way, according to your own national traditions. From now on you are paddling your own canoe."

That was Stalin's 'line' during those first two years after the war, before the cold war got under way. But even then there was a widening gap between his words and deeds.

"What," I asked Beneš, "do you think is going to happen to your unique experiment here of advancing quite rapidly towards Socialism by democratic and parliamentary means, through a national coalition in which the Communists are the leading and far the biggest party? After the toughest period of reconstruction is over and the foundations of the new society have been laid, will this coalition separate out into a Government and Opposition according to normal parliamentary practice, although on the basis of both sides accepting the essentials of the new society? Or will the Communists at some point kick over the traces and make themselves dictators?"

Beneš replied that, with the elimination of the classic obstacles to the working of parliamentary democracy in a capitalist society, in the shape of the quisling parties and big businessmen and the Civil Servants and Army officers who had backed them, all swept away in the downfall of Hitler and the revolutionary aftermath, he thought even the Communists would decide they could achieve the social changes they wanted by constitutional means. "But," he added, "democracy can survive here only on condition that those who were allies in the war remain partners in the peace. If the Great Powers can pull together in peace all will be well with us. But if the rifts already beginning to show widen, and the Powers fall apart and quarrel, our compromise cannot survive, and we shall have to choose between Russia and the West. In that case we will choose Russia."

I asked why. "We will do so," replied Beneš, "because the choice for us Czechs and Slovaks will not be between Russia on the one hand or France and Britain on the other. For if France and Britain quarrel with the Soviet Union, they will start rearming Germany—and we do not want another Munich."

That was in September 1946. Between then and 1948 I visited Czechoslovakia frequently and took a lively interest in the economic reconstruction and plans of that country, partly because it was an example of Socialism being built by democratic methods and partly in connection with the campaign some of us in the Labour Party were waging to develop trade with the People's Democracies and the Soviet Union.

At the same time, naturally, I was more than ready to talk with anyone in those countries who was willing to listen about what their Governments ought to do to improve their relations with the West, and particularly the Labour Government. I will give two instances here, because they played a part in the subsequent Slansky trial and cast some light on what were the relations between the Soviet Union and the 'satellite' People's Democracies at that time, and the impact of Western policy.

The first instance was the Marshall Plan. When the Governments of the People's Democracies were debating the question of whether or not to attend the Paris Conference for launching the plan, I wrote to Zdenek Fierlinger, the Deputy Prime Minister, who was an old friend from Geneva days when he was the Czechoslovak Permanent Delegate to the League of Nations and a member of the Czechoslovak Social Democratic Party. I argued that either the Marshall Plan was a piece of humbug and there was no serious intention of allowing Communist-ruled countries to benefit under it; in which case the Czechs, by attending the Conference, could help to show up the swindle and educate the American and British public who believed the offer was sincere. Or it really was genuine, in which case they would stand to benefit by going to Paris. Or it was a mixture, in which case they could support what was genuine and show up what was humbug. So that on any hypothesis they ought to accept the invitation!

If they did, I suggested, they should take their stand, first, on the principle that help should go in the first place to ex-allies and only afterwards to ex-enemies. (The French, I explained, were bound to support that, and it would be very difficult for anyone to resist. And that would preclude the Americans from giving the lion's share of help to Western Germany.) Secondly, they should insist that the Economic Commission for Europe of the United Nations, which had only just been set up to do the very kind of job for which the United States was now promising assistance under the Marshall Plan, and in which the Soviet Union and Eastern Europe, as well as the Western countries and 'neutrals', were represented, should be designated as the body to apply the Marshall Plan. That too, I argued, would be difficult to resist and would obviate most of the causes for hesitation on the part of the Socialist States.

Fierlinger told me afterwards that he had received my letter half an hour before the Cabinet meeting to discuss the issue and had read out most of it in the Cabinet. It had played a considerable part in determining the decision to attend the Paris Conference. The Czechs had thought at the time that the Russians, although they themselves had pulled out their strong delegation (sixty in all, headed by Molotov), would let the Czechs do as they thought best. Instead, Stalin told the Czechs they must choose between the U.S.S.R. and the West, and if they went to Paris would be regarded as having cut themselves off from the Socialist camp. So the Czechoslovak delegation went home again.

This was disappointing, but hardly surprising. For Oscar Lange, the Polish economist and former Professor at Chicago University, and then a member of the P.P.S. (the Polish Socialist Party), had told me soon after the event how angrily the Soviet delegates had, behind the scenes, opposed the idea of an Economic Commission for Europe when he put it up on behalf of the Polish delegation at the General Assembly of the United Nations. The Poles had had their way that time, but clearly Stalin, who was boycotting the auxiliary organisations of the United Nations, feared and distrusted any genuine economic co-operation between East and West.

The second instance was after the February *coup d'état*: one day Kratochwil, also a former Social Democrat and at the time the Czechoslovak Ambassador in London (he is now an *émigré*) rang me up from a public telephone booth and asked whether he could come home to see me, in strict confidence. When he arrived he explained that he had just been appointed one of the Czechoslovak delegates to the General Assembly meeting in Paris and was anxious that his country should play a constructive and conciliatory part. "You know our boys are apt to be a bit crude and raw. I think that, without running counter to the principles and the aims of the policies of the Soviet Union and the other Socialist States, one should be able on some issues to take a line that could build a bridge between their views and those of reasonable people in the West. You were so many years at Geneva that you know your way about in this kind of thing. Can you help me to go through the agenda of the General Assembly from that point of view?"

It had, of course, often been my duty as a League of Nations official to give delegates just the kind of help and 'technical' advice that Kratochwil was asking of me—namely, help in applying their countries' policies to the matters on the agenda in such a way as to elicit the maximum of agreement, or to play a part in reconciling opposing points of view. I said I should be delighted to try to do as an amateur what I used to do professionally, but, of course, then I was 'on the inside' and knew all that was going on, which was not the case now. Kratochwil and I had several talks on the subject, and I finally wrote memoranda for him on four points on the agenda which he took with him to Paris.

Those four memoranda and the letter to Fierlinger were later to turn up in the Slansky trial in strangely altered and sinister guise, as I shall tell below, because it helps to explain what the trial was really about. By that time, of course, Stalinism, responding to cold war pressures, had grown into an ugly and stifling tyranny in Czechoslovakia.

The February 1948 *coup d'état* caused a furore in the West. "We have the example of Czechoslovakia before our eyes," cried Winston Churchill to the Conservative Party Conference at Llandudno in October 1948, "where Stalin has perpetrated

K

exactly the same act of aggression in 1948 as Hitler did when he marched into Prague in 1939." If so, the Russians must have done the job with an army of invisible men. For there was no action, either diplomatic or military, by the Soviet Government, from start to finish.

I went out as soon as I could to investigate what had happened on the spot. The facts, some of which I was able to check from British Embassy sources, were as follows: the two-year plan adopted in 1946 by all the parties in the coalition, of which the principal author was the Economic Committee of the Communist Party that dominated the coalition, was drawing to an end. There had been failure in certain sectors, notably that for private enterprise, as well as extensive diversions of man-power and materials through the black market and a deadlock between the parties on social issues that had held up action for months.

The Left in the coalition demanded further measures of socialisation, whereas the Right became progressively tougher in their resistance, not uninfluenced by the fact that the forces of the Right were growing stronger in the whole Western world. And, of course, the Stalinists and tough boys in the Czechoslovak Communist leadership were chafing at the restraints and freedoms of democracy and spoiling for an excuse to establish the 'dictatorship of the proletariat', i.e. to make themselves dictators.

Finally, the twelve non-Socialist Ministers (i.e. half the Cabinet) resigned over a relatively trivial issue. The British Catholic weekly *The Tablet* of March 6th, 1946, was right when it said that their resignation in the latter part of January took place because they intended, "there can be no doubt, to force the resignation of the whole Cabinet and to secure the formation of a new coalition without the Communists, as had been done in France and Italy."

That was certainly the way the Left in the coalition also saw the situation. But they further remembered that this had happened in those two countries because they needed economic aid, and the United States let it be known that such aid would be forthcoming only when the French and Italian Communist parties had been expelled from the governing coalitions. Czechoslovakia too had been refused the American loan for which it had asked, but the United States Ambassador in Prague, Mr. Steinhardt, who had returned from the United States the day after the crisis broke, publicly announced, as reported, for example, in the *New York Herald Tribune* of January 20th, that he had not abandoned hope that Czechoslovakia might yet qualify for the benefits of the Marshall Plan.

These suggestions were strengthened by the programme of the resigning ministers, who assumed they would be called upon and could form a coalition without the Communists. After that they intended to hold a snap election, instead of waiting for the appointed date, which was the end of May. For they believed that they could win an immediate election, but that by May the Communist Party might secure a clear majority.

Part of their calculation was based on the partial split in the Czech Socialist Party at their conference in Brno the previous July, when the right wing (encouraged, incidentally, by Transport House) pressed the Party to part company with the Communists.

But in face of the crisis the Left regained command of the Socialist Party and joined with the Communists, the trade unions, and left-wing groups in the other parties in staging armed workers' demonstrations in the streets, with slogans demanding that President Beneš should refrain from calling upon the resigning ministers to form a new Government and proclaiming that the revolution was in danger and that Czechoslovakia would not be another Greece.*

Finally, Beneš yielded and the Communist Party became virtual dictators, after winning what was not only a 'coupon' election as in 1945, but a 'single list' election on the best Soviet models.

No doubt the Soviet Government was privy to what was

---

* Where the Western Powers were conducting a war of intervention against a Communist-dominated but broadly-based people's front that had been the backbone of the resistance movement against the Germans, on behalf of right-wing elements that included out-and-out collaborators, quislings and Fascists.

happening. But there was no Soviet official action of any sort. What happened was due to the operation of internal Czechoslovak social forces, although the clash between them was made sharper by the competing pressures of the cold war.

In June 1948 came the break between Tito and Stalin. In 1949 I was excommunicated by the Cominform countries, including Czechoslovakia, for saying Tito was right to resist Stalinist dictation, and in 1952 was pilloried in the Slansky trial as the 'veteran spy' and agent of the Anglo-American Intelligence Services who had been the go-between between the "Slansky centre" and the Western Powers. I had transmitted instructions to Slansky, the Secretary of the Czechoslovak Communist Party, to overthrow Socialism and restore capitalism in Czechoslovakia under the guise of Titoism and, still following Tito, to tear Czechoslovakia out of the Socialist peace camp and put her into the American war camp. I was supposed also to have set up similar centres in the other People's Democracies—and all this in close conjunction with Tito and his Fascist agents, as well as the British and American Intelligence Services.

It was queer to read in the reports of the trial detailed confessions by people I had known in London and Prague to things that neither they nor I had ever done. What I found significant was that all this was mixed with some of the things that had actually happened, but in strangely distorted forms.

Thus Frejka was condemned as a traitor for his 'national Communist' line. But it was the official Party line in 1946 and 1947. He told me at the time that the Czechoslovak Government were anxious to trade with both the capitalist West and the Socialist countries on a fifty-fifty basis, so as not to be wholly dependent on either. Clementis told me the same thing. This the Government at the time considered to the national advantage, on both economic and political grounds. Now it had become 'Titoism' and treason.

Again, the publicly available information in the shape of reports, Press handouts, etc., on Czechoslovak economic planning and progress, which had been given to me on various occasions, now figured as espionage reports and proofs of treasonable relations with the Western intelligence services. The four memoranda I had prepared for Kratochwil, at his request and for the purposes mentioned above, turned up as instructions sent to Foreign Minister Clementis, in order to provoke a break between Czechoslovakia and the Soviet Union (although Clementis had in fact turned down Kratochwil's proposals that he should take the line suggested). The letter to Fierlinger, giving reasons why the Czechoslovak Government should give conditional support to the Marshall Plan idea, became instructions to Slansky to send a delegation to the Marshall Plan Conference for the purpose of separating Czechoslovakia from the Socialist camp and paving the way for her becoming a vassal of the United States, etc., etc.

I was, of course, asked by the Press to say what I thought of these confessions and charges. I was also given facilities to broadcast comments on the trial in Czech. I said flatly that the trial was a frame-up, that its ultimate object was to brand all attempts at national independence and democratising Communist régimes as being Titoist treason, and that this was done on directives from Stalin. But I added that this had in no way weakened the case for peaceful coexistence: on the contrary, these evil things were largely the products of the cold war; the forces for democracy and freedom within the Socialist camp could gather strength and ultimately prevail only in the context of peace, trade and friendly relations.

I came to Prague with all these experiences in the background, eager to talk with old friends and find out from those who had actually been in jail on the false charges of conspiring with me, what had happened to them, how they were made to confess to a pack of lies and rubbish, and what they thought of things now.

On arrival I was met by an invitation to dine at his home with my old friend, Fierlinger, who had remained Deputy Premier all through, but had at one time been in the danger zone. He embraced me and said, "Thank you for not changing." Me: "?" Fierlinger: "When all those dreadful things were said about you here I wondered, 'Is he going to join the ranks of our enemies now? It would be so natural.' I waited with breathless interest to hear what you had to say, and when you said it you hadn't changed in the least."

We settled down for an afternoon's talk. As in all my other talks in Prague, the progress of de-Stalinisation, the meaning and origins of the Slansky trial, and events in Hungary were the main topics.

Fierlinger, like Novotné, the Party Secretary, whom I met later, was at pains to make it clear that he did not quite agree with Tito's view that the trouble in Hungary was the result of the régime not making sufficiently rapid and sweeping concessions. "Nor do I quite accept the view that the Slansky, Rajk, and Kostov trials were the results of Stalin's attempt to strike down potential Titoism—although there are elements of truth in that. Rakosi and the others were small 'native' Stalins trying to take advantage of the situation to dispose of rivals and come out on top. Rakosi actually played with the idea of going to war with Yugoslavia, in order to make himself the Stalin of Central Europe. Sometimes Stalin himself even tried to curb the zeal of some of these little Stalins. I think perhaps it would be going too far to say that the Soviet political police infiltrated and dominated their counterparts in the People's Democracies, although no doubt M.V.D. agents helped the local Stalins and their police. But we have started to clean up all that and will see the business through, although in our own characteristic fashion, gradually, without drama and incidents."

Looked at from London, the Slansky trial bore such a strong resemblance to the great Soviet treason trials in the '30s, as well as to the recent trials of Kostov in Bulgaria and Rajk in Hungary, that they all seemed to be prompted from the same source and conducted by the same methods. It had certainly been common practice after the war for the governments of the People's Democracies to send administrators and planners, including officers of the political police, to the Soviet Union for training. At the time of Tito's break with Stalin the Yugoslavs had found out a great deal about how their own political police had been infiltrated by Soviet agents and the dual loyalties of many of its members, particularly those who had received Soviet training.

From 1945 on, the Soviet authorities, both military and

civilian, had taken into their service thousands of Yugoslavs, not least those in the political police. These agents were sometimes forced to enter Soviet service by various forms of blackmail (i.e. knowledge of something they had done which gave their Soviet employer an unbreakable hold on them); sometimes they were confused in their loyalties and made no distinction between their loyalty to Soviet Communism as represented by the Soviet secret police officials and their own native brand. The idea of a break between the two parties had never entered their minds; when it did, many in this category remembered they were Yugoslavs and reported their Soviet connections to their official superiors. But others were perfectly clear about it that in their view their loyalty to the leaders of the Soviet Communist Party came before everything, even their loyalty to their own country and its Communist Party and Government. And many did not know what to think—and so lay low and said nothing. The Yugoslavs found it a big and difficult job to 'purge' their police force and administration of these categories of Soviet agents.

In Prague I learned that something similar had happened in the Czech political police—with the difference that there had been no clean-up worth speaking of. This 'unreconstructed' police force was regarded by some of those I spoke with as constituting a serious danger for the future. "These men," said one friend to me, "are utterly unscrupulous. They would be just as ready to frame any of the present leaders as they were to arrest, torture and liquidate Slansky and other victims of the great treason trial and numerous purges up and down the country, when thousands of people disappeared into jail, without anyone knowing why or what had become of them."

There was also ample confirmation of the fact that the initiative as well as the methods came from Moscow and that the object was to wipe out 'national' Communism. Tito had given Stalin a good fright and Stalin's reaction was to tighten up, crush the slightest symptom of national independence in the Parties of the People's Democracies, and brand what as recently as 1948 had still been an official Communist 'line' in those countries, as 'Titoist-Fascist treason'.

Most of the victims who were jailed or shot as a result of the

Slansky trial did quite clearly belong to the category of 'national' Communists. Some had also been in the West during the war, others were ex-Spanish international brigaders (suspect categories everywhere during the Stalin era). But Slansky himself and his faction did not fit into this category, for he was a 100% fanatical Stalinist.

I heard a macabre account of how he had set out to find a "Czechoslovak Rajk" and was trying to build up Madame Schwermerova, a prominent Slovak Communist whose husband, killed in the war, had been a national resistance hero, for that role. But in the course of questioning her and the others arrested at the same time, with the object of establishing connections between them and the great Titoist-Fascist-Western Agents plot that the police had to construct out of whatever materials were to hand, the interrogations took a turn that ended by implicating Slansky. He did not know that the Czechoslovak Rajk he was so anxious to manufacture would turn out to be himself, that what he had started would end by finishing him, and he would go down to history as the classic case of a man hoist with his own petard.

It was now officially admitted that Slansky had not done the things of which he was accused, but he was still denounced as a bad hat, who had told the political police not to be afraid of learning from the methods of the Gestapo, and who was plotting to gather power into his hands and make himself the successor of Prime Minister Gottwald, already a very sick man with not long to live. This tended to confirm the view that the Slansky trial was the outcome of the Stalinist purge getting mixed up with a faction fight within the Czechoslovak Communist leadership, and that someone else got at the political police and turned their guns on Slansky, at the very time he thought he was working them for his own ends.

A stranger once came up to me as we were leaving after a lecture, wrung my hand and said he was delighted to meet me, because he had heard so much about me and in a way, although we had never met before, I had meant a great deal in his life. He had gone before I could ask him to elucidate. But a friend explained: "That poor devil has just come out of four years in prison for allegedly plotting with you."

I talked with a number of people who had been imprisoned after being made to confess to acting as my agents in alleged counter-revolutionary espionage activities in Czechoslovakia. I asked them how they had been made to say these things.

"Very simply," said one friend. "First they keep you from sleeping for a long time and keep on questioning you, alternately bullying and cajoling, and above all keeping it up ceaselessly day and night through relays of interrogators. After a longer or shorter time, perhaps a week, perhaps a month, even three months, you are reduced to a condition when you can no longer think straight; your mind goes fuzzy and queer and your will is confused. When they have got you into that condition they start appealing to your Party loyalty. They explain that the cold war is the same as a military war, where sometimes it is necessary to sacrifice a detachment in order to save the rest of the regiment. The Party asks you to sacrifice yourself by confessing to what they want you to say, in order to help the Party to defend itself in the cold war.

"By that time you are in such a mental condition that you can't spot the sophistry and you give in and say, 'Right. I'll say whatever you like.' Then they produce a written confession with the questions of the public prosecutor and your answers all complete, and you have to learn the whole thing by heart. When you have learnt it they rehearse you with a stop-watch to see that you speak at a normal conversational rate."

One man told me further how when his case was reviewed prior to his being rehabilitated, the examining magistrate had asked him how it was he had made this confession if it was untrue. He explained the procedure and was told, "Comrade, what you say may be perfectly true. Personally, I don't doubt you. But where is your proof? How can you show this is what really happened?"

"That's easy," was the reply. "I can still remember my confession word for word."

"I recited it to him with the prosecutor's questions and all," said the man who told me this. "He was convinced but horrified. 'Comrade, that was three years ago. How can you still remember it? You ought to forget such dreadful things.' "

"I told him it was connected with such awful things that I would never forget it as long as I lived. And you know, I still remember it."

With that he looked down and began in a gabbling monotone, with the Prosecutor's questions and his answers, word perfect, to recite the confession he had made nearly five years before to committing treason as my agent. It was an eerie and almost unbearable experience.

I said, "Good God, man! That is exactly like Weissberg's *Conspiracy of Silence*."

"Yes, I know. When I first read that book I didn't believe it. Now I know it's true."

He, at any rate, had not been tortured physically. But others were. One man explained to me why the people who succumbed most easily to this technique were the intellectuals. They were complicated and sensitive and could be broken down morally, confused mentally and convinced by sophistry more easily than those of simpler and robuster build.

"Only one man I know of," said one friend to me, "never confessed and never signed anything, although for a year he did not sleep more than two hours out of twenty-four and they made him starve and freeze, beat him up, broke some of his ribs, and subjected him to every indignity and outrage. But he was as strong as a bull, a worker with a simple and indestructible faith in the Party. To him the Party was something good and true and nothing on earth could make him believe that these bad men who were doing such terrible things spoke in the name of the Party. He thought that somehow he had fallen victim to villains, and if the Party only knew it would be all right. And so they could not break him, because they could not break into his inner citadel, suborn his faith to their own ends."

These real-life extracts from *Darkness at Noon* and *Conspiracy of Silence* bear witness not only to the horrors of the system, but to the power of faith in Communists, which is glorious and terrible, a miracle and a portent, rooted in the strongest and finest things in human nature, moving mountains—and capable of bearing nightmare fruit. Not one of the many of those I had talked with, who had almost literally been snatched from the jaws of death after years of devilish assaults on human decency and dignity, was a broken man. None had lost his faith that out of the revolution would in the end come a society in which there was equality and freedom.

The very man who told me how he had been made to confess was full of hope about the future, and said that in the light of what was happening in Hungary he, like many others, felt they should support their Government. "It may be stick-in-the-mud and bureaucratic, slow to release, slower still to rehabilitate those falsely imprisoned in the Slansky trial and slowest of all to move towards more democracy and political freedom—but such as it is we prefer to take our chance with it in the present situation."

CHAPTER ELEVEN

The Impact of Hungary

I ARRIVED IN PRAGUE on October 27th, a few days after the Poles had induced the Kremlin delegation to Warsaw to accept their national revolution and just as the Hungarian tragedy was entering its brief hopeful phase—the formation of the Nagy Government, the withdrawal of Soviet forces from Budapest and the announcement of the negotiations for their total withdrawal from Hungary. The peak point came with the October 30th declaration from Moscow about the willingness of the Soviet Government to withdraw their forces and advisers from any of the People's Democracies who felt they were no longer needed.

Then came, on October 31st, the thunderclap of the Anglo-French ultimatum and attack on Egypt, and immediately after that the reversal of Soviet policy and second occupation of Budapest.

These events stirred Czechoslovakia to its depths. The papers were full of reports of factory and other meetings in many cities and towns denouncing the 'counter-revolution' in Hungary and expressing fervent support for the Government. That, of course, was the official 'line'. But even those I talked with who were 'agin the Government' confirmed that the people were rallying to the Government because they were frightened by the spectacle of Soviet tanks bombarding Budapest and Anglo-French tanks bombarding Port Said. They thought another war was around the corner. There was a run on the shops in Prague. Housewives were telling each other, "The Germans are coming back."

The Government did not improve matters by trying to keep

the nation in the dark about what was happening. That was
of course a futile effort. Polish broadcasts were universally listened to and Polish papers were sold out within an hour or
two of arrival (Czechs and Slovaks can understand and read
Polish, and *vice versa*). The same thing happened to Hungarian
papers, for there is a Hungarian minority of half a million in
Slovakia and most Slovaks over forty speak some Hungarian
because they had to learn it at school. Anyone in Prague
who knew Hungarian in those days was in great demand for
listening in to the Government and rebel broadcasts from
Hungary.

The Government went extraordinarily far in their Canute-
like efforts to keep out the tide of news flooding into Czechoslovakia. The grandiose posthumous rehabilitation of Rajk in
Budapest, with the many speeches and the crowd of several
hundred thousand, was given exactly fifty words in an official
communiqué appearing three days later. When *Pravda* described
the rising in Hungary as due to counter-revolutionary bands
instigated by the West, etc., the Czechoslovak Press reproduced
its article. But it was silent when the Hungarian Communist
Party's official organ, *Szabad Nep*, published a sharp retort
denouncing the Soviet view as nonsense and saying that the
Hungarian workers and people had revolted against the evils
and excesses of the Rakosi régime.

The Czechoslovak papers printed *Pravda*'s attack on some Polish
papers, but not their spirited replies. Gomulka's sensational
speech at the 8th Plenum, which heralded the Polish revolution, was not reported at all. I asked one of the top men in
the Party why. He said it was because they did not quite
agree with his views, particularly with his references to democratisation of the Party, which they regarded as dangerously
vague and sweeping. But they did not wish to differ publicly
with him and so decided not to publish. I asked (I fear in
a spirit of mischief, for I knew the answer) why they did not
simply publish it as a piece of straight news without comment.
The official looked embarrassed and said, well, no, they could
not quite do that; it would be difficult, and so forth. "You
mean," I interjected helpfully, "that if your papers simply
published what he had said without comment it would be

assumed that the Party leaders agreed with Comrade Gomulka ?"
He admitted that that was the position.

Now all of this, of course, is felt as scandalous and outrageous
by a great many people in Czechoslovakia, who are used to
Western standards of democracy, political freedom, independence of the Press and Courts, etc. Nevertheless, there was a
real rallying to the Government as a result of Soviet aggression
in Hungary and the Anglo-French attack on Egypt (everyone
I discussed the subject with, whether official or unofficial, for
or against the Government, connected the two events). The
reasons for this pro-Government feeling seemed to be two-fold:

In the first place there are no Soviet forces in Czechoslovakia, and so one of the main reasons for Hungarian revolt
and Polish dissatisfaction is absent. At the same time, there is
a national pro-Russian tradition, whereas in both Hungary
and Poland the tradition is anti-Russian. The Czechs remember
how, before the war, when they were an advanced democracy,
the Western Powers had no hesitation whatsoever in holding
them down on the chopping-block while Hitler carved them
up. On that occasion the Soviet Union offered to fight on their
side if they decided to defend themselves, even although she
was not formally obliged to do so, because the French had
torn up their Treaty of alliance with Czechoslovakia, and the
Soviet alliance did not become operative unless the French
acted on theirs. After the war, when Czechoslovakia, under
Beneš as President and Masaryk as Foreign Secretary, still had
a very real measure of democracy, the Western Powers, as the
Czechs and Slovaks saw it, treated her as an enemy because
she was building Socialism, and thereby showed once more
that their professions of devotion to democracy were humbug.
The Western rearming of Germany and the encouragement
of the rise of the old militarist, nationalist, fascist elements in
that country, so dreaded and hated in Czechoslovakia (and
Poland), was one more factor in determining the Czechoslovak
attitude towards the Polish and Hungarian revolutions, the
feeling that in all the circumstances it was a lesser evil to stick
to their Government and the Soviet alliance.

The second reason is economic: in Hungary and Poland
there had been exploitation by the Soviet Union, top-heavy

and over-centralised industrialisation and bad mistakes in planning, the whole adding up to great economic distress for the workers and the population generally. This factor too is absent in Czechoslovakia, where planning has been more efficient. The Czechs have also been more adroit and successful in conducting their trade relations with the U.S.S.R. As a result, the Czech standard of living is considerably higher than the Hungarian and Polish, and steadily improving.

This is not all due to the superior efficiency of Czechs and Slovaks: whereas Poland suffered fearful damage in the war and had six million killed, and Hungary also suffered great damage and had very little industry to start with, Czechoslovakia emerged from the war with more industrial plant than she had started with, for the Germans had imported a good deal of industry into the country.

But it is the facts and not the reasons for them that count. I discussed the standard of living with one young Czech economist, who made out a good case for his view that the Czechoslovak workers are little if any worse off than their British counterparts. He told me that he considered that the "true" exchange rate for such comparisons, judged in terms of the purchasing power of the crown in relation to wages, works out at 40 crowns to the £1. This is midway between the official rate of about 20 to the £1 and the tourist rate of 60 to the £1. The latter rate, he explained, is intended to attract tourists by making it relatively cheap to live in good hotels and buy freely. It is a sort of bonus for their *valuta* (foreign currency).

Using this "true" exchange rate, he claimed that the somewhat higher costs of food and clothes are largely offset by lower rents. The rent of his own centrally heated flat of four rooms, kitchen and bathroom was £5 per month, with light and heating. (Housing is regarded as a social service, and rents are little more than nominal.)

Another large factor in the standard of living is the scale of social security benefits. Evshan Erban, whom I first met when he was Secretary of the Trades Union Congress, and this time as Minister of Social Security, was rightly proud of the new and comprehensive Czechoslovak social security law, which he was engaged in piloting through its last stages in Parliament. He claimed that it was the most advanced social security law in the world, being ahead even of that of Sweden and much more advanced than ours.

Be that as it may, it is certainly an impressive and exciting social experiment, comprising old age pensions, widows' pensions, disability pensions, family allowances, sickness and maternity benefits, funeral allowances, grants on the birth of a child and free medical care. All this, together with spa treatments, holiday camps and special holiday rates for trade unionists, adds up to a bold and comprehensive scheme which is non-contributory, being financed out of the revenues of the State.

In its general lines the scheme is based on the Soviet model, but the scales are much higher and there are many extra amenities. In the Czechoslovak scheme, too, full basic pensions begin at sixty for men and fifty-five for women, provided the pensioner has completed twenty years of work in categories one and two or twenty-five years in category three.

All pensions are calculated as a percentage of average earnings in a period before retirement of either five or ten years, whichever is most favourable for the pensioner. Up to £600,* average yearly earnings are reckoned in full for calculating the pension; above that amount and up to £1,500, one-third of the average earnings are added to the £600 in calculating the pension. This would mean, for instance, that a man with average earnings of £1,500 a year would have his pension calculated on the basis of £900 (i.e. £600 plus one-third of the additional £900).

In the first category are those who do dangerous and highly skilled work, such as, for instance, miners and air pilots. Men and women in this category, who have reached pensionable age after twenty years' work receive a pension at the rate of 60% of their average annual earnings. They get a further 2% on those earnings for each year worked after completing the required twenty years. A Category 1 old age pensioner who goes on working after attaining pensionable age receives the full old age pension in addition to his or her earnings, if still working in the same category. For the next five years the pension is

* All figures calculated at the 'true' rate of 40 crowns to the £1.

increased by 4% of the average yearly earnings and subsequently by 2%. The maximum pension is 90% of the average annual earnings.

In Category 2 (heavy labour) the basic old age pension after twenty years of work is 55% of the average annual earnings over the preceding ten or five years, with a further 1·5% of those earnings for each year worked after the completion of the required twenty. Pensioners who continue to work after pensionable age receive one-third of their old age pensions in addition to their earnings, with an increase equal to 4% of their earnings for each year of work up to sixty-five (sixty in the case of women), after which it increases by 1·5% of annual earnings. But the full pension is paid in any case as from sixty for women and sixty-five for men.

In Category 3, twenty-five years of work is required to qualify for the full basic pension. The pensioner who works on receives one-third of his or her basic pension if still employed and gets an annual increase in the pension equal to 4% of his or her earnings, up to the age of sixty for women and sixty-five for men, after which they are paid their full pension and, if still working, can increase it, so long as they are employed, by 1% of their annual earnings.

The maximum pension in Categories 2 and 3 is 85% of the average annual earnings for the ten or five years preceding pensionable age.

The minimum wage is £10 a month and the minimum pension for someone in the lowest category, who has worked less than twenty years by the age of sixty-five, is £7 10s. a month.

Disability pensions are reckoned on the same principles and according to the same categories. After fifteen years an employee is entitled to a 50% disability pension in all three categories. After that the rate of increase varies, going up most rapidly for Category 1. The maximum after forty years' employment is 75% of average annual earnings in Category 3, 85% in Category 2, and 90% in Category 1. The minimum and maximum invalidity pension is the same as in the case of old age pensions. There are also provisions for those who have been partly incapacitated, and for a 'wife's pension' when through poor health she cannot do her household work and is not gainfully employed nor in receipt of a pension.

Sickness insurance depends on average daily wages and length of service, from a minimum of 8s. a day up to a maximum of £2 10s. Maternity benefits are paid for eighteen weeks on similar principles, with a maximum of £2 5s. a day and a minimum of 8s. a day.

There is a grant of £16 5s. on the birth of each child and a funeral allowance of £25.

Family allowances are calculated monthly and rise per child with the number of children. Thus for the first child the allowance is £1 15s. a month; for two children £4 5s.; three children £7 15s.; four children £12 5s.; five children £17 15s.; six children £23 5s.; seven children £28 5s.; £5 10s. a month for every additional child.

The Czechoslovak people, it will be seen, already have a good deal to lose in standard of living and welfare State terms. The workers are very conscious of that fact. I spent an afternoon with the Trades Union General Council. They referred with pride to the relatively high standard of living and said their main task was to raise it still higher. They did not approve of the Yugoslav, Polish and Hungarian experiments in workers' management, which they thought too unorganised and unco-ordinated, and preferred large scale State planning as in Czechoslovakia [and the Soviet Union!].

However, they insisted that this State planning was becoming more decentralised and that the trade unions were taking a bigger and more active part in planning, from the national down to the factory levels, both in working out and in applying and controlling the plans. The functions of the trade unions included the administration of social security and public health policies, as well as responsibility for organising recreation and providing amenities for workers. Within the trades union organisation more and more was being left to the initiative of individual unions. These changes had been developing and gathering momentum ever since the 20th Congress of the C.P.S.U.

They claimed that even before that there had been no fundamental mistakes. But on secondary matters, such as the actual running of the factories, safety precautions, canteens and amenities, the collective agreements between trade unions and factory directors had not always been properly carried out. But now, if the workers themselves saw anything wrong, it was becoming easier, through their factory committees, shop stewards, etc., to insist upon matters being put right.

The 20th Congress and its revelations of the consequences of the 'personality cult' had come as a great and painful shock to them. But, they assured me, the 'personality cult' and its abuses had never gone so far in Czechoslovakia [shades of Slansky and the others done to death or jailed in the great trial and the purges!]. Gottwald and the other leaders had always been popular and respected, and Gottwald himself was a very modest man who had always opposed any attempt [and the attempts were certainly strenuous and prolonged] to turn him into an object of the 'personality cult'.

[True, he was a comfortable old Vienna carpenter who liked his pipe and his pot of beer and had a sense of humour. But under it he was a fanatic and in any case had to be tough and tricky in that *galère* or go under.] The workers soon understood when it was explained to them why and how the 'personality cult' was wrong as a system of thought and action. They were now conducting the Party and the Government along the lines of collective leadership supported by inner-Party democracy and the active participation of the masses.

All this was the official view, which I was to hear again with minor variations from a rising young Party member whom I met on another occasion. This young man was at pains to explain how systematically and thoroughly the Government and Party leaders were setting about the business of 'getting rid of the consequences of the cult of personality'. They would see the job through, he said, but wanted to avoid drama, crises and excesses as in Poland, not to mention Hungary. Slow but sure was their motto. But the job had to be done. The Slansky trials and all they stood for ran counter to the national character. There was a bit of Schweik in every Czech, and it accorded ill with the grimness and rigidity of Stalinism.

What made this man's remarks significant was that, I learnt later, he had, during the Stalinist period, been unpleasantly zealous in persecuting and denouncing victims of the Slansky trial and purges. So that his remarks showed how the wind was blowing.

Up to a point the unofficial views corroborated the official 'line': it was true, I was repeatedly told by old friends and new that concessions were being made and the work of de-Stalinisation was progressing—but only slowly and reluctantly. The present leaders had killed off all the prominent 'national' Communists and were all tarred with the Stalinist brush. Only one of the first-rank leaders was guiltless of direct participation in the framing of Slansky and the others.

It was clear that the top Party leaders were hanging on as tightly as they could because—as one of them admitted to me— they feared that 'give the devil an inch and he'll take an ell'— i.e. give the people a little freedom and they'll ask for a lot more. The students and the 'intellectuals' had already been doing too much of that. Nevertheless, they would have to go on, for something had been started in the Soviet Union that had now spread to the rest of the Communist world and had set in motion forces too powerful to arrest. The main support of the Stalinists were those in the West who magnified every fault and difficulty and were trying to encourage the reactionaries in the literal sense who dreamed of the violent overthrow of the existing régimes with Western help. In this connection the *Voice of America* and *Radio Free Europe* came in for drastic criticism and were contrasted with the B.B.C., whose 'objectivity' and sobriety were much appreciated.

The resistance to democratisation and more freedom, I was told, was particularly strong in the middle ranks of the Party, where there were many who held official positions that they had taken over from those who had been 'purged'. These, when they were released and rehabilitated, readmitted to the Party, etc., found that their jobs and homes were occupied by intruders who pulled every wire to hang on to what they had got.

But the pressure was strong and getting stronger, even in the Party, not to mention the people at large. As a rather grim and formidable ex-Spanish brigader, who had formerly held a high position, was then jailed, and had now been rehabilitated and given what he regarded as a piffling job, said, "I have never seen the Party so united as it is to-day—against its leaders."

I spent an evening with Party Secretary Novotné, and his right-hand man, Hedrich, I speaking Russian and they sometimes Russian, but mostly Czech. In his forties, fair, with an intelligent, sensitive face, Novotné is the one top leader who was not directly involved in the Slansky case and the accompanying purges and minor trials. But he has made up for it since in the orthodoxy of his views about the necessity for Soviet leadership in the Socialist camp, and his condemnation of Polish 'national' Communism and Yugoslav Titoism. Hedrich, round-faced, spectacled, very much an *apparatchik* (Party machine man), was amiable, but left most of the talking to his chief.

Both were very worried about developments in Hungary and told horrifying stories about how the Nagy Government was losing its grip; the more concessions it made the greater the demands for fresh concessions: it was torn between right-wing opportunists and left-wing fanatics; the Army was crumbling and most of it had gone over to the insurgents; terrorist bands were murdering Communists wholesale; there had been pogroms of Jews. The country looked like slipping into chaos.

Novotné concluded that it was wrong to make Rakosi the scapegoat for everything—but he was a little vague as to just what he meant by that remark. The only thing clear was that he disagreed with Tito's analysis that the Stalinists in the Hungarian Party should have been got rid of and sweeping concessions made much earlier. If anything, his views seemed to be the opposite—that concessions should have been made more slowly, doled out more parsimoniously, authority clamped down more rigidly, so as to prevent the situation getting out of hand.

"Here," said Novotné, "we are keeping a tight hold on the situation and have the full support of the workers, who do not want us to get into that kind of mess. But the work of cleaning up and reform will proceed to the end. Meanwhile, working-class standards are rising, the peasants are even better off than the workers and our 1953 monetary reform has been a great success."

While I was with Novotné and Hedrich the news came in that Britain and France had sent an ultimatum to Egypt. They wanted to know what it meant. I had to tell them that I did not begin to understand. (I didn't want to mention the obvious fact that it looked like a put-up job, to give the British and French Governments the excuse, for which they had long been manœuvring, to attack Egypt, overthrow Nasser and occupy the Suez Canal.) The only thought that occurred to me was the old saying, "Whom the gods would destroy they first make mad."

The next day I called on our Embassy and tried to find out what had happened. Sir Anthony Eden, however, in his hurry, had omitted to inform our representatives abroad, and I found the whole place in a flap and everybody asking what had got into the Government. One young man told me it seemed so crazy that he was sure the Government had some special knowledge of which we were ignorant, because they obviously must know what they were doing. I said, "My boy, if you will pardon me for addressing you in such terms, you are still young and idealistic and suffer from the delusion that those in power know what they are up to. I have been around a long time and shed that delusion many years ago. I know from bitter experience that when our rulers appear to behave like damn' fools it is because they really are being damn' fools. There never is any convincing explanation or secret knowledge anywhere that justifies their conduct."

Nowhere so strongly as in Czechoslovakia did one feel the contrast between the forces of democracy and freedom burgeoning below the surface and the régime on which they were pressing. In the Soviet Union the régime is tougher, but it has advanced a long way as compared with Stalin's day, is moving with the times and the relatively modest demands from below, and has patriotism on its side.

In Yugoslavia there has been a 'national' revolution which gained the country complete freedom on the international plane, and although developments at home have stuck halfway they have nevertheless advanced to that halfway point before sticking. And there the immense prestige and popularity of Tito act as an elastic buffer between the pressure of popular discontent and the resistance of the régime.

But in Czechoslovakia there has been only a modest gain in freedom since the 20th Congress, and there have been few changes in personnel on any level in the Party. Moreover, even quite young people can remember back to the much greater measure of freedom and democracy they enjoyed from 1945-8, and everyone in his or her forties or older can remember back to the days of Thomas Masaryk and Beneš, when Czechoslovakia was one of the freest democracies in Europe. The régime will have to move fast and far to satisfy the people's demand for democracy. This is not Russia or the Balkans, but Central Europe. Prague the Golden is one of the great monuments of European culture. Czechoslovak history is an integral and important part of the history of Western civilisation.

I left for Warsaw on November 2nd, feeling divided and depressed. On the one hand I passionately longed to fly home and get into the fight the Labour Party was waging so magnificently. On the other, it was clear even from afar that Poland was the key to this whole complex process of the new birth of freedom in the Communist world, and if I missed going there this book would be *Hamlet* without the Prince of Denmark. By that time it was clear too that the whole world situation had darkened suddenly and we looked like being in for another round of the cold war.

I left with the words of a Czech friend—one of those who had been released after four years in jail and made to confess on trumped-up charges, but who had not lost his faith—ringing in my ears: "Do you realise that on the Labour Party rests the responsibility for saving world peace? Don't let the United Nations be destroyed. It is our only hope."

CHAPTER TWELVE

Warsaw Lives Again

FOG AND SNOW STORMS held up the Warsaw plane on Prague Aerodrome until late in the afternoon, so that it was night when we arrived. Stefan Litauer and Clem Kemplicz, old friends from Geneva and London, were at the airport. Litauer, small, grey, wise and witty, is an international journalist, known almost as well in London, Paris and New York as in Warsaw or Geneva. He was a Minister in the new Poland, fell into disfavour during the Stalinist years and is now Foreign Editor of that lively daily, *Życie Warszawy* ("Warsaw Life"). We first met at Geneva in 1928 and have been running across each other ever since from time to time in various parts of the world. Kemplicz, also a journalist, was in the Polish Embassy in London just after the war. Tall and lean, he hides enthusiasm and faith under a quiet manner spiced by dry humour and ironic wit.

"If you had come a week ago you would have found a jubilant Warsaw. Now you find us tense and worried," was Stefan's first remark. "What the Russians are doing in Hungary and you British in Egypt has suddenly made our position tricky and anxious."

Kemplicz took me to dinner and started the proceedings by drinking my health with the toast, "Here's to the Fascist beast." That struck the right note—it showed appreciation of the abysmal silliness of Stalinism, which is as important as its sheer beastliness. And it was as I had hoped. For although the Polish Communists, like the rest, succumbed to Stalinism, they never went so far as the other People's Democracies. They never had any big treason trial like those in Bulgaria, Hungary and Czechoslovakia. They did not kill off Gomulka and his supporters, i.e. the 'National' Communists, although they jailed them. Nor did they forget that Stalin had slaughtered most of the leadership of the Polish Communist Party in 1937 as "national deviationists". And their national pride and tradition were engaged on the side of independence.

Next morning we took a drive around the city, a ghost town come to life. For I remembered it from pre-war days as a noble and beautiful city, one of the capitals of Europe. Then I saw it again in 1946, when it was one vast rubble heap and the scorched roofless shells of what had been houses, mute and terrible witness to the obscene madness that was Hitler. For three months the Nazi robots had systematically, block by block, razed this great city to the ground, homes, historic buildings, churches, everything, as a punishment for having dared to rise and fight against his army of occupation. Hitler swore that never again would the Poles live in their capital—and the Poles vowed they would, whatever it cost and however inhuman the effort.

So in 1946 there were tens of thousands and soon hundreds of thousands living in holes among the ruins, piling the heaps of rubble into peasants' carts with their bare hands and carefully saving all the unbroken bricks. In 1947 there were a few buildings; in 1948 quite a lot more. And now, when I came back after eight years, there was a city again. There were still ruins and rubble heaps here and there, but Warsaw is once more one of the great cities of Europe. A good deal of it is new, but some of the famous buildings and the whole of the medieval old town have been restored exactly as they were —hence the eerie feeling that all round me were ghosts that had come to life.

It was during my 1946 visit that I first came to know Cyran-kiewicz, the present Prime Minister, Oscar Lange and other leading members of the Polish Socialist Party, as well as the then leaders of the Polish Communist Party, Bierut, Gomulka, Berman, Hilary Minc and others. There was a very strong desire in those days among the Communists as well as the Socialists that Poland should be a bridge between East and West. They wanted to be on close and fraternal terms with the Labour Party and were bewildered and disappointed at the hostility towards them of the Labour Government, which was backing the returned London *émigré* and right-wing Peasant Party leader, Mikolajczyk.

Julian Hochfeld, one of the younger intellectuals in the Polish Socialist Party, and a disciple and close friend of Cyrankiewicz, wrote an open letter to a "Comrade in the Labour Party" published in the Polish Socialist Party's newspaper, *Robotnik*, in which he tried to explain his Party's position so that it could be understood by Labour folk: "The bond between us is the idea of democratic Socialism. We should also feel bound to each other by a common freedom from prejudice and desire for peace. But our roads must be different. We, like you, have Socialism as our aim. But we have not yet passed the stage when the conflict of ideas is bitter. Our history has not yet allowed us to break altogether with what in your history were the pioneering days of the Elizabethan adventurers, the fanaticism of Cromwell's republicans, with their horrifying cruelty at times to opponents and criminals, and so forth. We must pass through this stage at lightning speed and catch up with history, which has not been kind to us, whereas your way is to move forward calmly with your famous British phlegm.

"You know that if the coming elections were to give a majority to your Tories they would not destroy all you had done while you were in power, nor take arms to prevent your return to office, and would probably not introduce fascism. But with us it is different. We *know* that if we once surrender power we would have to win it back again, not from Conservatives, but from Fascists, not by ballots, but with bullets, gaining courage for the life-and-death struggle from the sacrifices of those who perished in prisons and concentration camps and on the gallows."

Polish Socialists and Communists co-operated closely after the war because they believed the unity of the working class was essential in face of the forces of Fascism and military dictatorship that had ruled Poland for fifteen years before the war and were deriving encouragement from the hostility of the West to the revolutionary régime.

"The Communists have taught us that Poland must choose between our two traditional enemies, Germany and Russia, and that for us, who want to build Socialism, the choice must be the Soviet Union as our ally, for both national and social reasons," said a Polish Socialist friend in 1946, "but we are teaching the Communists the need for patriotism, for loving our own country and its traditions and prizing its independence."

The fusion of the two parties was long and carefully prepared. Unlike Czechoslovakia, where the Social Democrats were much weaker in numbers and spirit than the Communists, the Polish Socialist Party was as big as the Communist Party and had a strong revolutionary tradition. "But," to quote my Polish Socialist friend again, "the Communists have the support of the Soviet Party and Government, whereas we do not have the support of your Labour Party and Government. If we did we could carry out the union of the two parties on a 50-50 basis and the resultant united Workers' Party would be recognised as a fraternal party by both the Labour Party and the C.P.S.U. As it is, the best we can hope for is that the whole thing will be done on a 40-60, or at worst one-third *versus* two-thirds basis, and that you will not treat our united Workers' Party afterwards as enemies."

The strong infusion of Socialists in the Polish United Workers' Party has been a considerable factor in keeping it from going all the way to Stalinism and for the strength of 'national' Communism in Poland.

In 1946 and 1947 I had two long talks with Hilary Minc, who was then Minister of Commerce, responsible for Polish economic policy. He afterwards turned into a tough Stalinist, which gives added interest to his views in 1946 and 1947—they illustrate the prevailing political climate at that time, the period of the 'false dawn' after the war.

"I know," said Minc, "that historical parallels are dangerous things, but I will risk one nevertheless: the French people paid a bitter price in the shape of civil war, intervention, terror and international war, for the fact that theirs was the first political middle-class revolution. But as a result, the rest of Europe was able to complete the change-over from feudalism to capitalism by milder means.

"The Russian people have paid a fearful price for being pioneers in social revolution. But now as a result the rest of us can advance to Socialism by gentler means. This is particularly true because the war was also a revolution and victory meant the downfall and disappearance of the big business men, bankers, landowners, Army and Police officers, judges, civil servants and teachers, who either turned quislings and threw in their lot with Hitler or were killed off and fled the country and were then replaced by his henchmen. Here in Poland, for instance, we have a clean slate, for there is nothing left of the machinery of the State, or of the landlords and big capitalists of the Marshal Pilsudsky and Colonel Beck dictatorships. Therefore, there is no reason why we should not advance to Socialism by peaceful means.

"Moreover, we shall, for a long time, have a mixed economy with a state sector for heavy industry, a co-operative sector for light industry and agriculture (although we shall have to go slowly and cautiously about the business of inducing the peasants to go in for collective farming), and a sector for small-scale private industry and trade. There will therefore be, if not classes, at least different economic strata in the country, and it would be logical that each of them should have its own political representation. So I see no reason why, after we have met the most immediate and pressing needs of post-war reconstruction, we should not have a system of Government with several parties and a Parliament in which they are all represented."

I heard similar views at that time from Dimitrov in Bulgaria and Duclos and Thorez in France (they expressed them publicly, too), and from some of the Czechs (but not from Slansky). But by 1948 the situation had changed: I followed developments closely through the eyes of Polish Socialist friends, whom I saw in London between visits to Poland. What happened roughly was this: as it became increasingly clear that Britain and the United States were determined to pursue an anti-Communist cold war,* which amounted, whether they admitted it or not, to interference in the internal affairs of the

---

* Contrary to popular belief, the cold war policy was initiated by the West, and its origins can be traced back to 1943. In fact, it was the resumption of a policy pursued more or less uninterruptedly by Conservative Governments since the Russian Revolution. For ample evidence on this point, see my Penguin book, *I Choose Peace*.

'People's Democracies', the great power security interests of the Soviet Union became an ever more obtrusive and oppressive factor in Stalinism. The 'false dawn' of 1946-7 faded as the Russians replied in kind to the West.

"The Communists decided," a Polish Socialist friend, now a member of the United Workers' Party, told me when he was in London in 1949, "that we didn't have as much time as we had thought, but must collectivise our economic life quickly. We could not afford to leave any capitalist sectors in our economy, for they might offer a foothold for Western encroachments."

The relation between the competing pressures of the cold war and the toughening of the Communist régimes was clear and close. It also, of course, accounted for the tightening of the bonds between them and the Soviet Union, and for the growing insistence of the latter that its leadership should be unchallenged and supreme in every field. It was Stalin's excesses in this respect that provoked the Yugoslav revolt—which Stalin attempted to meet by still further tightening his grip on his satellites and starting the intimidation, branding and purging of 'national' Communists. The vicious circle of the cold war, which had touched off McCarthyism in the West, fostered the Red super-McCarthyism of Stalin in the East.

Stalin's death was hailed with relief in Poland. The prompt quashing of the case against the Kremlin doctors, the indictment of the accusers and the massive gaol delivery that followed were signs of the times not lost on the Poles. They promptly released 30,000 political prisoners—including Gomulka and Herman Field—and began reviewing the cases of 70,000 others (almost all of whom have since been released).

The revelations of Khrushchev's secret report on Stalin (which is no secret to the Poles—not only was it 'legally' discussed at every level in the Party throughout the country, but a black-market edition was at one time being peddled in Warsaw), and the whole tone of the public debates and decisions of the Congress gave the green light to the powerful forces in the Polish people and Communist Party that wanted big changes. It released long pent-up forces that have been growing and gathering momentum ever since, like a snowball rolling down a hill.

At first the changes were gradual, almost imperceptible. A new note crept into Polish broadcasts—less jargon and more plain speech, less uniformity and more variety, an occasional fresh thought, even a note of criticism and human emotion. The Press too began to speak a little more freely. All this was the outcome of a constant struggle within the broadcasting services and newspaper offices, enlarging the opportunities that the changing situation afforded, and discovering the limits of the new freedom by trial and error.

"We did not get freedom overnight, you know," said Teliga, a tall, well-set-up ex-Battle of Britain pilot with the high cheekbones, blue eyes and fair hair of a true Pole. He had returned to Poland after the war, suffered persecution during the Stalinist period and was now editing a trade union journal on his way to better things. "Newspapers gradually won more freedom for themselves by writing more and more boldly. Every now and again someone would get into trouble for it, and then the rest of us would back him and there was a lot of argument and shouting—but each time the Government yielded a bit more. Now we can say pretty well anything we like, although of course, as patriotic Poles, we want to help our Government in its struggle for national independence and not say anything that would make its position more difficult. That is why one of the cracks in Warsaw is: 'What's the difference between the Polish and Yugoslav Press?' The answer is: 'The Yugoslav Press may criticise the Soviet Union, but not the Government. Our Press may criticise the Government, but not the Soviet Union.'"

In Poland, as in Hungary, an alliance between the students, mostly Communist Party or Youth members, and the workers grew up that became the most dynamic factor in the situation. For weeks and months the students sent flying squads into the factories, held joint meetings with the workers, helped them to formulate their grievances and press their case, explained what was going on and why, and joined with them in demanding more freedom. The famous newspaper *Po Prostu*,* which won

---

* *Po Prostu* is literally 'Simply', or 'Quite Simply'. But 'Straight Talk' or 'Speaking Plainly' would render the flavour of its title more adequately. And it certainly lives up to its title.

all the prizes for journalistic excellence, besides being the most courageous and outspoken paper in what is becoming a very lively Press, was started and is run by students.

The first overt sign of the fermenting social discontent and national resentment, and the first test of the new forces, was the strike at Poznan in June 1956 that turned into a large-scale riot. This, like the similar events in Berlin in 1953, showed how strong the pressure was from below and how dangerous and difficult it might be to loosen the tight hold of the régime on the people.

But the response from the Government showed that the process had gone too far to be reversed. The Poznan outbreak was taken by the Prime Minister and others as a sign that something was badly wrong in the condition of the working class and the way they were treated.

A thorough investigation was set on foot, and the workers were promised redress of their grievances. The ring-leaders of the revolt were arrested, but their trial was perfecly fair, as attested by Western lawyers who attended it, and their defence turned into an indictment of the régime.

Although they had admittedly killed, sometimes very cruelly, members of the Polish Security Police, relatively light sentences were passed in the few cases brought to trial and the charges against the rest were dropped. In particular, Prime Minister Cyrankiewicz categorically rejected the 'Stalinist' contention that the instigators of the trouble were Western agents and counter-revolutionary elements, although this was the version put forward in *Pravda* (that did not, however, prevent the theoretical organ of the C.P.S.U., *Kommunist*, as late as September 1956, bringing in the Poznan trial as an example of anti-Communist infiltration and subversion by Western agents).

Meanwhile, Gomulka, after being released, was readmitted to the Party, as were others who had been imprisoned with him. The new forces, in the country, the Party and the Press, that had triumphantly passed the Poznan test, grew stronger day by day.

CHAPTER THIRTEEN

The Polish Revolution

THE NEW FORCES were strong enough by August to create a deadlock in the 7th Plenum of the Central Committee. A reasonable view of the Poznan riots was taken at this Plenum, which laid down lines of policy for the future that took account of the new mood. But the Plenum did not make any drastic criticism of the past nor take any bold decisions about rehabilitating and taking back into leading positions in the Party, Gomulka and the others who, the Plenum now admitted, had been unjustly condemned.

The Stalinists in the Party—known as the 'Natolin Group' from the village in which their leaders met—had been obliged to yield on points of policy, but were strong enough to resist the drawing of any practical conclusions or making any disconcerting revelations about the past and the realities of the present. The proceedings of the Plenum were kept secret.

But the very fact that there was deadlock and dissension prevented any lead being given from the Politbureau to the rank and file in the Party, seething with discontent and rebellious moods. Consequently, the new forces grew stronger and stronger and the Politbureau made bigger and bigger concessions to them. This was the background to the historic 8th Plenum, when what the Poles called the 'break-through' occurred.*

Even before the Plenum met on October 18th the papers announced that the Politbureau had decided to co-opt

* They also call it 'the Polish October', 'the Polish revolution' and 'the Polish Renaissance'.

Gomulka. These developments greatly alarmed the Soviet Communist leaders.

Their disapproval was shown on one plane by an article in *Pravda* condemning the allegedly ant-Socialist, counter-revolutionary and anti-Soviet tendencies in the Polish Press. The article was supposed to be written by the Warsaw correspondent of *Pravda*, but according to the Poles who knew him, he had not written it—nor, indeed, knew anything about it until it had appeared in print and indignant Polish friends began to put him on the mat.

The Polish papers mentioned by *Pravda* were not slow in replying, nor did they display a meek and contrite spirit. Although observing the courtesies of debate, except for some acid references to their absence in the Soviet article, they dealt vigorously with the substance of the charges and in their turn counter-attacked the arrogance, xenophobia and lack of understanding displayed by the *Pravda* article's author.

By this time, Soviet apprehensions had assumed more sinister forms than *Pravda* polemics. On the one hand, Soviet tanks in West Poland went out 'on manœuvres', which quite accidentally and coincidentally, of course, according to the Soviet official version, began to gather in a big semicircle around Warsaw. On the other hand, a high-power delegation from the Soviet Presidium, consisting of Khrushchev, Mikoyan, Kaganovich and Molotov, arrived by air on October 19th, not only uninvited, but unheralded and unannounced, and wanted to attend the meeting of the Plenum. The Poles told them politely that the Plenum was a private inner-Party affair where they were not in the habit of receiving fraternal delegates from other countries. At the same time, the Polish Politbureau reported to the Plenum that the Soviet visitors had arrived and asked for an adjournment until they had been received by the Politbureau.

One delegate wanted the Central Committee to elect a new Politbureau before adjourning. But the majority agreed to the proposal that the discussion should be conducted by the old Bureau with the addition of Gomulka. When they met at six that evening the then Party Secretary, Ochab, asked for a further adjournment until eleven o'clock the next morning. "I

M

should like to inform you, Comrades," he said, "that our
Political Bureau and the Soviet delegation have been talking
for several hours in a very business-like way. The subjects we
have been discussing include the fundamental problems of the
relations between our two States and Parties, as well as the
development of the situation in Poland, which is causing deep
anxiety to our Soviet comrades."

The discussions went on until four that morning at the
Belvedere Palace, and were at times stormy. Khrushchev
began by saying: "We have shed our blood to liberate your
country and now you Poles want to sell it to the United States."
At the same time, Marshal Rokossowski, the Polish War
Minister, who, as a Warsaw worker, had joined the Red Army
in the Revolution and risen to be a Soviet Marshal, and who
owed his position in Poland solely to Stalin's pressure, ordered
the Polish troops near Warsaw out "on manœuvres". His object
seems to have been to effect a junction with the Soviet tanks in
order, if necessary, to take Warsaw by force.

But he soon found out he could not rely on his troops. On the
other hand, General Komar, who was in charge of the Government Gendarmes, or Security Troops, 60,000 strong, made it
clear that he would use them if necessary to fight for the
Government—and there was every chance of Rokossowski's
forces joining them. He also supplied the workers of the Żeran
automobile factory, the biggest in Warsaw, with arms and
munitions. They stood to arms for three days and nights in the
factory. An armed workers' militia was formed from the various
factories. It patrolled the streets and broke up several meetings
which hot-heads were trying to turn into riots against the
régime and the Soviet Union.

At a public meeting of 16,000 people, mostly workers and
students, a delegation of students was elected to go and find out
what the troop movements meant and report back to the
meeting. Not satisfied with the explanations of local Party
officials, they insisted upon being received, and were received,
by a member of the Politbureau. They came back and reported
their talk with Cyrankiewicz.

The explanation that the troops had gone out on manœuvres
was received with howls of derision and the Polish equivalent

of 'Tell us another'. But the boos and howls changed to cheers when they announced that the troops had been ordered back to barracks, and the cheers rose to a roar of applause when the students quoted Cyrankiewicz's final remark: "Rest assured Comrades, that Polish soldiers will never shoot at Polish workers."

When the Soviet delegation discovered that on the one hand they would have a second Warsaw rising on their hands if they attempted to coerce the Poles and that this would spread throughout the country, and, on the other, that the Gomulka régime was solid, its line was popular, and it was determined to remain the ally of the Soviet Union and cultivate friendship between the two peoples, as a matter of vital interest to Poland in the face of the menace of a rearmed Germany laying claim to Polish territory, they accepted the Polish revolution. And in the usual Russian way, once they had accepted the accomplished fact, they did so wholeheartedly and handsomely.

The joint statement issued after the talks was most cordial. The Russians promised to review Poland's economic grievances and to give substantial aid and invited the Polish Politbureau to pay a return visit to Moscow.

After these exciting events the 8th Plenum duly reassembled at eleven on the morning of October 20th. Its proceedings opened with a speech from Gomulka, newly co-opted to the Politburo and First Secretary Designate to the Central Committee. It was he who, with Prime Minister Cyrankiewicz and the 'sitting' First Secretary and Chairman of the Plenum, Ochab, had been in the forefront of the long tussle with the Soviet delegation that ended in the famous victory.

"When, seven years ago, I addressed the November Plenum of the Central Committee, I thought that I was speaking to its members for the last time" were his opening words.

He was referring to the 3rd Plenum, when Stalinism 'broke through' in the Polish Party almost as suddenly and dramatically as the break-away from Stalinism at the 8th Plenum. While in Warsaw I was shown the verbatim records of the 3rd Plenum. They made sinister reading. Nearly every speech contained more or less veiled charges against Gomulka of being not only 'subjectively' a 'nationalist deviationist', but

'objectively' a Titoist and so a Fascist and foreign agent. There
was the clank of chains and the tramp of firing squads in those
speeches. For that had been in the year—1947-8—when the
vicious circle of the cold war had begun to revolve in earnest.
Stalin's reply to the 'Truman Doctrine' was to attempt to
toughen and consolidate the Soviet bloc and to put down with
an iron hand those who might be tempted by the Yugoslav
example to dream of national independence.

And now here was this bent, grey little man with tired eyes
behind round spectacles, and a benign face like an emaciated
Slav Mr. Pickwick, back again, proved right by history, the
symbol and hope of the new forces, instinct with Polish tradition and national feeling, that were welling up from below and
breaking through the surface. A worker and originally a
member of the Polish Socialist Party, expelled for being too left,
Gomulka joined the Communist Party, but escaped the
holocaust of 1937, when Stalin 'liquidated' most of the émigré
Polish Communist leaders in one of his purges. At the end of
the war he returned to Poland from Moscow with the 'Lublin
Government, as the Secretary of the Polish Communist Party.
He then became Secretary of the United Workers' Party of
Poland resulting from the amalgamation of the Communists
and Socialists, until he disappeared in 1949, first into house
arrest and then into jail.

Gomulka reminded the Central Committee that at its 7th
Plenum it had made his return to the Politbureau conditional
on his attitude to its decisions. On the whole he thought that
their decisions had been correct. But unfortunately they had not
been carried out. Nor had the 7th Plenum faced the facts of
the situation.

With this, Gomulka launched into a blistering analysis of
the mistakes made in the six-year plan and the evils of Stalinism. The claim to have raised the standard of living by 27%
was nonsense that merely infuriated the workers, who knew
only too well it was not true. In the basic coal industry increased
production had been accompanied by lowering of productivity
per man-hour of labour, and had been obtained only by
making the miners work overtime, including Sundays, on a
scale that was exhausting and demoralising them and could not

go on. The production figures for collective farms showed a lower productivity than in the individual farms, in spite of State assistance to the former.

Gomulka drew a gloomy and unsparingly truthful picture of the great economic difficulties of the country and the desperate poverty of the Polish people. "The key to the solution of this tangled pile of problems," he concluded, "is in the hands of the working class. Everything depends on the workers, to-day and to-morrow, and the attitude of the working class depends on the policy of the Party as conducted by its leaders and on the capacity of our Government and of the whole machinery of the State.

"Recently the workers gave a painful lesson to the party leadership and the Government. The workers of Poznan, in resorting to the weapon of the strike and demonstrating in the streets on that black Thursday of June, cried with a great voice: 'Enough! We cannot go on like this! Turn back from this wrong road!'

"Never and nowhere have workers resorted frivolously to strikes in order to defend their rights. Least of all did they do this without serious reasons in the Polish People's Republic that is governed in their name and in the name of all who toil. Quite clearly their cup of suffering had overflowed.

"The workers of Poznan were not protesting against the Polish People's Republic, nor against Socialism, when they demonstrated in the streets. They were protesting against the evils that had spread so widely in our social structure and that had caused them so much suffering, against the perversion of the basic principles of the Socialism in which they believe.

"To the workers the hope of a better life is bound up with the idea of Socialism. They have fought for Socialism from the moment they became politically conscious. And when history put power into the hands of their representatives the workers put all their enthusiasm and energy into realising the idea of Socialism.

"The working class is our class, our unbreakable strength. The workers are ourselves. Without them, without the confidence of the workers, none of us could do anything or would represent anything besides his own person.

"The attempt to present the painful tragedy of Poznan as the work of *agents provocateurs* and agents of imperialism was politically naïve in the extreme: such agents may be at work at any time and anywhere. But never have they been able to determine the attitude of the working class. If foreign agents and *agents provocateurs* could really make the workers do their bidding, the enemies of the Polish People's Republic, the enemies of Socialism, would have a much simpler job and could easily attain their aims. But the point is that this is not true. . . . Foreign agents, *agents provocateurs* and reactionaries have never been able, are not able, and will not be able to make the working class do what they want.

"The causes of the Poznan tragedy and the profound unrest and discontent in the whole working class are to be sought in ourselves, in the leadership of the Party and in the Government. Inflammable material has been accumulating for years."

They must, insisted Gomulka, tell the workers the whole truth, however bitter. And he did, in this and other speeches. There is a quality in them that can be compared only to Winston Churchill's broadcasts in the darkest hours of the war. There was the same shining confidence that if the people were told the truth they would understand and rise to the emergency.

The Polish people rose as worthily as had the people of Britain. "At last someone is telling us the truth" was the universal reaction to Gomulka's speeches and is the foundation of his immense popularity.

Gomulka was equally outspoken about the need to democratise the Party by introducing free discussion and election by secret ballot to all party offices. "You have no idea how far a little democracy goes," one Polish Communist told me. "Some of us have been protesting against all kinds of petty tyrannies and abuses by bureaucrats and local Stalinists, and as the freedom of the Press increased were writing articles on the subject. Up to now the officials we were gunning for either ignored the criticisms or even quite illegally made difficulties for the papers printing our articles, or for those who distributed them. But now they are shaking in their shoes, for they know that the rank and file are going to elect in their place those of us who have been raising hell with them." There is a great shake-up going on inside the Polish Communist Party and the Stalinists are rapidly being voted out of their positions.

The Trades Union Congress too was a stormy affair, with heated contributions from the floor, and ended in practically the whole of the Polish Trades Union General Council being voted out and replaced by new men.

Some of Gomulka's most drastic remarks were on the subject of the "personality cult":

"It is no use trying to reduce the personality cult to the defects of Stalin as an individual. The personality cult was a certain system, prevailing in the Soviet Union, that was grafted on to practically all Communist parties and to the countries in the Socialist camp, including Poland.

"The essence of this system consisted in the creation of a unified hierarchical ladder of cults. Every cult had its own sphere within which it functioned. In the bloc of Socialist States Stalin stood at the apex of this hierarchical ladder of cults. All who stood on lower rungs of the ladder did obeisance to him. The ko-tow to Stalin was performed not only by the other Soviet party and Government leaders, but also by the leaders of the Communist and workers' parties of the countries in the Socialist camp. The latter, i.e. the first secretaries of the Central Committees of the parties of the various countries, sat on the second rung of the ladder of personality cults, and in their turn were enveloped in the garment of infallibility, wisdom and omniscience. But their cult extended only to the frontiers of their countries, where they stood at the head of the national ladder of cults. Their cults could be called only reflected glories, borrowed gleams. They shone like the light of the moon. Nevertheless, within their own spheres they were omnipotent, and so in every country the ladder of cults extended from the top to the bottom. The head of the personality cult knew everything, could do all things, solved all problems, directed everything and took all decisions within his own national sphere of activity. He was the wisest of men irrespective of what personal knowledge, capacity, or merits he might possess.

"This was bad enough when some sensible and modest man was enveloped in the garments of the cult. He generally felt ill at ease in this outfit. We may say that he was ashamed of it and did not want to wear it, although he could not altogether divest himself of it. For no director of any party organisation could work normally, even when he worked collectively with all who shared responsibility for the leadership, because in the political system of the personality cult, the conditions for normal work did not exist.

"But it was worse and produced wholly evil results when some narrow-minded, stupid bureaucrat or rotten careerist was endowed with the honour and glory of the power and the worshipful rights of the cult. For such men buried Socialism, unwittingly but with deadly efficiency.

"In the system of the personality cult a party as a whole could function independently only within the limits of obedience to the leading cult. If anyone tried to go beyond those limits his comrades would threaten to exclude him. If a whole party was at fault the other Communist parties would ban it with bell, book and candle. Was it possible in these circumstances for the relations between the People's Democracies and their parties on the one hand, and the C.P.S.U. and the Soviet Union on the other, to be based on the principles of equality. Obviously not. The system of the personality cult made that impossible. For it was a highly organised system that crushed every independent Socialist thought.

"The system of the personality cult deformed men's minds and the way of thinking of party leaders and members. Some believed and were convinced that the only infallible interpreter of the science of Marxism and the only man developing and enriching this science correctly and showing the one right road to Socialism, was Stalin. Consequently everything not in accord with his ideas and directives must be harmful, must involve a deviation from Marxism-Leninism, must be a heresy. Others, although cherishing doubts, were certain that any attempt to utter their views publicly not only would make no difference, but would lead to very unpleasant consequences for themselves. Still others were indifferent to anything except how to land a cushy job or dig themselves in in the comfortable positions they were already enjoying."

It would be quite wrong, insisted Gomulka, to think that all the evils of the personality cult were due solely to the Soviet

Union. This was the source from which they originally came, but Poland had developed quite a lot of these evils on her own account and there would have to be a thorough clean-up of the party and the régime and fundamental reforms to put an end to these evils for good and all.

Even before the 8th Plenum the Stalinist heads of the Polish Political Police had been dismissed and there had been a purge of its personnel, its numbers had been reduced and its powers severely limited. The Security Commission of the Politbureau was abolished and the whole institution put directly under the Home Office.

There were some horrifying revelations at the 8th Plenum as to just how vile the methods of this political police had been. A good deal of what was said led to the inference that the Polish police, like the Yugoslav police (and all this came out after the break with Moscow) had been infiltrated with N.K.V.D. agents and infected by Stalinist methods.

Particularly dramatic and revealing was the duel between Berman, who had been in charge of the Polish political police, and his accusers at the Plenum. Leon Wudski began the attack. He complained bitterly that many comrades now blamed everything on the system, but "the system was created by people and people can change it or end it. It was possible not to accept the system, or if we had to accept it, we could at least have changed some things in it, adapted it to our conditions. After all, surely there were Communists with strong characters who were still moved by moral considerations, and even if they did not dare to oppose it, nevertheless could within the system have behaved like Communists, like human beings? Unfortunately, obviously some could not and others did not care. At any rate, those who did oppose were broken and thrown into gaol as enemies and traitors, and those who tried to behave like human beings were either dropped or themselves retired. In any case there were too few of either category. The majority made their peace with the system, made snug nests for themselves at the warm and full breasts of the Beria system and sucked in and made themselves drunk with power, with all its perquisites and privileges. All moral considerations ceased to function."

It had been easier, Wudski said, under the half-fascist régimes of Marshal Pilsudsky and Colonel Beck, to intercede with a Minister on behalf of men unjustly imprisoned, than to secure justice for innocent comrades who had fallen victims to the personality cult system.

"During the years 1950-1, I, a member of the Presidium of the Central Control Commission of the Party, could do nothing to help even comrades of whose innocence I was passionately convinced. When my brief-case was overflowing with tears and sufferings, I decided to go and see one of the secretaries of the Party. I first knocked at the door of Comrade Zambrowski, so as to bring a few cases of this sort to his attention, such as people arrested on the street and let out after seven days of observation incapable of living. They had to be taken to the lunatic asylum. They went there so as not to fall into the hands of the Secret Police. They pretended to be mad. Even decent people were so shocked and horrified that they fled abroad simply to escape our system."

"For months I tried in vain to see Zambrowski," continued Wudski. The nearest he could get was a request from a lady secretary to put what he had to say in writing. Then he tried Bierut, with the same result, except that this time he did commit one case to writing. That led to months of telephone calls and ended with another fruitless interview with a lady secretary. Finally, he had tried to approach Berman himself, but when he suggested it, "the secretary looked at me as though I had asked for a ticket to the moon". Those were the methods of the system!

"Comrade Berman has been giving us the benefit of his self-criticism," Wudski continued. "He has accused himself of lack of co-operation with his colleagues, of ignorance and of insufficient supervision. Comrade Berman belonged to the Politbureau Commission for security questions and knew nothing of what went on there. The whole town knew that people were being murdered, that there were dungeons in which people for three weeks on end were standing in excrement up to their ankles. The whole town knew that Różanski [a high police officer] was himself, personally, tearing out people's fingernails. The whole town knew that people were being drenched in cold water and then stood out in the frost. But Comrade Berman—

a member of the Commission for security questions—did not know. . . .

"I ask you, Comrade Berman, who was supposed to know about these things and whether you did not know how your secretary, Comrade Anna Duracz, was treated, you who knew about her every move.*

"Two years ago the whole family of Theodore Duracz went to Comrade Berman to try and get her out, but Comrade Berman could do nothing. Comrade Berman could remove Różanski, as he told us in his self-criticism. Różanski, who was a high dignitary of the secret police and treated prisoners by his own hellish methods—but he could not help Anna Duracz!"

Wudski then gave cases of people who had, as punishment for minor ideological deviations, been expelled from the Party and practically condemned to starve by being forbidden to write, and went on:

"I also remember, Comrade Berman, your speech at the time of the trial of Rajk, when you said you would look here for our own Rajks. That was at the meeting of the Central Committee held to demonstrate solidarity with the butchers of Rajk. . . .

"Knowing your position in the Party, there is only one possible conclusion: either you really didn't know what went on in the Political Police, in which case you are incompetent to occupy any position of public responsibility, or else you really did know, and in that case the Party must, I think, draw some far-reaching conclusions. This also applies to the other members of the Security Commission."

In his reply Berman linked what had happened in Poland closely to the whole history of developments in the Soviet Union and in the U.S.S.R.'s relations, both with the Socialist States and the capitalist world, that was referred to by Khrushchev in his report to the 20th Congress. "Political dissensions and quarrels," he said, "tragically degenerated into the morbid and destructive psychosis of persecution mania about plots and conspiracies . . . in connection with the conflict with Yugoslavia, the Rajk trial and the general worsening of the international situation in the years 1949-50."

* *Darkness at Noon* in real life!

As for his own attitude between 1949 and 1953, explained Berman, it had been due to several causes; first, "the monstrous and oppressive hand of 'Berianism' weighed heavily on events. It led to the cynical falsification of facts, to the extracting of confessions under duress, to dreadful methods of examining suspects, to moral and physical torture. What made it extremely difficult to grasp what was happening was the mingling of slanders and morbid fantasies with grains of truth, amidst complicated situations, clues and facts that reflected the class fight and the hostile activities that in fact had been going on."

"In the second place, these difficulties were aggravated by the lack of any real co-operation or contact between the members of the Politbureau's Security Commission [presumably because they all suspected or were afraid of each other]. Nor did they have effective control over the political police [presumably because the latter was infiltrated and dominated by men in the service of the Soviet police]. In any case, the Military Intelligence Service [in the Communist countries no distinction is made between military intelligence, the Secret Service, counter-espionage, and such functions as those exercised by M.I.5 in this country and the *Deuxième Bureau* in France] functioned independently and was not even formally under the control of the Security Commission."

In the third place, said Berman, he himself had been under suspicion because of the Field case.*

"When Noel Field was in Poland in 1948 he asked for an interview with me," said Berman. "I refused then, because I

---

* Noel Field was a U.S. State Department official seconded to the Disarmament Section of the League of Nations Secretariat—where I made his acquaintance—who during the war worked for the U.S. Office of Strategic Services, secured the release of a good many leftists in Vichy concentration camps through the Quaker and other relief organisations just after the war, and was first condemned by the Anti-American Activities Committee for being a Communist and later arrested in Czechoslovakia (his brother Herman was arrested by the Poles) for being a Western agent. Both were released in the post-Stalinist gaol-deliveries. Herman received substantial compensation and joined his family in London. Noel sought political asylum in what was then still Rakosi's Hungary, and his subsequent fate is unknown.

did not know him. Afterwards, through Anna Duracz, who worked in my secretariat, he sent me a letter. Field knew Comrade Anna Duracz from Paris in 1945, because on coming out of a camp she found herself in Paris and was given help by various humanitarian societies to which Noel Field also belonged. Comrade Duracz considered Noel Field to be a man of honesty and principle and told me so, so that I accepted his letter. In it he asked me to explain that he was innocent of the charges being made against him, in recognition of his services to the anti-fascist movement in previous years. Obviously, there was nothing I could do in that matter.

"In the Rajk trial in 1949, Field, who was treated as the chief American spy, admitted that he had sent me a letter and had known Comrade Anna Duracz in 1945. These matters came to the knowledge of Beria and of Stalin himself, and from that moment began the most terrifying persecution and charges of espionage and treason directed at me.

"Stalin intervened directly in the question of Anna Duracz. I opposed her arrest to the end, because I was profoundly convinced of her innocence. Comrade Bierut defended me against the slanderous charges of espionage with the utmost energy and devotion—over a series of years, because the pressure was constantly renewed. . . . There can be no doubt that if Comrade Bierut had not put up such a stout defence, the best I could have hoped for to-day would have been posthumous rehabilitation.

"How all this must have affected my work is obvious. I asked several times to be removed from having any concern with security questions. . . . As I have already explained, the painful cases I have mentioned were being dealt with in the conditions of intense pressure from 'Berianism', originating in the highest central organs, through advisers, military intelligence and public pressure organised on a great scale in the Budapest, Sofia and Prague trials."

The case of Herman Field, he explained, had been dealt with in the atmosphere prevailing between the Rajk trial in the spring of 1949, the Slansky trial in November 1952, and subsequent events. "The methods being used by Różanski in these cases only came to our knowledge later, when a few who had been suspected without cause were set free." The Military Intelligence service had "by the most perfidious and brutal methods fabricated the question of conspiracies" out of a number of cases in 1949 that were themselves dubious, but, in the prevailing atmosphere, had to be examined. What military intelligence had concocted then, served as the justification for arresting Spychalski [who was War Minister before Rokossowski and is now his successor] in May 1950 and "in 1951, on a wave of confessions generated during these proceedings, Comrade Gomulka himself was arrested".

Berman said he had protested in vain against these proceedings. "As you know, the pressure from Beria to organise a trial in this matter had gone on for a long time and never relaxed. The first attempts were made during the Rajk trial in 1949. Then it was renewed in brutal and provocative fashion during the Slansky trial, when representatives of our Party were invited, for reasons that are all too clear. An attempt was made to achieve this aim by the nonsensical confessions connecting Comrade Gomulka with the fictitious diversion allegedly organised by Zilliacus and others. This was at the end of 1952."

This interchange between Berman and his accusers bears out the previous information from Yugoslav sources as to the ways in which Stalin, through his political police and advisers, instigated and helped to organise the great treason trials in the People's Democracies that were his idea of the way to consolidate the Socialist camp in face of the growing Western menace, and to deal with the sympathy felt for the Yugoslav revolt in the satellite countries. But it also shows that the whole system was not as highly organised and centrally conducted as is often supposed in the West. There was a little 'play' in it and some opportunities for resistance to it by Communist Parties who were prepared to put up a fight. The fact, as Berman pointed out, that Bierut and others had successfully resisted his arrest and the handing over of the cases of Spychalski and Gomulka to military intelligence, accounted for their having survived (although in the case of Berman it seems pretty plain that he bought his freedom, if not his life, by doing their dirty work for the Stalinists).

After these exchanges in the Plenum, Berman was dismissed from the Politbureau, the Central Committee and the Party. His fate, however, is an indication of the change in Poland since the Stalin era. For he is now living in retirement, finished so far as public life is concerned, but not persecuted.

Equally significant was the 8th Plenum's decision to invite back into active co-operation and treat as comrades those ex-members of the Polish Socialist Party who had refused to join the new United Workers' Party formed jointly by the Polish Socialists and Communists. There is no question of a new Social Democratic Party, because there is no room for two working-class parties, although some reality has been restored to the Peasant Party and the Progressive Party. But there is no longer a ban on being openly and uncompromisingly a Social Democrat.

Gomulka, in his 'programme speech' to the 8th Plenum, drew up the lines of future economic, social, Party and State policies with the same uncompromising clarity and courage as he had exposed what was wrong. He insisted in particular on the need for maintaining the authority of the Communist Party, while democratising its structure, as the guiding force for introducing the reforms and meeting any attempts to abuse the new freedom by those who wanted to overthrow the régime and go back to capitalism or even fascism. He was equally emphatic about the need for maintaining the Polish-Soviet alliance and Soviet troops in Poland till the international situation had radically changed, and to cultivate friendly relations between the two peoples and parties, which he said had been impossible during the Stalinist personality cult, but could and would develop in the conditions of freedom and equality between the allies.

Gomulka's next move was to call a monster public meeting on October 24th in the chief square in Warsaw. It is estimated that between 300,000 and 400,000 people listened to him on that occasion. "It was an act of fantastic courage and faith in the people," said one Polish friend. "The whole city was in a state of wild excitement, and it was touch and go whether the crowd would not get out of hand. But his courage paid and was a further victory for our bloodless revolution."

"In the last few years much evil, injustice and painful dis-illusionment have been our lot in Poland," was how Gomulka began, as the sea of faces froze into breathless silence. "The ideas of Socialism, steeped in the spirit of human freedom and respect for the rights of the individual, in practice have been sadly stained and distorted. Words have not been borne out by deeds. The grinding toil of the workers and the whole people did not yield the expected reward. I believe profoundly that those years have gone for good and will never return. The 8th Plenum of the Central Committee of our Party has reached a turning point in its history. It has begun a new era in our long endeavour, in the history of the building of Soci-alism in Poland, and in the history of our people."

The leadership of the Party had told the people the whole bitter truth, holding back nothing, he continued. They were going to tear up by the roots the evils of the era that had passed and go forward on the road to democracy, into the kind of Socialism best suited to the Polish people. They would not allow anyone to remain in responsible positions who had had a share in the mistakes and evil deeds of the past. (Cheers.)

On the other hand, they would not allow the enemies of Socialism and of the friendship and alliance between Poland and the other Socialist states to wreck their position and pro-spects. Poland's relations with her Socialist allies must rest on complete equality of rights and full freedom for each to exer-cise its sovereignty without hindrance.

"Our meeting with the delegation of the C.P.S.U. resulted in our Soviet comrades understanding the political situation in Poland better than they had before. The First Secretary of the Central Committee of the C.P.S.U., Comrade Khrushchev, assured us that he saw no reason why the mutual relations of our two parties and States should not develop on the prin-ciples indicated by the 8th Plenum of our Party.

"Every specific issue concerning our internal affairs has been settled in accordance with the views of our Party and Govern-ment. It depends only upon us whether and for how long Soviet specialists and military advisers will still be necessary in our forces. At the same time we obtained from Comrade Khrushchev the assurance that Soviet forces on Polish territory will return in two days to their stations, where they remain on the basis of international agreements and of the Warsaw treaty.

"Their presence is closely connected with the existence of Soviet forces in the German People's Republic. So long as N.A.T.O. bases exist in Western Germany, a new *Wehrmacht* is being built up there and Chauvinism and claims to our territory are being encouraged there, the presence of the Soviet Army in Germany is in accordance with our highest reason of State."

There were ovations for everything Gomulka said concerning Poland's new-found freedom and national independence, but only a polite scattering of applause for his insistence on the necessity for the Soviet alliance and for maintaining Soviet forces in Poland. It was on this point it was feared the crowd might get out of hand.

Next Gomulka turned to the Party officials. They were summoned to a national conference on November 4th and Gomulka's speech to them was broadcast. I sat with Clem Kemplicz and his family and listened in to it. It had that same Churchillian quality as his other speeches of courage and shining confidence that the people will understand and rise to the occasion if they are told the truth. And this time too they were certainly treated to some home truths about Poland's present position and what must be done. But mostly it was devoted to giving the Party activists, apparatus and cadres their marching orders—telling them how to tackle the jobs that lay ahead. Democracy, he told them, must begin with themselves. He explained exactly what he meant by that, including full and clear instructions about how to conduct Party elections at every level so as to make a reality of free discussion and the secret ballot. He told them that the security police had been purged of Stalinists, its numbers and powers drastically reduced, and its functions strictly confined to combating espionage and similar activities against the State and the people. He described what should be the new 'democratic' relationship of the Party to the people and the Government, and concluded with an appeal to patriotism as well as to the ideal of Socialism.

N

His analysis of the history of post-war Poland makes a fitting close to this chapter:

"There are two clear stages in the post-war history of our Party," he told the conference. "The first began in 1944 and was abruptly closed at the August session in 1948 of the Central Committee Plenum." [This was when Stalinism and the cold war 'broke through', as they had done almost simultaneously in the other People's Democracies, after the proclamation of the 'Truman Doctrine' and after Stalin had reacted to the resulting Yugoslav revolt by stepping up the pressure and starting the treason trials.]

"The second stage, which began then, faded out gradually as from 1955. In the beginning this process hesitated and fluctuated a good deal. What gave it a powerful impetus and caused it to develop at increasing speed was the 20th session of the C.P.S.U., and in particular the speech of First Secretary Khrushchev at the private session of the 20th Congress [this, of course, was the famous secret report on the 'Consequences of the Personality Cult']. What also had a considerable influence on this process was the rehabilitation of the Polish Communist Party, which in 1937 was falsely and slanderously accused and dissolved by the Communist International [and, he might have added, most of its leaders 'liquidated' on Stalin's orders].

"These external factors, however, merely helped to set in motion the tremendous internal forces that had been exerting ever greater pressure for the ending of this second stage in the life of the Party and of the whole Polish people. The tragic events in Poznan and the 7th Plenum of the Central Committee of our Party will be looked back on as decisive steps on this road, the beginning of the end of the second stage in our history after the war.

"Great changes in the life of the people and events of historic significance always have some date attached to them. I think that it would be correct to describe the 8th Plenum of the Central Committee of the United Workers' Party of Poland as the date on which the new, that is the third, stage in the post-war life of our people and Party began. The former stages have gone and will never return."

CHAPTER FOURTEEN

Problems of the New Poland

A FEW HOURS in Warsaw early in November 1956 produced repeated evidence of the truth of Litauer's remark at the airport. Events in Hungary and Suez were in everybody's mind, and everyone was anxious about how they would affect the Polish Revolution.

On October 30th the Russians had announced that the necessity for maintaining Soviet forces and advisers in the People's Democracies needed reconsideration in the light of the fact that these countries had developed their own cadres of military and civilian experts. The Soviet Government were accordingly, said the Declaration, prepared to enter into discussions with any of the People's Democracies that wished to raise the question of the reduction or withdrawal of Soviet forces and advisers.

This declaration delighted the Poles as well as the other People's Democracies. A couple of days later the Polish Press published a declaration by the Chinese Party strongly supporting this line and expressing the warmest approval for the changes in Poland and the policies proclaimed by Gomulka and the others. The Poles attached great importance to this Chinese support, which they considered powerfully strengthened their position in Moscow. There have indeed been stories that it was partly Chinese representations in Moscow that induced the Soviet leaders to accept the national independence of Poland with as good a grace as in the end they did.

But there was a gasp at what many not only in Poland but abroad regarded as Gomulka's foolhardy courage when he calmly took the Soviet leaders at their word and sacked

Marshal Rokossowski and the Russian or Stalinist advisers and officers in the Army and Air Force. Rokossowski, it is true, had received only twenty-three votes in the Central Committee on the last-minute nomination of him (by one of the 'Natolin Group') to the Politbureau. But it nevertheless seemed a bold move to remove him and replace him by General Spychalski, who, until quite recently, had been in prison for 'national deviationism' and worse.

The places of the dismissed men were filled with Polish officers who had, like Spychalski, been cashiered or even jailed for their un-Stalinist views. Among them were many Air Force officers who had been Battle of Britain pilots. Teliga went through the list with me, pointing with pride and joy to those of his old comrades who had at last come into their own after years of hardship and persecution. He also told me how disappointed he was at having received no reply from any of his former British messmates and comrades in battle, who had now risen to high positions in the R.A.F. and to whom he had sent telegrams telling of these promotions of old comrades.

The dismissal of Rokossowski was greeted with unfeigned joy by most Poles. The news came through too late for the last edition of the Warsaw evening paper, *Express Wieczorny*. They decided to bring out a special edition. But all their newsboys had gone home. So they recruited a voluntary staff, mostly students, who ran through the streets in the night with their papers calling "Come and pay 20 grosz for Kostia's single ticket to Moscow." ("The students know their Polish history," said one friend to me. "They remember that the Czarist general who held down Poland after the 1830 revolt was Grand Duke Constantine, the Czar's brother, and transferred the contemptuous nickname Kostia of that much-hated man to Konstanti Rokossowski.")

I found one Pole, an ex-officer, who felt sorry for Rokossowski: "You know," he said, "if he had refused to obey orders and not moved his troops he would have been vindicated in twenty-four hours, and become as great a man as Gomulka—perhaps even greater, because we Poles are fond of marshals' uniforms. But his military training and Communist discipline were too much for him—he blindly obeyed orders.

It is said he was in tears when he received his order of dismissal and exclaimed: "During all my years in the Soviet Army the Russians called me 'the Pole' because I was proud of my Polish origin and still talked Polish even when a Soviet Marshal. And now the Poles call me a Russian and will have none of me. Where do I belong?"

This was, however, by no means the prevailing mood. Few tears were shed over Rokossowski's fate, particularly when the news came through that he had immediately been given high office again in the Soviet Army.

Then came the inevitable Warsaw wisecracks, this time couched in terms of the Olympic Games, which just then were much in the public mind: "Who is the champion long-jumper? Rokossowski, because he jumped from Warsaw to Moscow."

"Who is the champion high-jumper? Spychalski, for he jumped from prison to the post of Minister of Defence."

"Who is the champion swimmer? Cyrankiewicz, because he kept on the surface the whole time."

The most popular crack of all was about Gomulka, whose name is a homonoym of a word meaning a "small cottage cheese". So the joke runs: "What is a greater miracle than the multitude being satisfied with five small loaves and two little fishes? The satisfaction of 28 million Poles with one Gomulka."

But the Anglo-French ultimatum to Egypt on October 30th and their bombing raids, followed promptly by the return of Soviet tanks to Budapest on October 31st, caused grave anxiety in Warsaw. In those early November days the tragedy of Hungary hung like a pall over Poland and like a sword of Damocles over the Government. I saw Hungarian flags here and there in people's windows and I heard about a student demonstration in Cracow: the students had been given permission to demonstrate, but on condition they did not shout slogans, so they marched through the city, quite silent, carrying Hungarian flags, while the crowds bared their heads. There were other more violent demonstrations too that were dangerous—one or two assaults on Soviet officers and soldiers, landlords in garrison towns on the frontier turning out the wives and children of Soviet officers who were their tenants, etc.

For the Polish and Hungarian peoples are very old and close

friends. Hungary was oppressed in the Austro-Hungarian Empire until she rose and gained her freedom, in the way the Poles had tried to do so many times without success. Their eighteenth-century social structures were akin too, so that Polish and Hungarian magnates saw eye to eye, as did the peasants and the workers suffering from similar oppressors. Polish friends told me that during the last War the Hungarian troops who occupied part of Poland behaved like friends and not enemies, helped the civilian population with food, and not infrequently also managed to help the Polish Resistance Movement.

It was no accident that the October 23rd demonstration in Budapest that started the Hungarian revolution was held in the square with the statue to Joseph Bem, the Polish General who had fought with Kossuth in the 1848-9 revolution in Hungary. The crowd carried Polish as well as Hungarian flags to demonstrate their sympathy and admiration for the stand Poland had just successfully made for independence and as a tribute to the past and the historic parallel commemorated in the square.

I was invited to a luncheon with some members of the Central Committee. Like everyone I talked with in Warsaw, they were convinced that there was a close connection between the Anglo-French assault on Egypt and the return of the Russians to Budapest after they had withdrawn from the city. As this is important, I may say that everyone, from Gomulka, Cyrankiewicz, and Foreign Minister Rapacki, with whom I discussed Hungary at length, on, took much the same view of the situation. It was based on firsthand information from Polish journalists, officials and others returning from Budapest and other parts of Hungary.*

As the Poles saw it, the Russians were faced with a genuine dilemma: having swallowed Poland's stand for freedom with considerable reluctance, but in the end with good grace, they were faced with an even bigger demand in Hungary. In Poland there had been no doubt that the Gomulka régime had nation-

---

* The Poles were sending plane-loads of medical supplies and blood for the wounded—there was such a rush to supply blood that the medical authorities had more than they could use.

wide support and was firmly in control, nor that, although determined to liberalise and democratise the political super-structure, it intended to go on building Socialism under the control of the United Workers' Party and regarded the Polish-Soviet alliance as a vital interest for Poland, in view of the German threat fostered by the West.

But the Nagy Government were asking Soviet forces to leave Hungary, had announced that they intended to leave the Warsaw alliance, and promised free elections that would certainly mean the Communist Party being overwhelmingly defeated. And on top of that, it began to look as though Nagy in his turn were being superseded. For every concession he made, fresh concessions were demanded. He could not rely on the Army, which had mostly gone over to the various revolutionary organisations. Reactionary and Fascist elements did mingle with the revolutionaries. There were pogroms of Jews; not only members of the hated Security Police, but their wives and families were done to death, sometimes very cruelly. The same fate met many merely because they were Communists.

The Polish leaders' view of what was happening in Hungary was, in fact, almost identical with the one Tito had given me, except that the Poles, unlike Tito, deplored the second Russian intervention as much as the first. The Czechoslovak leaders had told me much the same, but I discounted their views because they were frightened of and hostile to the Hungarian revolution from the start, and approved of Soviet intervention, whereas the Poles and Yugoslavs wanted the revolution to succeed and Soviet occupation to end.

But, said the Poles—and later I found this was also the Yugoslav view—the Russians were faced with the prospect that not only Stalinism but Communism itself would go down in the Hungarian revolution, and the régime that ultimately emerged, after more or less prolonged and bloody disorders, might be 'Christian Democratic' or something of that sort. They both scouted the idea that Fascism and the old order could come back—it was too late for that; the peasants would never give up·their land to the Church or the landowners, and the workers would not surrender the factories and mines to private owners, even if any were left. On top of that Nagy had asked for the

withdrawal of Soviet forces and announced that Hungary
proposed to repudiate the Warsaw treaty of alliance with the
U.S.S.R. and to become a 'neutral' state, like Austria.

For about twenty-four hours it looked as though the Soviet
Government were prepared to accept even that. In the declaration issued on October 30th the Soviet Government promised
to discuss with the People's Democracies whether they wished
to go on availing themselves of the services of Soviet civilian
and military advisers and to retain Soviet troops on their
territory, and to withdraw them if their presence was no
longer desired.

The Anglo-French attack on Egypt, by a dramatic and
devilish mischance, came at exactly the moment when matters
trembled in the balance at the Kremlin and transformed the
situation: to the Russians it looked as though Britain and
France had decided to end the attempt to work out forms of
co-operation and peaceful co-existence with the Soviet Government, for which the new leadership in Moscow had made so
many concessions. The alternative to the Anglo-French 'go-it-
alone' policy would have been to go ahead with the resolution
moved by the United States and endorsed by the Soviet Union
in the Security Council. That would have been the beginning
of East-West co-operation in this area, and Khrushchev would
at last have been able to point to some success for his conciliatory policy. Instead, the Russians now felt they had been
slapped in the face—Britain and France were treating them as
a negligible quantity in the Middle East and were attempting
to destroy Nasser, whom the U.S.S.R. had been backing.

In the circumstances, the cold war was on again and the
attempt to get away from rival alliances and positions of
strength seemed to have failed. In that perspective what
guarantee was there that a neutral non-Communist Hungary
would not speedily become a bitterly anti-Soviet, anti-Communist Hungary, joining N.A.T.O. and allowing Anglo-
American bases on its territory?

Even if Hungary did not join the Western camp and remained neutral, there was still the possibility that the Polish
and Hungarian examples would be followed in Eastern Germany. That could lead either to the Russians crushing the

revolt, at the risk of Western Germany becoming involved, which would touch off the third world war; or else the Soviet Government would yield for the third time—and then an 'independent' Eastern Germany would join Western Germany more or less on Adenauer's terms, i.e. united Germany would remain a member of N.A.T.O. and rearm in earnest, with the help of the West, for the recovery of the territories ceded to Poland. The whole balance of power in Europe would have changed to Russia's disfavour and the Soviet Government would have suffered crushing blows to its prestige.

The Poles saw all this and admitted that the situation was exceedingly difficult for the Russians. Nevertheless, everyone with whom I discussed it agreed that however great the risks of any alternative, what had actually happened was the worst possible solution. "Better even reaction in Hungary than Russian intervention," said one of my Central Committee hosts. "For in the former case it would be the responsibility of the Hungarian people and a disgrace to the Hungarian workers. But Russian intervention is a dishonour to Communism everywhere." The others agreed. One expressed his bitter regret that there had been no Hungarian demand for Polish volunteers. "We could have raised fifty thousand men in a day," he said.

"Imre Nagy should have refused office until the Soviet forces had been withdrawn and he should have armed the workers," commented another. "His trouble was that he did not trust them. That was why he kept making more and more concessions to the right, until he was helpless and his Government broke up." Another agreed and added that revolution was a difficult job and one should know how to do it.

The one point on which there was unanimity was that the only way out now was to work for a general European settlement involving the withdrawal of both Western and Soviet forces from Germany, and the latter from Poland and Hungary as well, and the supersession of the rival alliances by an all-European treaty. At this point, of course, I produced the Labour Party's Blackpool Conference resolution on Germany and read it to them. I enlarged on the policy behind it, in the light of Conference speeches and those made in the House. They said, yes, that was the kind of thing they had in mind, but they thought there should be a collective guarantee of Poland's and Czechoslovakia's frontier with Germany.

That was the general view, although the top leaders I discussed the matter with did not really feel enthusiastic about the unification of Germany at all, and insisted that there should be limitation and control of German armaments at a very low level and guarantees against any German resort to aggression. But they all agreed that the only way out was through an all-European treaty, which in some way would supersede and replace the rival alliances and would include provisions for the reduction, control and limitation of armaments and withdrawal of forces. They thought too that the new Labour policy could become the basis for negotiating such an agreement.

The Government's great problem, while I was in Warsaw, was to prevent the feelings of sympathy for Hungary overflowing into demonstrations of hostility to the Soviet Union that might endanger the country's independence. A resolution was moved in one institute—but promptly quashed—censuring the Polish delegate at the General Assembly for having voted against the General Assembly majority resolution on Hungary. "Such a pity," said a member of the Polish United Nations Society to me, "that when for the first time public opinion is really interested in how we vote at the United Nations, we should have had to go against popular feeling in this way."

"It wasn't pleasant to have to make this decision," said a member of the Polish Government to me. "But after all, what good would it have done to vote for the General Assembly majority resolution? It wouldn't have helped Hungary and it would have jeopardised our hard-won independence." He also implied that they had been disappointed at the rather wishy-washy attitude of the Yugoslavs, who they had hoped would give a lead.

There was a dramatic debate in the editorial board of one of the live-wire youth papers that have brightened up the Polish Press and galvanised Polish public opinion: "Better to die on the barricades than to live with the shame of not standing with our Hungarian comrades," cried a girl of eighteen. "Yes, we could do that, I know," replied a woman of thirty. "I fought in the Warsaw rising when I was your age—you were too young to remember all that. When we began, the whole people were for us, enthusiastically and with all their hearts. But in the end they hated us and cursed and reviled us, because they held us responsible for the destruction of our city by the Germans. That too is something we must reckon with." That view carried the day.

I found some Poles a little puzzled and touchingly proud at how much restraint and discipline they had shown in this crisis. "I knew we Poles were always rather good at risings and last stands, dying on barricades and all that kind of thing," said one to me, "but this lark of behaving with restraint and common sense is something new. We've become almost British!"

Others took a tougher view, and compressed their wry bitterness into another of the wisecracks for which Warsaw is famous. This one ran as follows: "The Hungarians are behaving like Poles, the Poles are behaving like Czechs, and the Czechs are behaving like swine" (the normal Polish attitude to Czechs and *vice versa* is that of a Spaniard to a Swiss. But in this case feelings were heightened by the canny pro-Stalinist and anti-Polish and anti-Hungarian revolutions attitude of the Czechoslovak leaders).

The attitude of the Catholic Church in Poland has been a great help in steadying the people amidst the shocks and changes of the new era. Thanks largely to Cardinal Wyszyński the Church after the war began to come to terms with the régime and even concluded, more or less against the wish of the Vatican, a kind of unofficial concordat.

This broke down with the onset of the Stalinist period. The Government did not keep the terms of its agreement and Cardinal Wyszyński was banished to a remote village and many of his bishops thrown into jail.

One of the first acts of the new régime was to put an end to all that. Cardinal Wyszyński returned to Warsaw in triumph. The bishops have returned to their bishoprics and the relations between Church and State are once more becoming normal. A mixed Government-Church Commission is going into the whole question of the relations between Church and

State, and is expected to produce some form of agreement or concordat.

A period has been set aside in State schools, during which parents who wish their children to have religious education can make the necessary arrangements. In practice, as Poland is a solidly Catholic country, this means that priests come to the schools to give religious instruction. Indeed, the boot is now on the other foot: parents who do not want their children to be taught religion are complaining that the other children set upon theirs and call them Communists!

There was remarkably little difference in the views on the situation expressed to me by two old friends, one a Communist, the other a Catholic, former great landowner and aristocrat, whose family is part of the history of East and Central Europe and Russia. They both said that Catholicism was the national and traditional religion of the Polish people, but that only a small minority were ardent in their faith or basically hostile to the régime. Catholicism was strong in Western Poland, which was formerly under Germany, because there it was the badge of Polish nationality, just as Protestantism was that of the Germans, and so became an integral part of Polish patriotism resisting Prussification.

The Church had realised, said both, that it would be as foolish to assume that Polish peasants would agree to return their lands to the Church, as it had been for the Czarist régime to rely on the supposed piety and devotion to the Little White Father of the Russian *moujik*. Peasants and workers who were Catholics did not want interference with their religious faith. But neither did they want the old order back under which they had suffered so grievously.

Both admitted that there were some members of the Communist Party who were also Catholics. But both had no use for them, regarding them as neither fish, flesh, fowl, nor good red herring. My Communist friend spoke contemptuously of members of the Communist Party who remained nominally Catholics in order not to upset their families or the community in which they lived. My Catholic friend spoke equally scornfully about Catholics who became nominal Communists for career reasons. Both were agreed that now the Church and the régime had made their peace with each other hybrid phenomena of this sort, in which they included the little 'tame' Catholic organisation "Pax" that had been fostered during Stalinist times, would disappear.

To Western concepts it does not seem unreasonable that membership of a political party should be determined by a man's political opinions and leave unaffected his philosophical convictions or religious beliefs. But that of course is not the basis on which the Communist Party functions. As the process of democratisation develops, however, the new social order becomes an accepted thing, the danger of counter-revolution recedes, etc., the Communist parties are likely to cool down into political mass parties that do not make such all-in demands on their members.

The Catholic community is once more free to publish its own newspapers, reviews, etc., and the 'All-Polish Club of Progressive Catholic Intellectuals', which was dissolved under Stalinism, has been started again. Its first meeting was devoted to a discussion of the economic problems of Poland.

The President, a nationally known Catholic writer, Jerzy Zawieyski, emphasised the fact that representatives of the club had been in touch with the Cardinal and that they had his entire confidence. He said it was not only a political but a moral duty in the present situation to have a sense of responsibility, to remain calm and to show common sense. The second task of the Catholic community, said the President, was to co-operate in carrying out the programme of the 8th Plenum.

Another Catholic speaker, Dr. Stomma, said that Catholics had an important part to play in the new situation:

"The overwhelming majority of the Catholic community is not Conservative. It agrees with the programme of the Party on such matters as sovereignty, the return to the rule of law, the practice of telling the people the truth, and publicity in public life. The October changes in Poland mean a new phase in the life of the people, and it is the duty of Catholics to play their part fully in it as active members of the People's Front."

A guest at this meeting was Wladyslaw Bienkowski, close friend of Gomulka and now Minister of Education. I met him, and found him fiery, tough, witty and prodigiously intelligent, and one of those Polish Communists who manage to combine the philosophy of dialectical materialism with humanism and a passionate belief in morality and principles—a grand man. He had personally brought back Cardinal Wyszyński and, although a Communist, is on excellent terms with the Catholic community.

He made a speech on this occasion defining Stalinism as the "dogmatisation of Marxism, which thereby ceases to be materialism. And so during the Stalinist period what we were oppressed by was not materialism but pure idealism," said Bienkowski amidst tumultuous applause. "To-day," he concluded, "both Marxists and Catholics want to go back in economic life to the working of economic laws and so to materialism in economics, which, of course, does not mean that Catholics have become materialists."

When I was there Gomulka's remark was going the rounds in Warsaw: "Well, when both Cardinal Wyszyński and Comrade Khrushchev approve of our programme, we must be right!" Another Polish leader said to me: "In the present situation Cardinal Wyszyński is a more reliable supporter of the Government than some of our own student hotheads!"

Although Hungary was so much in the forefront of people's minds, there was also a good deal of feeling and discussion about the Anglo-French attack on Egypt. The first feeling was overwhelming surprise, giving way in a day or two to indignation and apprehension. "Your Government has knocked out our moral prop abroad," said one Pole to me. "We know the Russians have no political morals and that the Americans regard us as enemies. But we thought you British were a decent and civilised country that wouldn't do this kind of thing."

Another Pole told me of the case of Mackiewicz, a recently returned *émigré*, who had been writing a series of violently anti-British articles in a Warsaw paper (presumably partly under the impression that he was working his passage and partly to relieve his feelings of the bitterness wrought by exile). "Up to now there have been indignant replies to him from Poles who were in England during the war or returned some years ago and love your country. Public opinion was with them. But now they have fallen silent and people are beginning to say, 'After all, Mackiewicz is right. Look at what they are doing in Egypt.' " Other Poles echoed the view I had heard in Czechoslovakia, that it was now up to Labour to defend world peace by preventing the destruction of the United Nations.

And so at a meeting arranged by the Polish United Nations Society, where I spoke on "Labour and Current World Problems", I said I did not know what Labour's official line on Hungary was, but I was pretty confident that it would be very similar to the views I had heard in Warsaw—namely, that:

(*a*) The Russians were faced with a real dilemma aggravated by the Anglo-French incursion into Egypt.

(*b*) They had in fact chosen the greater evil, thinking it was the lesser, and what they had done was not only a crime in point of international morality, but a first-class political blunder.

(*c*) The way out lay through a general European settlement on the lines to which the Labour Party had committed itself in its Blackpool Conference resolution on Germany (which I read again).

As for the Anglo-French attack on Egypt, it was a violation of the Charter by aggression and therefore an international crime. It was also a blunder, the political equivalent of leading a cavalry charge into a quicksand. Labour had taken its stand on loyalty to the Charter and was offering strenuous opposition to the Government. I assured my hearers that Labour would never allow this or any Government to get away with violating the Charter by aggression, and reminded them of the stand Labour had taken to stop intervention in Russia and the Labour Party's world peace loyalty proclaimed in 1934. I said I did not think it would come to anything as tough as this, because Labour's power was now so great that its mere refusal to support the Government or to forgo industrial claims in order to make things easier for the Government would be enough to put an end to the Egyptian adventure. It was only by taking the obligations of the Charter seriously that we could find a basis for active peaceful co-existence and negotiated settlements in Europe and Asia that would put an end to the feud and the competition in armaments between the Communist and non-Communist worlds, and leave the social and political structure of each country strictly the internal affair of its own people. Every true friend of Poland in Britain would understand why it was necessary in present circumstances to maintain the Soviet alliance and would hope that, given freedom and equality in their mutual relations, the ancient grudge between the two peoples would fade away.

That address got me into a bit of an argument at our Embassy in Warsaw. But I still think I was right in contending that I had in fact helped to uphold the honour of our country and rekindle confidence in it among those of our friends in Poland who were beginning to doubt.

I also went counter to official policy in attending the Soviet Embassy reception on the anniversary of the Revolution on November 7th, which the Western Governments had instructed their Embassies to boycott (for the British and French Governments, who themselves were in breach of the Charter in Egypt, to take this line was surely a classic case of the pot calling the kettle black). When I met the Soviet Ambassador I told him that I disagreed strongly with Soviet policy in Hungary, but I had come because I would not in any circumstances be a party to reviving the cold war.

I had a very good chauffeur home from that reception: coming out at midnight, I could not find the car that was supposed to be waiting for me, but ran across Prime Minister Cyrankiewicz, who said he would give me a lift. He drove me back to the hotel. "I always drive myself. My wife says I am a better chauffeur than Prime Minister—anyway, I always know I have another job to fall back on if I lose my present one."

Just before leaving, I attended the first meeting of the last session of the Sejm before the elections under the new law. It began with the Finance Minister, Jendrychowski, presenting the budget for the new five-year plan. The next speaker was Oskar Lange, Chairman of the Finance Committee of the Sejm, who made a detailed, constructive, but at times drastic criticism of the report and presented the Finance Committee's alternative views. After that, the matter was thrown open to debate.

But before that came an "interpellation" by an M.P., who was the Mayor of Kattowice and complained that the Government had promised the town and region so and so many thousand tons of potatoes by a certain date. They had already overrun the date by a month, delivered only just over half what they had promised, and most of them were frozen. What did the Government propose to do about it?

The Government were mercifully given till next day to think up the answer to that one, which was delivered in a tough, straight-from-the-shoulder style that would have done credit to the House of Commons. Evidently the new spirit was already at work.

While I was sitting in the gallery listening to the proceedings, a man took his place beside me whom I had last seen in Stockholm in 1949, when he was Polish Ambassador there. "I am an *émigré* now," he told me, "and it was all your doing. Don't you remember, when we met you had just come from Yugoslavia, and we talked at great length about Tito's stand against Stalin?"

I did indeed remember that talk, for while stoutly defending the Cominform line, as he was in duty bound to do, he had been reasonable and willing to listen. "Well, you convinced me, and as a result I resigned from my job. But I have come back now to see what is happening—you know the Government have introduced a new rule by which Poles who have left the country may come back freely to find out for themselves what conditions are like. And if they like them, they are welcome to return. I do like what I have seen, and I think I shall come back for good."

I checked with Polish friends afterwards, who said it was perfectly true about the new rule, and it had been introduced with a dual purpose: in the first place, by letting anyone who wanted to, whatever his past record and views, visit the country and go away again without let or hindrance, they had cut the ground from under the feet of a lot of hostile propaganda among Polish *émigrés* and made it easy for those who wanted to come back to do so. The Government, of course, retained the right to refuse to allow *émigrés* who were out-and-out enemies of the régime to return permanently, and they could do no serious

o

harm on a visit. On the other hand, they did not want *émigré* Poles who had become accustomed to higher standards of living in the West to come back full of good intentions and rosy illusions, and then to become disappointed and bitter when they found that life was still hard and standards of living low.

"Let them come and find out for themselves what things are really like," said one Polish friend, "then if their patriotism impels them to return all the same, they will be coming back with their eyes open, knowing what to expect—and they will be very welcome."

I was invited to the big celebration at the Palace of Culture, the Soviet gift to Warsaw, in honour of the anniversary of the revolution. The building in itself is a notable structure and the interior is very fine. Besides, as a Polish friend said: "It really is very useful." But in order to introduce Polish national touches, the Soviet architects have added a number of ornaments and excrescences of one sort or another which lend colour to the Polish jibe that the whole thing looks like a wedding cake. Amidst the somewhat plain and severe architecture and low horizons of Warsaw it sticks up like a sore thumb. It represents a genuine gesture of goodwill by the Soviet Union to Poland, but not many·Poles regard it in that light.

It had been feared that the hall would be half empty, for the first time, on the occasion of the celebration. But perhaps owing to the special efforts made, the place was packed as usual. The speeches no doubt differed from the past, for they stressed how much Poland prized her independence (invoking the appropriate Leninist principles of course), as much as the importance of the Polish-Soviet alliance and the achievements and place in history of the Russian revolution.

After the ceremony I went back to his home with Premier Cyrankiewicz—after a decent show of reluctance; it was late and he had had a heavy day. But he said it was his first free evening for a long time and he wanted to enjoy it by talking with an old friend. Julian Hochfeld, a close friend of the Prime Minister, was there too, just returned from lecturing at the Royal Institute of International Affairs in London. There he had expressed much the same view as Tito, that the Soviet Union and People's Democracies hold no monopoly of Socialism and should learn about the approaches to Socialism and ideas about Socialism in the West, and have friendly relations with the Labour, Social Democratic, and Progressive parties of those countries.

Our talk covered a great deal of ground and was, of course, informal and private, as well as lasting until late at night. But these are the main points that were made by the Prime Minister or Hochfeld, or both: first, pride at the discipline and unity displayed by the Polish people and appreciation of the 'line' taken by Cardinal Wyszyński in his sermons preaching the need for calm and discipline and doing one's job (as distinct from striking or demonstrating), as a patriotic duty, and for charity among Poles as a religious precept with a poignantly topical political application. For the first time the Government and the people were united and Polish leaders enjoyed the unaccustomed sensation of finding that they were popular. There had been a great rallying of the people to the régime during and after the 8th Plenum.

But—and this was the second main point—the break with the past in Poland would have been impossible without an easing of the cold war, as well as the example set by the 20th Congress of the C.P.S.U. The continuation of the cold war was the greatest obstacle to the advance of democracy and political freedom in the People's Democracies. "Here in Poland we have been able, thanks to the relaxation of international tension, to achieve our national independence in a very full measure. But we cannot change the international pattern nor be completely free until it has been changed. An agreement between the great powers and a general settlement in Europe is the only way to complete our freedom and to open the door to freedom in the other People's Democracies. If the cold war gets worse again as a result of Hungary and Egypt, our position will once more become precarious and anxious."

I heard again the view that the Anglo-French plunge into Egypt had tipped the scales the wrong way in Moscow and determined the second occupation of Budapest. Labour's Blackpool resolution on Germany was cautiously approved.

I drew attention to the policy—very similar to that of Labour—and the prospects of victory in the next election of

the German Social Democratic Party, and suggested that if
Germany were united on their terms and with them in power,
the Socialised economic foundations of Eastern Germany
would be preserved and we might in a few years have a Socialist Germany with a very different outlook from Adenauer's
Germany, which represented the last stand of the old guard.
Even with Western help I doubted whether they could survive,
for Germany could no longer be a great power in military
terms any more than Britain and France, and being plumb in
the middle was bound to be atomised in any war between the
two camps. A lot of Germans understood this and had had
enough in the last war, anyway.

We agreed that the development of Socialism and of 'func-
tional' internationalism through the United Nations was the
only hope for Europe and the thing to work for, and it was only
in this atmosphere and in these conditions that democracy and
political freedom could take root and spread where they did
not yet exist, or in the long run survive even in the West, apart
from the contingent risk of extinction in the war that the cold
war would sooner or later bring upon us by accident if not by
design.

Hochfeld told me he was translating Rosa Luxemburg's
pamphlet on the Russian Revolution, in which she had with
uncanny accuracy foretold how the party structure devised by
Lenin would in the end lead to bureaucracy and dictatorship.
As the German original is practically unobtainable he was
working on a French translation he had found in Paris. I asked
him whether he had thought of translating Trotsky's history
of the Russian Revolution, but he said it was not a serious
enough analysis from a Marxist point of view—more like a
novel.

It is indeed as exciting as any novel—but I suspect a reluctance to entertain the idea of translating it was part of the
general feeling that it would be imprudent to try the Russians
too high. Trotsky is no longer regarded as an ex-foreign agent
in the Soviet Union, but he has certainly not been rehabilitated.

High appreciation was expressed for the sobriety, objectivity
and wise counsel of the B.B.C., which had been helpful all
through the crisis in sharp distinction to Radio Free Europe

and the Voice of America, about which ·there is only one
opinion in Eastern Europe and the Soviet Union: they are
frankly out for counter-revolutionary upheavals in all these
countries and never count the cost or the consequences.
Their broadcasts are slanted accordingly. That, of course, is
Mr. Dulles' 'drastic and dynamic' (to use his own words)
policy of "anti-Communist liberation", of which Mr. G. F.
Kennan, formerly head of the Policy Planning Staff of the
State Department and United States Ambassador in Moscow,
has said that it is a policy that would lead to war.

Premier Cyrankiewicz said it was a relief to feel that now he
could talk freely and without reservation to Labour comrades
visiting Poland. "I don't mean you, of course. I have always
been able to say what I thought to you." One of his last remarks
was: "One day, as we put more democracy into our Socialism
and you put more Socialism into your democracy, we shall
meet halfway."

If all goes well we shall. But since November 1956 the path
looks steep and thorny. The international situation has grown
no better and the Polish people are already chafing at the limits
of their new freedom. Over Hungary and the whole question
of the relations between Socialist states the Poles and the
Yugoslavs are loosely allied, in more or less open opposition to
the rest, with the Italians keeping a foot in both camps and
the Chinese acting as 'middle-line' mediators. The Poles, to
their relief, were not invited to the meeting at Budapest
attended by Khrushchev, Malenkov, and the faithful Czechs,
Rumanians and Bulgarians, which endorsed the Soviet line
on Hungary.

The Chinese Foreign Minister Chou En Lai's visit to Warsaw
looked outwardly like a disappointment, for he seemed to be
urging the Poles to come closer to the Soviet views, both on
Hungary and on the need for closing the ranks and accepting
Soviet leadership in the 'Socialist camp', in face of the renewed
cold war threat from the West. But privately the Poles claim
to be highly satisfied with his visit, for they say he made it
quite clear that China would go on supporting Poland in her
stand for independence, while begging them to observe a
statesmanlike prudence and restraint in the present critical

international situation—which coincides with the view of the Polish leaders.

"If only China were in the United Nations," said a Polish delegate on his way to the General Assembly whom I met on the airport (I knew him before), "she would be on the same line as we, because she could make her own contacts, stand up for her own interests and see things for herself. Whereas now she is isolated and dependent on the Russians for information about the rest of the world as well as for defending her interests in the councils of the nations, for economic aid and military support."

The Polish revolution, like all revolutions, has aroused high hopes that must be at least partly satisfied, and has released energies that must be harnessed to constructive purposes, if the dynamic of the revolution is not to ebb or turn into dangerous channels. The revolution cannot stand still without beginning to slip backward. It must press forward. But the road ahead is strewn with difficulties and mined with dangers.

There is first of all the fact that very many people are desperately poor and have to work till they drop to keep alive. Gomulka gave a warning that no great and rapid improvement could be expected, and that to increase consumer goods and raise the standard of living the Polish people would have to produce more. But he did promise alleviation of the conditions of the poorest sections of the community, and notably to do something for the miners.

Nevertheless, the Government must show results soon, or the tremendous enthusiasm it has aroused will begin to turn sour. The immediate and central problem is to raise coal production, because coal is Poland's key export and much in demand from countries that can deliver what she needs in return—namely, machinery and equipment, particularly for the coalmining industry, but also for other industries. At least as urgent is the shortage of raw materials, which creates bottlenecks and frequent stoppages in Polish industry. Cars, trucks and tractors are badly needed too, as much for agriculture as for industry.

The Soviet Government have given some very real help by supplying grain, by cancelling debts and making good the losses incurred by the sales of coal to the U.S.S.R. below world

prices, and by granting credits. But the Poles need a great deal
more help and would like the West to grant them long-term
low-interest credits and conclude trade treaties that would give
them what they need to raise their own production, in which
case they could pay back whatever they had borrowed, for
Poland's potentialities are great. The Poles do not want any
political strings attached to economic or financial help, and
believe that the best way of holding the balance even and
retaining their independence is to do business both with the
Soviet Union and the other Socialist states on the one hand,
and the West on the other.

There is still a tough struggle ahead before the Communist
Party is thoroughly de-Stalinised and democratised. Not a few
of the 'Natolin Group' are fanatical enough to want the Polish
revolution to fail and even to encourage ugly things like Polish
Chauvinism and anti-Semitism in order to help wreck the
great experiment and go back to Stalinism. The fact that to do
so would produce a situation analogous to that in Hungary and
might even bring on a world war, does not deter them.

Their number is however diminishing day by day, for most
members of the Polish Communist Party have heeded Gomulka's appeal to stop thinking in terms of the groups and
factions that divided the Party before the 8th Plenum and to
judge Party comrades only by their words and deeds since the
great change.

But other and even more dangerous forces are moving under
the surface. As one Polish friend said to me, "More democracy
and political freedom will for a time mean anti-Semitism
rearing its ugly head again." That has already happened and
many thousands of the 60 odd thousand Jews left alive in Poland (out of 3 million or so—Hitler slaughtered the rest) are
now applying for passports to emigrate to Israel. The Polish
Government is putting no obstacles in their way and are being
generous about their taking their property with them.

It is the habit in the West to talk of all the Communist-
ruled countries as though they were free democracies before
the war. This is true only in the case of Czechoslovakia. Poland
had democracy on paper after the First World War, but it
was quickly snuffed out by Marshal Pilsudski. After his death

the semi-fascist dictatorship he had established was continued by Colonel Beck. Chauvinism, megalomania (a desire to restore Poland's pre-war eastern frontiers and even dreams of going back to the boundaries of the eighteenth-century Polish Republic, which took in most of the Ukraine), fanatical and almost insane hatred of both the Soviet Union and Germany as hereditary enemies, anti-Semitism and hostility to democracy were rife in pre-war Poland.

It is foolish to imagine that the opposition to the present régime consists wholly of frustrated democrats longing for more freedom. In this field the Gomulka régime, on the contrary, has the support of practically everything liberal in Poland. The opposition to the Communist régime as such— as contrasted with those who accept it but want to reform it in the direction of more democracy and political freedom— comes mostly from sworn enemies of democracy, racial equality and peaceful relations with Poland's neighbours.

This fact makes more difficult and risky the aim the Party leadership have set themselves of democratising the régime. For sooner or later that process will become incompatible with the Party retaining control. It is bound to reach the point of no return, i.e. the point beyond which the Communist Party could no longer gather all power into its hands again even if it wanted to, because so much would have been yielded to the other parties in the People's Front and to the elected representatives of the people in Parliament and in the Government. The Communist Party would no longer have the last word.

"We will cross that bridge when we come to it," said the Polish leaders whom I questioned on this point. Meanwhile, it is their avowed intention to give the single chamber legislature (the Sejm) more work and power and to make it in reality and not only on paper the law-making and controlling organ of government.

In the short run, the success of the Polish Revolution depends on improving the people's standard of living. That in turn requires help from the West, in addition to that already being obtained from the Soviet Union. In the long run, the fate of Poland hangs on the success of East and West in composing their differences and negotiating a European settlement.

CHAPTER FIFTEEN

The Great Controversy

THE HUNGARIAN TRAGEDY sparked off a great debate in the Communist world that began with an argument about what had actually happened in Hungary, who was responsible and what ought to be done, but soon swelled into a debate on fundamental issues: at home the monopoly of power of the Communist Party and the dictatorship of the proletariat have had to be defended against critics, as has State ownership and control in industry against workers' management, producers' co-operatives and ideas resembling guild Socialism. In international affairs the whole idea of maintaining the Socialist group or bloc and the Soviet claim to leadership within it has been challenged, as has the twin idea of treating the Communist ruled states as representing all the Socialism there is in the world.

The Yugoslavs have, from the beginning, made the running in this controversy, partly because they have ever since 1948 taken their own line both on how to build Socialism and on what should be the relations between Socialist states, and partly because they feel free to speak their minds and have done so with vigour and point. When I saw Tito in October 1956 he said the Yugoslav Communists were not prepared to sit around for another twenty years while the Russians re-made all of Stalin's mistakes over the past twenty years, which they had themselves denounced at the 20th Congress. He was going to start fighting all this and was convinced the Yugoslavs would win because there were such strong forces arrayed even in the Soviet Union against Stalinism.

The first phase of the controversy was the letter already

mentioned from the C.P.S.U. to the Communist parties of the
People's Democracies, warning them against taking Yugoslav
Socialism as their model, because it had been distorted by the
capitalist powers during the years Yugoslavia depended upon
them, and the Yugoslavs had adulterated it with social democracy. Then came a whispering campaign in the capitals of
the 'Socialist camp' saying that Yugoslav influence was to
blame for the Polish and Hungarian revolutions.

The second phase began with the publishing of these charges
in a long article in *Pravda* by Enver Hoxha,* the Secretary
of the Albanian Communist Party. This thoroughly roused
the Yugoslavs, never remarkable for meekness, who had not
forgotten the violent hostility of the Albanian Party leaders
throughout the Yugoslav conflict with Stalin.

Velko Vlahovich, in *Borba* of November 15th, 1956, poured
scorn on the idea that Yugoslavia possessed such magic power
that she could make the rain fall or the sun shine in Poland
and Hungary, where there was more industry, the cultural
standards were higher and the working class had longer
traditions than in Yugoslavia. This was idealism, not Marxism.
He poked fun at Hoxha's 'hill-billy' Marxism, but was concerned at the fact that his article had appeared in *Pravda*,
although it took a line contrary in many respects to the decisions
of the 20th Congress of the C.P.S.U.

Tito Speaks

The third phase opened with a big speech by Tito to young
Party workers at Pula on November 11th, 1956. It was reproduced in its entirety by the Chinese and Polish Party organs
and brought all the basic issues into the controversy.

Tito began by holding the Soviet leaders largely responsible
for the fearful abuses of the Rakosi régime and for the failure
to replace him by Imre Nagy and bring in the reforms in the
summer before it was too late. He also said the first Soviet
occupation of Budapest was a wellnigh fatal mistake. But he
severely blamed the Nagy Government for its failure to fight
the growing counter-revolution that was swamping what had

---

* Pronounced Hodzha.

been a national rising largely under Communist and working-
class leadership, and suborning it to its own ends. In the resulting situation he thought the second occupation of Budapest
was a lesser evil than the alternative of counter-revolution,
civil war, foreign intervention and a possible world war.

The Russians, he said, were in a difficult position and realised
they had roused the whole Hungarian people against them.
Soviet soldiers were engaging in the fight reluctantly and with
heavy hearts. The whole thing was not due to a deliberate
act of Soviet policy.

The root of the trouble was that the Soviet leaders had so
far not been prepared to apply to all the Socialist States the
principles of freedom and equality laid down in the Bulganin-
Tito and Khrushchev-Tito declarations of June 1956. He had
noticed on that occasion and later in the Crimea that whereas
they had learnt to respect the Yugoslavs' desire for freedom
and equality, because they were tough and united, their régime
was solid, they had won power by their own efforts and they
had stood up to Stalin, the Soviet leaders took a different view
of the other People's Democracies, whose governments they
had helped into the saddle. This was a big mistake, because
"the same elements that produced Yugoslav resistance in 1948
exist in Poland, Hungary and other East European countries. . . . We warned them that they existed in all other
countries too, and that they might break out as they had in
our country, and in that case it would be much more difficult
to remedy the situation.

"When Stalin died the new Soviet leaders saw this folly
had led the U.S.S.R. into a blind alley and left her in a very
difficult position, both in foreign and domestic affairs, and
that the same was true of the People's Democracies, because
Stalin's methods had been treated as Holy Writ and forced on
them too."

The Soviet leaders at the 20th Congress had rightly repudiated Stalin. But they were "wrong in talking as though what
was wrong was only the cult of his personality. Because the
personality cult is in fact the product of a system. They have
not conducted a campaign against that system, or in so far as
they have, they have kept quiet about it and claimed that as

a whole they have done everything right, but that Stalin in his last years grew old and began to go a bit crazy and make mistakes. From the beginning we have said that the issue is not simply the cult of personality but the system that made the personality cult possible, that these are the roots of the evil against which we must strike our heaviest blows, because this is the most difficult part of the job. Where are these roots? In the bureaucratic apparatus, the methods of administration, the so-called one-man management principle, the ignoring of the desires and importance of the working masses. . . .

"But we did not take this Soviet attitude too tragically because we noticed that . . . it had been imposed on some Soviet leaders by others who still clung to their old Stalinist positions, and that the internal evolution of the Soviet Union may still bring to the top those who want a more rapid and resolute democratisation of the country's internal life, the abandonment of all Stalinist methods, and new relations between Socialist states. We also noticed that developments in this sense were extending into foreign policy. From all we saw and from our conversation it was plain that these elements are not weak—they are strong.

"But this internal process of development in a progressive direction, toward the abandoning of Stalinist methods, is being obstructed by some Western powers, which by their propaganda and incessant repetition of their demand for the 'liberation' of these countries, are interfering in their internal affairs and preventing the rapid development and improvement of relations between these countries. Because interference has developed on such a scale, through broadcast propaganda, sending of materials by balloons, etc., as to make the Soviet Union fear that if it left these countries altogether and gave them the same status as Yugoslavia, the results might be damaging. They fear that in that case reactionary forces might get the upper hand in these countries."

This fear, said Tito, showed that the Soviet leaders had no confidence in the Socialist and revolutionary forces within the peoples of these countries. That was the root error of Soviet policy toward the People's Democracies. But he believed that the bloodshed in Hungary and the fearful sacrifices of the

Hungarian people would open the eyes of their Soviet comrades to the impossibility of going on like this and that Hungary would prove the last tragedy.

"We must work in the very closest contact with the Polish Government and Party, and help them in every way we can. Together with our Polish comrades, we must fight against the tendencies appearing in various other Parties, both in East and West. Comrades, that fight will be a hard and long one, for what is at stake is nothing less than whether the new line that began in Yugoslavia and which was in part adopted in the decisions of the 20th Congress of the C.P.S.U., shall triumph in Communist parties everywhere. The issue is whether this new line will win or whether the old Stalinist line will again get the upper hand. Yugoslavia must not retire into her shell. We must be active in every direction, not by attempting to undermine these countries from within and to provoke negative excesses, but in the field of ideas, through contacts and conversations, so that the new spirit will triumph. We must not be afraid of openly criticising what is no good in other parties."

Pravda *Answers Tito*

After some preliminary skirmishing between the Belgrade *Borba* and the Soviet Telegraph Agency (Tass), *Pravda* on November 23rd published a 6,000-word reply to Tito entitled "For the Closer Unity of the Forces of Socialism on the Basis of Marxist-Leninist Principles". This article, courteous in tone, makes a full statement of the Soviet view (and the version of the facts on which it rests) on all the issues raised by Tito's speech.

It begins by drawing attention to the Soviet-Yugoslav agreement to discuss all their differences with the utmost frankness, in a friendly, comradely spirit, and says this is a correct principle, and it welcomes discussion—but thinks that Tito was more frank than friendly.

The article admits that the rising in Hungary was due to the explosion of the "banked up discontent of the workers, who rightly demanded an improvement in the government of their country, and a raising of the standard of life of its people.

There is no doubt that the responsibility for the Hungarian events lies with the former State and Party leadership of Hungary, headed by Rakosi and Gerö. They made bad mistakes in dealing with the problems of building Socialism, both on general political issues, on economic questions and in the field of culture and education. The leadership of the Party, headed by Rakosi and Gerö, lost touch with the rank and file and with the people, and knew nothing of what the workers, the peasants and the intellectuals were thinking and feeling. Legality was grossly violated (the Rajk trial and a number of other trials where many honest party members and servants of the State suffered unjustly)."

This account, it will be observed, does not mention that Rakosi and Gerö had been exported from Moscow, imposed on Hungary, kept in power and incited to commit their worst excesses by Stalin.

Pravda's account of the actual outbreak and course of the Hungarian rising does not differ much from Tito's, but alleges that the "counter-revolutionary elements were organised in advance, had their directing military centre and their forces ready and placed in position for overthrowing the Government, as well as units assigned to seize the arms stores and the objectives marked for attack. They had mobilised means of transport and set up distribution centres for collecting and handing out arms." Nagy is accused not only of being wavering and weak, but two-faced: "On the one hand he declared that bringing in Soviet troops was necessary to put down the counter-revolutionary forces, and on the other he encouraged the active resistance of counter-revolutionary elements and kept in touch with them." (In fact, of course, it was not Nagy, but Gerö who behind his back, and against his will, called in the Soviet troops, and the 'counter-revolutionary elements' with which Nagy kept in touch were mostly the Workers' Councils, partly the Small Holders and Social Democrats.)

Even after the 20th Congress of the C.P.S.U., continued *Pravda*, Rakosi had claimed that all was for the best in the Hungarian Party, and there was no need for reforms and changes. This had caused serious discontent in the Party, to which the leadership went on turning a deaf ear and a blind eye. "It should be added that for some months there was open agitation and propaganda against the Party and the Government in the Press, in some literary and student circles, etc. In this propaganda, side by side with justifiable criticism of the leadership, there were more and more nationalist and Chauvinist opinions, demands for a return to bourgeois democracy and anti-Socialist feelings, which were often put forward under the guise of contrasting the 'Yugoslav road to Socialism' with the experience of the whole Socialist camp, including the experience of the S.U."

Pravda ends its account with the curious, almost wistful, remark that "When everything is quiet again in Hungary, when life has resumed its normal course, the Hungarian working class, peasantry and intellectuals will without doubt understand our action better and appreciate it more justly. . . . When order has been restored in Hungary and its Government considers that the further presence of Soviet forces is unnecessary, the Soviet Union will not in any circumstances insist on keeping its troops in Hungary."

Pravda, of course, makes the most of Tito's admission that there was a serious danger of counter-revolution in Hungary and that the second Soviet intervention was on the whole a lesser evil. It accuses the Yugoslavs of interfering in the internal affairs of other Socialist states by criticising their Communist parties and of attacking the structure and foundations of Soviet society by condemning bureaucracy and centralism in the C.P.S.U. and saying that they had produced Stalinism. The Yugoslavs, says *Pravda*, are arrogant, and claim that only their way to Socialism is the right one. But workers' management, in spite of some successes, has produced fragmentation of economic planning and relies too much on market relations. Yugoslav agriculture is chaotic, still below pre-war production. For some years Yugoslavia obtained economic help from capitalist states who wanted to aggravate the dissensions between Socialist states. This was not a road to Socialism that others could or should adopt.

Pravda deplored Tito's remarks about the struggle between Stalinists and anti-Stalinists, which had been hailed with joy in the capitalist world. It accused the Yugoslav comrades of occasionally cherishing views inconsistent with Marxist-Leninist theory and lacking in loyalty to the principles of proletarian internationalism. It warned them against starting quarrels and sowing disunity in the present critical situation when the counter-revolution in Hungary and the Anglo-French attack on Egypt had revealed the renewed danger of imperialist aggression. "The events in Hungary were the first major outbreak of Fascism in the whole post-war period and showed that the threat of Fascism has not yet passed. In these circumstances the supporters of Socialism must be united and on their guard."

Borba's *Rejoinder*

Borba, November 27th, complained that *Pravda* had not given Soviet leaders a chance to read what Tito had really said, but gave them a garbled and incomplete account. Its main charge was that Tito's speech had played the game of international reaction. "Does *Pravda* mean by this that because international reaction exists there must not be any open discussion or constructive criticism between Communists, that they may not face facts and speak the truth?"

Pravda was running away from the unpleasant fact that some Communist parties were neither correcting the mistakes of the past nor taking the new line proclaimed at the 20th Congress of the C.P.S.U. Why did *Pravda* publish Enver Hoxha's article, which not only libelled Yugoslavia, but contradicted the decisions of the 20th Congress?

Instead of attacking Tito for speaking of the desperate courage with which the Hungarian people fought for their freedom, *Pravda* should have asked itself why this had happened. "What are the causes of this broad and deep anti-Soviet feeling in Hungary? Why did it reach such a pitch that the Hungarian people did not care about anything, if only they could put an end to the unequal relations between Hungary and the Soviet Union? Must we not think seriously about these things, analyse them, and tell the whole truth? Yes, the whole truth —so that we can learn the necessary lesson!"

The Poles Take a Hand

At this point the Polish Press joined in the argument: *Try-buna Wolności*, the weekly organ of the Central Committee of the Party, wrote that Tito's view of the Hungarian rising was much the same as that of the Polish Party, and warmly endorsed his statement that the Poles and the Yugoslavs must work closely together. The importance of Tito's speech was that he had started the discussion on great issues of principle. was criticising the positions adopted by the Soviet and some other Communist parties, and had pointed out that the 20th Congress of the C.P.S.U. had laid the foundations for correct relations between Communist Parties. *Trybuna Mazowiecka*, which is the organ of the Warsaw Regional Committee of the Polish United Workers' Party (a strongly anti-Stalinist body), vigorously criticised *Pravda's* article, while welcoming its declaration of willingness to engage in discussion on these issues. In particular it rejected *Pravda's* contention that the Hungarian rising could be ascribed to Fascist and reactionary forces which had been organised beforehand. No doubt reactionaries did join in the great revolutionary movement in Hungary, but to attempt to reduce this enormous tragedy to Fascist provocation was completely unjustified and unreal, and *Pravda* was quite in the wrong when it accused Comrade Tito of 'exaggeration' because he had said that the whole people took part in the revolutionary struggle. If the whole thing had been the work of a few Fascist bands, Hungarian resistance would have been over in a few hours, instead of lasting for days and weeks, and counting its victims by thousands. As for *Pravda's* statement that the responsibility for the explosion in Hungary lay with the Rakosi and Gero Party leadership, *Trybuna Mazowiecka* said it doubted whether it was possible to put all the blame only on the leadership of the Hungarian Party.

On the very day *Pravda's* article appeared another Polish paper, *Życie Warszawy*, made an outspoken attack on Soviet policy in Hungary, which it said was zigzagging back to Stalinism. It poured scorn on the Soviet allegation that the Hungarian revolution was really a counter-revolution started by Western agents and American money. The heroic Hungarians,

P

said the paper, were fighting for the same thing as the Poles, namely freedom for their country. It said the Hungarian rising was essentially a working-class and people's protest against intolerable conditions, like the Poznan riots in June. It was a revolt on a national scale against Stalinist violations of every people's right to build Socialism in their own way and without interference and oppression from outside.

The Czechs Support Moscow

The next development was a resolution by the Central Committee of the Czechoslovak Communist Party, after two days' secret session, in which a whole paragraph was devoted to condemning Tito's Pula speech, on what were now becoming familiar lines. *Borba* of December 10th pointed out that, as usual, the speech was condemned although neither in the resolution nor in the Czechoslovak Press had there ever been any mention of what Tito had actually said.

Borba *Sums Up*

This resolution, said *Borba*, was merely a link in a lengthening chain that had been forged over several months. "As we know, the thing began with the sending out of a secret letter expressing doubts about the Yugoslav Communist League, saying that it displayed social democratic tendencies and was not a wholly Marxist-Leninist organisation. Although all this was about Yugoslavia, this letter was not communicated to the Yugoslav Communist League. After that came newspaper articles, and then interpretations of Comrade Tito's speech at Pula that rested on falsifications of what he said. The latest step is the resolution of the Central Committee of an East European Communist Party. With that the attacks on our country have gone beyond newspaper articles, and assumed the form of an official document by a Communist Party.

"In view of all these things—the distortion of Comrade Tito's speech, the nature of the charges made and the official form given to them, it is impossible not to feel that we have here a typical case of renewing the methods adopted in the days of the Cominform."

The Kidnapping of Nagy

The next stage in the controversy was the kidnapping of Imre Nagy and the others who had taken asylum in the Yugoslav Embassy in Budapest. The Yugoslav Government had obtained a promise of safe conduct and return to their homes for them, but they were seized the moment they left the Embassy. This still further angered the Yugoslavs: the kidnapping was carried out by Soviet officers at the orders of the Soviet High Command, and the victims were spirited away to Roumania. At first lies were told by the Kadar Government, who said they had of their own free will decided to seek asylum in Roumania. The Yugoslavs pointed out that while in their Embassy in Budapest, Imre Nagy and the others had expressly said that they did not want to go to Roumania, but if not granted freedom to return to their homes, preferred to seek asylum in Yugoslavia.

Although holding the Hungarian Government responsible for this flagrant breach of the agreement, the Yugoslavs knew perfectly well, of course, that the Soviet High Command was the villain of the piece. They drew the conclusion that after all the Kadar Government were mere puppets and the Soviet authorites were running the country, just as in the worst times of Stalin.

Kardelj Gets Tough

This act, and pressure from below in the Party and in the country generally, about which more will be said later, accounts for the even stiffer tone adopted by the Deputy Prime Minister, Kardelj, in his speech to the Yugoslav Parliament on December 7th.

Perhaps the Yugoslav League of Communists, he admitted, had in the past not paid enough attention to the interdependence of economic and political factors and in particular to the fact that it was impossible to conduct an economic policy demanding tremendous efforts and sacrifices from the whole people and at the same time to expand democracy in the social and political system, without pause or risk. But "we have in principle and practice long ago finished with the Stalinist claim that in order to assure the development of Socialism it is enough that the Communist Party should have power and then 'build Socialism' through a State political and planning machine, that is, that it should build factories, collectivise agriculture, and fix wage scales—all in the name of the leading part it is called upon to play. We look upon building of Socialism as a much wider and more complex movement which only partly depends on the conscious purpose of those in leading positions."

Communist parties, he said, could only lead their countries if they truly represented and reflected the moods of the people they led, and particularly the working class, and changed with the times. "If a party does not understand that, then, no matter how much it beats its Communist breast, brags about its Marxism-Leninism and appeals to its historic role of leadership, it will in fact be an obstacle to the development of Socialism. It may even become a reactionary force if it obstinately persists in behaving like this. To believe that the mere fact that a Party calls itself Communist guarantees that its rule will be progressive and democratic is a bad anti-Marxist mistake.

"That was made very clear in Hungary. Here an anti-democratic system of despotic bureaucracy for years carried out the arbitrary policies of one clique against the will of the great majority of the people. That in the end led to armed revolt, in which the main forces of resistance were the working class, that is, the very class which alone can be the architects of Socialism in the Hungarian nation. In this the most important point is not who took advantage of this revolt of the working class, and in the name of what slogans it spontaneously rose against something that had become socially intolerable and reactionary. What is much more important is to note that in this case a political system in the name of Socialism became in fact an obstacle to the further development of Socialism, to such a point that it drove the working class, that is the main motive force in any Socialist movement, to armed resistance, because this class had no other way of getting what it desperately wanted."

Kardelj derided the Soviet contention that the Hungarian rising was a counter-revolution, organised from outside and taking advantage of 'mistakes' of Rakosi and Gerö that could be corrected after the counter-revolution had been defeated, without changing the bureaucratic system that was the root of the evil. That was merely a pretty poor attempt to appease guilty Communist consciences because "who can believe that the working class, 11 years after their own victory, have become counter-revolutionary? Even admitting for the sake of argument that this could be true, it only raises the question whether the workers should be punished for this, or whether the political system should be changed which reduced the workers to the tragi-comic position of fighting against their own historical interests. In any case this line of argument leads only to the absurd conclusion, which has nothing to do with Socialism, let alone Marxism, that some party or government can build Socialism without the working class or even against the workers."

In fact, argued Kardelj, "The Hungarian workers acted blindly and spontaneously, but nevertheless they acted as Socialists. True, they were, to a great extent, in their views on the organisation of the State, democracy and political and party relationships, influenced by various petty bourgeois abstract and liberalistic phrases. But at the same time they took their stand solidly on the defence of the social ownership of the means of production."

They had even tried to change State ownership into more advanced forms of social ownership under working class management, and to link up the workers councils into a nation-wide system. This could have been the basis for a new start with Socialism in Hungary. Instead, the Hungarian Communist Party had been split between Stalinists and petty bourgeois liberals. At the outset the second Soviet intervention had seemed possibly a lesser evil than the alternative. But only on condition that it resulted in "putting an end to further bloodshed and made it possible to set up a government and go in for a policy in Hungary that would, on the basis of a change of political system, rally all the Socialist forces in the country and give the workers power to influence public policy, through the workers councils and similar working class bodies, such as they had never yet enjoyed. Only such positive results could justify

Soviet intervention. If these results do not follow the act of intervention stands condemned by history."

What had happened in Hungary was the tragedy of a Socialist movement, but to an even greater degree a lesson and a challenge to international socialism. Kardelj made a spirited defence of the Yugoslav form of socialism, with its workers' councils and system of local and provincial elected committees, as the best form of socialist democracy, avoiding the extremes of either 'capitalist pseudo-democracy' or of 'Stalinist bureau-cracy'.

"I must add that in my opinion it was not the question of socialism but the balance of power in the present international situation that was the main reason for Soviet intervention in Hungary. Any moderately realistic observer must come to the conclusion that, given the present international situation, Soviet intervention was inevitable the moment internal developments in Hungary were such as to invite intervention from other quarters and to open the door for the establishment of Western political bases in Hungary. Such a situation would have had the gravest effect on the present balance of power in Europe, would have provoked very serious disturbances and might even have threatened European peace. Various 'Free Europes' and similar institutions, as well as nationalist hotheads in Hungary itself have practically confirmed these apprehensions. There can be no doubt that these considerations have necessarily influenced our own position, let alone that of the Soviet Government."*

Pravda *is Indignant*

Pravda held its fire till December 18th, when it replied with an article that was the strongest attack yet, not only on the Yugoslav position but on the neo-Communist outlook that

* The fear of severing the ties of friendship with the Communist world and so losing all bargaining power between the two camps, and nervousness about a reactionary Hungary emerging that might, in alliance with the West, lay claim to former Hungarian, now Yugoslav, territories, have been the 'reasons of State' for the ambivalent attitude and veerings and tackings of Yugoslav policy towards the Hungarian rising and the Kadar Government.

has been encouraged by the 20th Congress of the C.P.S.U.:

"In the last few weeks a bitter struggle has been developing throughout the world between international reactionary bourgeois ideology and Communism. The dark forces of reaction are trying to use the events in Hungary in order to mount a new crusade against Communism, in order to traduce the Communist movement, rouse dissension in it, influence the unstable and wavering elements that at one time or another have joined this movement, restart the 'cold war', and poison the relations between the peoples with suspicion and hostility.

"Obviously, in the conflict that is developing, no one who calls himself a supporter of Communism can adopt any 'middle line'. Any attempts of that sort can only mean greater or smaller concessions to the ideology of reaction. That is the relentless logic of the class struggle."

Comrade Kardelj's speech in the Yugoslav Parliament of December 7th, said *Pravda*, was an illustration of this truth, for he attempted to adopt a 'third line', but merely succeeded in demonstrating that no such line exists.

Pravda fiercely attacked what it called Yugoslav 'revisionism' (an even worse charge in the Communist political vocabulary than 'idealism'). Kardelj had practically come out against the dictatorship of the proletariat. *Pravda* quoted Lenin on Soviet rule and the dictatorship of the proletariat as being the fundamental principles of a Communist-led social revolution. It also quoted Lenin on the impossibility of exercising the dictatorship of the proletariat except through the Communist Party.

It accused the Yugoslavs of claiming that their own road to Socialism was the only correct one. 'As for the old idea that factories and other enterprises should be taken out of the hands of the Socialist State and handed over to groups of workers, the Communist Party of the Soviet Union has long ago passed the stage of polemics on this subject; under the leadership of Lenin the Party, as far back as the 10th Congress in 1921, decided that such demands were anarcho-syndicalist and contradicted the methods of Marxism."

Pravda was contemptuous of Kardelj's claims for workers' management and the other peculiarities of Yugoslav Socialism and quoted the West German Foreign Minister, Herr Von

Brentano, at a N.A.T.O. meeting as saying that the Western powers should encourage the spread of Titoism in the People's Democracies as a "more hopeful approach than direct incitements to overthrow their régimes". This of course is interpreted by *Pravda* as indicating that the Western powers look upon Titoism as an indirect way of overthrowing Communist régimes!

Significance of the Pravda Article

The most significant part of this article is that it begins by pointing to the revival of the cold war and the alleged aggressive intentions of the West and proceeds to draw the conclusion that there is no such thing as a 'third path' between Soviet-led Communism and American-led capitalism and that the only road to Socialism is the one proclaimed by Lenin of a Communist-led revolution and the dictatorship of the proletariat, embodied in its advance guard, the Communist Party. This comes close to contradicting what Khrushchev said in his Central Committee report to the 20th Congress on the importance for peace of the 'uncommitted' states and the variety of paths, including that of Parliamentary democracy, to Socialism. Khrushchev, of course, related these conclusions to an analysis of the world situation that drew attention to the slackening of tension in the world, the growing strength of the forces of peace and the fact that war could be averted.

By December 1956 Western Communists were taking a hand in the great debate and left-wing Socialists like Pietro Nenni, who had hitherto remained allies of the Communists, made even more drastic criticisms. Although most of the French and some of the Italian Communist leaders spoke up for Moscow, the orthodox were, on the whole, getting the worst of the argument with the heretics.

Far Eastern Reinforcements

That is presumably why Moscow felt it necessary to call in reinforcements from the East: on December 30th two whole pages, with a two-column overflow into the third page, of *Pravda* reproduced in its entirety a vast leading article from the

Chinese Communist Party's organ, *Jen Min Jih Pao*, with the snappy title, "Further Reflections on the Dictatorship of the Proletariat in the Light of History".

Tito's speech, says this leader, raised a number of issues requiring an answer on such basic questions as the road to Socialism and evaluation of Stalin's merits and mistakes, the struggle against the opposite evils of dogmatism and revisionism, and the need for the international solidarity of the workers in all countries.

The last issue, in the Chinese Party's view, is the background and frame for dealing with all the others:

"When we consider these questions to-day we must start with the fundamental and all-important fact of the antagonism between the imperialist aggressive block and the peoples of the world." This contention is illustrated by a review of Communist China's relations with the West, which to the Chinese appear as a series of aggressions and armed interventions with the object of overthrowing their government.

"We have always been of the opinion that our enemy is our best teacher. To-day Dulles is again giving us a lesson . . . he is now demanding of the imperialist world that it should put its conflict of interests with Communism above all other conflicts, that it should direct its energies and efforts to 'changing the character of the Communist world' to the 'disruption' and 'destruction' of the Socialist system headed by the Soviet Union. Although all this no doubt will turn out a vain enterprise, nevertheless the lesson for us is most useful. We have always stood and continue to stand for the peaceful co-existence of Socialist and capitalist countries, for peaceful competition between them, but nevertheless the imperialists, as before, keep on trying to destroy us. That is why we must never forget that the bitter conflict between our enemies and ourselves is the class war on a world scale."

Faced with this situation, the Socialist countries formed a camp of which the main support and defender was the Soviet Union. There were, of course, necessarily variations of detail in each country in working out the processes of transition from capitalism to Socialism. "But from the point of view of the fundamentals the road of the October Revolution represents the universal law of revolution and reconstruction at a certain stage in the development of human society. This is not only the highway along which the proletariat of the Soviet Union has passed, but also that along which the proletariat of all countries will have to press forward if they are to achieve victory."

It will be observed of course that this view, like the one in *Pravda* previously quoted, but even more emphatically, contradicts most of what Khrushchev said at the 20th Congress about the multiplicity of the roads to Socialism, including that of parliamentary democracy and constitutional action.

The editorial praises Stalin's great work as the builder of Socialism and the defender "of the Leninist heritage from the enemies of Lenin—the Trotskyites, the Zinovievites and other agents of the bourgeoisie". This contradicts what Khrushchev said in his secret report (and it was repeated in the subsequent public declaration of the Central Committee quoted in an earlier chapter) about Lenin's efforts to have Stalin removed as Secretary-General and his warning against him in his will. It also contradicts the horrifying revelations in Khrushchev's 'personality cult' report about Stalin's murder of most of the Party leaders from Lenin's day, and Khrushchev's emphatic declaration that the people who were killed were not agents of the bourgeoisie or enemies of the people, but simply men who disagreed with Stalin. He specially mentioned Zinoviev, Kameniev, Bucharin and others, contrasting Lenin's treatment of them with that of Stalin.

Again the article, although it does speak of Stalin's grave mistakes, violations of legality, etc., in fact undamns Stalin with faint dispraise, in startling contrast to what Khrushchev in his secret report said about the disastrous consequences to the Soviet Union and its relations with other countries, and the hideous cruelty and injustice of Stalin's orgies of torture and slaughter.

"If we look at the matter broadly we can only say to those who insist on talking about 'Stalinism' that 'Stalinism' is above all Communism, Marxism-Leninism. That is its fundamental characteristic. But it does contain some extremely serious

mistakes that need to be corrected radically and that go clean
contrary to Marxism-Leninism."

This way of looking at it is made the premise for the conclusion that it is wrong to treat those guilty of Stalinist mistakes
on the same footing as class enemies. The Yugoslavs are accused
of doing just that—they are given the 'fraternal advice' not to
exaggerate, to strengthen the international unity of the Communist ranks and not make it easier for the enemies of Communism to sow confusion and dissension.

The leader admits that Stalin's 'mistakes' in the last years
of his life became so big and lasted so long that they affected
the whole life of the State and will take years to eradicate.
But it deplores the fact that even some Communists have got
into the habit of calling the correction of Stalin's mistakes "the
struggle against 'Stalinism', the struggle of the so-called 'anti-
Stalinists' against the 'Stalinists' ".

The next section of the article tries to strike the happy
mean between 'dogmatism', of which it admits Stalin was
guilty, and 'revisionism', of which it accuses not only the
Yugoslavs, but other unnamed Communists whom it calls
"some unstable elements in the ranks of Communism". These
elements "are trying to weaken or reject the dictatorship of the
proletariat, to weaken or reject democratic centralism in the
Socialist countries, to weaken or reject the leading role of the
Party. . . . In no circumstances is it permissible to oppose
Socialist Democracy to the dictatorship of the proletariat and
to confuse it with bourgeois democracy."

A couple of columns are devoted to refuting these heresies
and their application to Hungary. Then comes the following
passage: "Among those who are revising Marxism-Leninism
under the guise of fighting dogmatism are people who have
simply ceased to draw the line between the dictatorship of the
proletariat and the dictatorship of the bourgeoisie, between the
Socialist system and the capitalist system, between the Socialist
camp and the imperialist camp. They believe that in some
bourgeois countries it is possible to build Socialism without a
proletarian revolution led by the political party of the proletariat, without forming a State led by this political party. In
their view State capitalism in these bourgeois countries is

already Socialism, and even human society as a whole is in transition to Socialism.

"But at the very time that they are conducting propaganda for these views, imperialism is actively preparing to 'disrupt' and to 'destroy' the Socialist countries that already exist, and is for this purpose mobilising all its 'moral', military, economic, diplomatic, and espionage resources. Bourgeois counter-revolutionaries, both those undercover in the Socialist countries and those who have fled abroad, are doing everything they can for the cause of restoration. Although the revisionist tendencies play into the hands of imperialism the actions of the imperial-ists are not on the side of revisionism, but bear witness to the bankruptcy of revisionism."

This sounds remarkably like an attack on Khruschev's references in his public report to the Central Committee on the possibility of advancing to Socialism by Parliamentary means. But it is in fact directed against the Yugoslavs, who are against the division of the world into blocs as well as being opponents of Stalinism.

The last section draws the conclusion from this view of the world that "for the sake of the cause of the proletariat in all countries, for common defence against the attacks of the imperialism camp, headed by the United States, for the sake of Socialism and the general raising of the economic and cultural standards of all the Socialist countries, we must continue to strengthen the solidarity of the workers of the world centring on the Soviet Union. . . . It must be plain that to-day, when the imperialists are conducting an all-out offensive against the ranks of Communism in all countries, the proletariat of every country must draw closer together. In face of a powerful enemy, words and deeds, no matter what they may be called, that act as an obstacle to the closing of the ranks of Communism internationally, can hardly be regarded with sympathy by Communists and workers of all countries."

The Stage Army of the Good

The next phase in the great polemic was a series of joint declarations with the C.P.S.U. by 'good' Communist parties

visiting Moscow, such as the French, Czechs, Bulgarians and
East Germans, ringing the changes on these arguments and
assertions, with more or less veiled attacks on the Yugoslav
position. These were accompanied by a swelling chorus of
articles and broadcasts in the Soviet Union and the 'loyal'
People's Democracies intoning the same refrain, with an over-
spill in the French Communist Press.

Borba *Re-states the Issue*

Borba dealt with all this incisively in an article on February
14th, entitled "Honest Discussion or Unprincipled Polemics?"

"In the last few months," it observed, "and particularly
after the October events in Poland and Hungary, a number of
articles have appeared in the Press of the Soviet Union and
some East German countries on such subjects as the relations
between Socialist countries, proletarian internationalism and
the dictatorship of the proletariat". But in spite of their pomp-
ous titles these articles had made no serious attempt objectively
to analyse the situation. They had merely rehashed the same
dead arguments and baseless assertions. The burden of their
song was the same in all cases. It was "the very simple proposition that Socialism is threatened by an offensive of the
reactionary forces and that therefore it is necessary to close the
ranks in the Socialist countries and Communist parties and to
rally round the Soviet Union. That and only that is the lesson
drawn from the tragic events in Hungary and from all the other
problems facing the working-class movement."

The authors of these articles and broadcasts "so far as they
can, deny the existence of internal factors that are obstacles to
the development of Socialism. They turn a blind eye to the
deep social roots of the Polish and Hungarian events and even
retreat from the facts admitted during and after the 20th
Congress of the C.P.S.U. They minimise, indeed virtually
deny, the evils of and damage done by the Stalinist policies, the
tangle of social phenomena that has been given the name of
Stalinism. This kind of line has even been taken recently by
some of the State and Party leaders of East Europe. . . ."

"The very word 'Stalinism' is deplored, and treated as

though it referred not to a reality but to a fiction, and those who oppose Stalinism are now accused of 'national Communism',* of wanting to weaken the unity of the Socialist countries, break up the Socialist camp, oppose the dictatorship of the Proletariat, and deliver Socialism to its enemies.

"Those who take this line have ceased to be Marxists and are now political pragmatists who are not interested in whether a proposition is true or false, but only in whether stating it might 'help the imperialists'. But in fact experience has shown that reactionary forces can function much more successfully in the conditions created by good old 'Stalinist' 'monolithic unity' than when there is freedom and equality in the Socialist countries and in their mutual relations."

Borba's article pointed out that the controversy had now crossed the boundary of ideological argument between Communist parties and was becoming a disagreement between Socialist states. The Soviet Foreign Minister, Shepilov, addressing the Supreme Soviet of the Union, had said that the U.S.S.R. wanted friendship and co-operation with Yugoslavia to continue to develop, but that this now depended mainly on the leaders of Yugoslavia, "where feelings are still being expressed that are not friendly and where there are even direct attacks by some elements on the Soviet Union and some of the People's Democracies".

Yugoslavia bore no responsibility whatever, objected *Borba*, for the original break with the Soviet Union, which had been all Stalin's work. Therefore the first move for healing the breach must naturally come from the country that had caused it, and now seemed again to quarrel with the Yugoslav position, which had remained unchanged before, during, and after the break and was still the same.

The Yugoslav Foreign Minister Speaks Out

The first practical effect of the 'inter-State' character the controversy had assumed was that the Soviet Government,

* The term 'national Communism' is resented and rejected by the Yugo-slavs (and the Poles), who claim they are better internationalists than the Stalinists, whom they accuse of Great Russian chauvinism.

without formally repudiating trade and economic aid agreements, entered into during Tito's visit in June 1956, began on a variety of pretexts to go slow with carrying out its undertakings. The help promised to the Poles also began to be doled out on a hand-to-mouth basis that meant it could be cut off at any moment and made the Poles more anxious than ever to get economic and technical aid from the West as well, so as not to be entirely dependent on their great neighbour. How far matters had gone was shown by the Yugoslav Foreign Minister Kocha Popovich's speech in the Yugoslav Parliament on February 26th, 1957. For it was a blunt answer to Shepilov's remarks and an equally blunt rejection of the fresh attempt made from Moscow at the end of January 1957 to induce the Yugoslavs to enter the Socialist camp, in view of the revival of the cold war.

The main new feature in this speech was that it talked for the first time at Ministerial level in terms of relations between States and vigorously pressed the Yugoslav objection to the division of the world into rival military, economic, political and ideological blocs, which, he said, by their very nature must act as obstacles to developing the policies of active peaceful co-existence, based on common membership of the United Nations and the obligations of the Charter.

Mr. Popovich was equally outspoken on the differences that had arisen between Yugoslavia on the one hand and the Soviet Union and some of the People's Democracies on the other, about the lessons to be drawn from the Polish and Hungarian revolutions and subsequent events. Once again, he said, whether consciously or not, the Soviet Government was using ideological arguments as "a convenient means for establishing the kind of international relationships that suit the Soviet Union. That is why a good deal of the so-called ideological polemic is being conducted on the wrong issues: such as the dictatorship of the proletariat, internationalism, solidarity of the workers in all countries, the theoretical possibilities of adopting different roads to Socialism, and so forth."

On these matters there could hardly be any argument on principles, but only on the way to apply them in each country, and the decisions of the 20th Congress and the Soviet declaration of October 30th had correctly laid down the principle that each country had the right to settle such matters for itself on the basis of full independence and equality.

"The real issue in the controversy, therefore, in my opinion, and as I have already said, arises out of the differences of view about our relationship to the 'Socialist camp.' "

Here Mr. Popovich repeated the objections of the Yugoslavs to joining the Socialist or any other camp, and recalled Khrushchev's words about the peace-loving unattached States as deserving of respect and making a big contribution to peace. No ideological arguments could make a serious case for the view that the 'camp' was a necessary form of international co-operation in which all Socialist states should take part. The whole campaign launched by the Soviet and some other East European leaders, was really directed against the fundamentals of Yugoslavia's foreign policy and the country's position of independence, which it intended to maintain, and was supported by assertions about the Hungarian rising that did not correspond to the facts.

Their friends and comrades in the Soviet Union and the other Socialist states, said Popovich, would have to accept the Yugoslavs as they were, including their firm determination to keep out of the rival blocs and to stand for their own views on Socialism and the relations between Socialist states. They should also realise that "all the difficulties in building Socialism are not by a long chalk due to foreign subversion and conspiracies. It is all the more necessary to understand that, since this is the only way of avoiding a relapse into Stalinism, which, it is our deep belief, did incomparably more damage to the cause of Socialism in the period after the Second World War than all the imperialist conspiracies taken together."

Pravda is Horrified

This last remark horrified *Pravda*. It was, said that paper, on March 11th, a monstrous conclusion that distorted truth. "What are we to think about such a statement by the Foreign Minister of Yugoslavia? In the Yugoslav Press the artificially constructed term 'Stalinism' is often used in order to decry the structure of Soviet society and the Soviet state, the policy of the C.P.S.U. and the Socialist camp. But how can anyone who calls himself a Communist make such attacks?

"Even if the Foreign Minister of Yugoslavia, K. Popovich, only meant to refer to Stalin's mistakes, that have been condemned by our Party, the mere fact of mentioning these mistakes in the same breath with the disruptive activities of the imperialists would seem outrageous and blasphemous to any Communist."

"This kind of comparison," thundered *Pravda*, "is an unworthy and miserable attempt to rehabilitate the disruptive activities of the imperialists and to throw mud at the Soviet Union and the whole cause of Socialism."

Pravda goes on in this strain for some time, depicting post-war history in the angels of light versus demons of darkness terms so beloved also of Western statesmen—but with the rôles reversed. The rest of the article, entitled "The Principles of Marxism-Leninism are the Foundation of the Foreign Policy of the Socialist Countries", takes issue with the Yugoslav objection to the existence of the rival camps:

"The Socialist States stand for the peaceful co-existence of all countries irrespective of their social and political structure, for their peaceful competition in economic and cultural matters and for the renunciation of force in the settlement of their differences. . . . As everyone knows, the Soviet Union, the Chinese People's Republic and all the other countries of the Socialist camp have consistently advocated and continue to advocate the disbanding of the military blocs, disarmament, and the establishment of a system of collective security. The Soviet Union long ago proposed that N.A.T.O. and all its subsidiaries on the one hand and the Warsaw treaty alliance on the other, which some Socialist states had to conclude in answer to the threat from the imperialist bloc, should be disbanded."

But in the world of to-day there was now a group of Socialist states, with the workers in control building a new social order and trying to strengthen peace, and a group of capitalist states, where the exploiting classes were in control and that were concerned to preserve the old social order, build up positions of strength and engage in an arms race.

Q

The Socialist states, argues *Pravda*, wanted to develop friendly and co-operative relations between these two groups, expand trade and human intercourse, work together in cultural and scientific matters, etc. "But of course it is impossible, without abandoning Marxist-Leninist principles, to regard the co-existence of states with different social structures as implying some kind of melting together of two opposing social systems —the capitalist and the Socialist".

That was apparently what the Yugoslav Foreign Minister wanted, said *Pravda*, and quoted his remark about the form-ing of a single world market. But "a world market is only a constituent part of the whole world economic system. So long as there are two economic systems in the world there must necessarily also be two world markets. That of course does not exclude economic relations, nor even a very wide measure of economic co-operation, between the two systems. But even the most favourable conditions for the development of economic relations cannot fuse the two opposing economic systems into one and re-establish a 'single world market'. Such a view of 'co-existence' has nothing in common with the principles of Marxism-Leninism."

The article ends by exhorting the Yugoslavs to remove exist-ing obstacles to and do all they can to strengthen Yugoslavia's friendship and co-operation with the countries of the Socialist camp.

The Wheel Comes Full Circle

The wheel came full circle in April 1957 with the declara-tions of Khrushchev and Tito—oddly enough, arising out of the visit to the U.S.S.R. of Enver Hoxha and Mehmet Shehu (the Khrushchev and Bulganin of Albania)—and Molotov's voice from the past. Of late, said Khrushchev at an Albanian Embassy reception on April 15th, international tension had increased because of 'imperialist aggression against Egypt' and the attempted counter-revolution in Hungary. "The situation in Hungary was very sharp—as sharp as Hungarian red pepper —but the plans of the counter-revolutionaries and international reaction have been defeated."

A few years ago relations with Yugoslavia, he continued,

had got into a bad tangle, and there were still certain difficulties and disagreements. But to-day these were greater between Albania and Yugoslavia than between the latter and
the Soviet Union, and the Soviet Party and Government
were doing all in their power to dispel all misunderstanding. He was an optimist and believed this could be achieved.
He hoped the Yugoslav people and their leaders also wanted
this.

"Some people disagree with the very idea of the Socialist
camp, and want to replace the expression itself by 'co-operation'
or some such word." But 'Socialist camp' was the exact and
appropriate expression for the relations between Socialist States
in a world where the two systems—capitalist and Socialist—
confronted each other. It was this that made it necessary to
"strengthen our positions and the friendship between the
Socialist nations and to consolidate the unity of our Socialist
camp. But both the capitalist and Socialist camps live on one
planet and cannot escape from it. That is why they must co-
exist and establish peaceful relations.

"We shall never take up arms to impose the ideas of Communism on anyone. . . . History teaches us the lesson that in
our day and age it is impossible to impose a way of life they
reject on a people fighting for their freedom."

Soviet Policy in Hungary is an odd commentary on this
statement, to say the least. But it should not be forgotten that
Hungarian freedom was crushed, not so much for the sake of
imposing (or maintaining) Communism in that country as for
strategic, national security motives—to prevent Hungary joining the other side in the cold war and/or setting Eastern Germany a dangerous example. That is, the prime motive of
Soviet policy in this case has been power-political, not ideological, although as usual it has been rationalised into ideological
terms.

Khrushchev went on to claim that in any case they did not
have to use force, because "the ideas of Communism express
the vital interests of the great majority of the people" and
"possess such enormous vitality that they cannot be destroyed
or even prevented from spreading by force of arms. Our ideas
will win the hearts of all mankind. History bears witness to

the fact that the attempts of the imperialists to stop the spread of Communism by military means are bound to fail."

Here Khrushchev cited the failure of British intervention in Russia and American intervention in China as cases in point, and concluded:

"Some people say that while he talks of co-existence, Khrushchev also insists that capitalism will perish and Communism will inevitably triumph. To that I can retort that for the last forty years the spokesmen of capitalism have been dinning into our ears that the cause of Communism championed by the Soviet Union is bound to fail and private enterprise will come into its own again even in our country. They claim that private enterprise is strong and will prevail. We say that the ideas of Communism are incomparably stronger and will inevitably triumph. That is why we never cease repeating; let us compete; let us co-exist in peace."

This is the quintessence of what the present Soviet leaders really believe. It is astonishing that they should, in face of the accumulating evidence that Communism, in anything like its present form, has an uncertain future even in the 'Socialist camp', let alone conquering the non-Communist world. But believe it they do.

Tito's reply, at the Plenum of the Council of the Socialist Alliance, on April 19th, 1957, was a pretty forceful reminder of the yawning gulf between this belief and reality. The whole world knew, said Tito, that Yugoslavia was once again in dispute with the Eastern countries, the countries of the Socialist camp. The Yugoslavs had repeatedly, in speech and writing, through the Press, at meetings and in official messages and declarations, made their attitude clear on the question of camps. "To-day I want to say that in this dispute too the main issue is that we have resolutely stuck to our view that we do not want to be included in any camp. We do not wish it, because Yugoslavia could then no longer play the part she is playing in the world, in which we can be independent and say what we think on all questions of domestic or foreign policy. It is this that upsets our Soviet comrades most of all.

"But we are profoundly convinced, in the light of experience, that our policy is the right one and that to change it would do

harm not only to us at home, but to the development of Socialism and the idea of Socialism in the whole world. Nor could
we by doing this help to lower the tension in the world. I
believe that one day they will become convinced that the
Yugoslav position will not change, that it serves a useful
purpose in the strained international situation of to-day, and
that it does not threaten the Soviet Union, but on the contrary is helpful to the U.S.S.R. and all those who want good
relations between nations and world peace."

He was sorry, said Tito, that the controversy had spread
from the field of ideological disputes between Parties into that
of disagreements between States. In particular he regretted
the unbridled campaign of lies and vituperation in Albania,
designed to stir up trouble among the Albanian minorities in
Yugoslavia. This was part of a concerted campaign in most of
the Socialist camp to belittle and denigrate everything in
Yugoslavia—her economy, workers' management in industry,
her political organisation, nationalities policy—in order to
attack her standing and influence as a Socialist country. In
the same quarter the Yugoslavs were being reproached for
defending themselves too vigorously when unjustly attacked.
But they had in fact displayed conspicuous self-restraint and
moderation. And now attempts were being made to saddle
them with responsibility for other people's mistakes.

"In regard to Hungary, for instance, they keep on obstinately insisting that we are largely to blame for what happened
in that country. There is not a grain of truth in that accusa-
tion. On the contrary, we warned them against the eventual
evil consequences of the policy of the Rakosi clique—and they
themselves recognised the danger and admitted to us that
Rakosi's policy had produced a very difficult situation. But
when it culminated in the tragic events in Hungary and their
consequences, which inevitably injured the prestige of the
Soviet Union throughout the world, they tried to shift responsibility from themselves on to us. That, of course, we could
never allow. We could never accept blame for a situation for
which we were not responsible in any way."

From the Soviet point of view, suggested Tito, the Yugoslav 'fault' would appear to be precisely their rebuttal of

charges implying responsibility for the consequences of the mistakes committed by the Soviet leaders. But it had been his duty to make clear the Yugoslav attitude to both the Polish Revolution and the Hungarian rising.

"You, who are more in touch with the masses of the people, know better than I how painfully for instance they were affected by what happened in Hungary. It should be easy to understand why Hungarian events made a big impression on our country and why we had to tell our people what they ought to know, so as to calm their minds. Obviously this meant saying things that were very unpleasant. But they were true. . . . However, that did not please our Soviet comrades. That is why they have reacted so sharply. They have written and circulated a whole series of articles that have appeared in all countries, both where Communists are in power and where Communist parties exist although not in power.

"Ought we now, under the pressure of a certain moral condemnation by these parties, to fall on our knees and confess that we have sinned, that we are wrong? No, Comrades, that we may not do. To-day we are responsible not only to our own peoples, but to progressive opinion and the working-class movement of the whole world. We are responsible both as a State and as a Party." What was at stake was nothing less than the whole issue of 'active co-existence'. That was why they could not and would not give way.

Many were asking, continued Tito, whether it was possible to trust the Russians at all, in view of the fact that after the grand reconciliation following upon the break for which Yugoslavia had no responsibility, they were once again being attacked. It was true, he said, that some of the Soviet leaders still could not rid themselves of their old ideas about the relations between Socialist states, and although they had done something to correct Stalinist tendencies, still allowed them to influence their policy toward other countries, and particularly to Yugoslavia.

But it would be wrong to think that the Russians could never again be trusted or to dramatise the conflict. It was necessary to look at the whole situation coldly and calmly. He had told Khrushchev, Bulganin and Mikoyan when they came to Belgrade on their reconciliation mission, that it would take long and would be difficult to restore confidence. But if both sides did their best and were patient it was only a question of time.

Unfortunately, the Russians had been impatient and impulsive. There had recently been an illustration of this.

"Whereas Khrushchev, a few days ago, spoke in a very conciliatory way in the Kremlin, and in my opinion spoke wisely and well, about the need for improving relations with Yugoslavia, so that we felt a gleam of hope that the change had already begun, that they already saw that they cannot go on this way any longer—and then suddenly Suslov spoke up and attacked us for alleged revisionism and national Communism.

"I ask you, Comrades, would there be any sense in our replying to this kind of thing and protesting that we are not enemies of Communism? Why, we *are* Communists! There is no such thing as national Communism. Suslov has borrowed this terminology from Western journalists, who have invented the expression 'national Communism' because Yugoslavia has stood up for her independence, for her own kind of internal development, and for an independent foreign policy. Suslov has taken advantage of this most incorrectly, for he knows it is not true, but uses it in his polemics against Yugoslavia in order to discredit us. And now, whom are we to believe, Comrades? To-day one man says one thing, and to-morrow another says something diametrically opposite."

Tito said the Yugoslavs would have to make it plain to the Russians that this kind of thing would not do and they must stop it, if they really meant what they said about improving relations between the two countries.

"I don't want to say, Comrades, that I am any great optimist, but nevertheless, I look calmly and with a good deal of optimism on all this and think that it is not something terrible and dramatic. From time to time we shall have to react firmly in order to contradict untruths. But nevertheless the day will come, and perhaps it is not so far away, when this incorrect, insincere and uncomradely polemic directed against us will die down."

That it has not died down yet, however, was made clear

by an article in *Pravda* of April 22nd, by Molotov, putting
with the utmost emphasis the Soviet view that in the conditions of the cold war a Communist country adopting a policy
of independence toward the Soviet Union endangered its own
existence.

"The ties of the Soviet Union with the other countries of
the Socialist camp are unbreakable. It is in their own mutual
interest. The successes of our country help their progress and
the advance of a small or a big Socialist country strengthens
the whole Socialist camp.

"A Socialist country cannot remain aloof from this fraternal
commonwealth of the Socialist countries. This would be not
only an outright refusal to co-operate in the strengthening of
the Socialist camp, to the delight of our class enemies—but
also a dangerous weakening of the country in question.

"All attempts at proving the reverse are empty words having nothing in common with the interests of the working class
and all working people. He who still cannot understand this
may be advised to read Lenin and every doubt in this respect
will be completely dispelled."

Unfortunately for the Stalinist old guard in the Kremlin,
of whom Molotov is the *doyen*, references to what Lenin said
in 1922 make much the same impression on irreverent *Kom-
somols* and even Party members of the younger generation, let
alone Communists in other countries, as appeals in this
country to what Gladstone said in 1892.

Those are the main lines of the great argument that is raging throughout the Communist world. The mere fact that this
great controversy is going on at all shows the immensity of
the changes in world Communism that have occurred since
the death of Stalin. In his day any such controversy would
have been unthinkable.

No less important is the fundamental nature of the issues
raised and the frankness with which they are being discussed.
It is clear that some Communists in the Soviet Union and
many Communists in the so-called People's Democracies, not
to mention those in the West, are facing such basic issues as
how to convert the 'dictatorship of the proletariat', which in
practice means the dictatorship of a more or less bureaucratic

and centralised Communist Party, into a genuine political democracy, based on something like economic democracy, through workers' management in industry and producers' co-operatives on the land. In international relations the controversy turns about the whole conception of a Socialist camp, as opposed to that of dissolving both camps in the United Nations.

The third fact of prime importance that emerges from the controversy is the use being made of the cold war and Western war preparations by the Stalinist old guard and their apologists in the Communist world to justify their opposition to a new birth of freedom.

CHAPTER SIXTEEN

Communism in Transition

The Soviet Union

THE GREAT CONTROVERSY shows the lines on which the present Soviet leaders are trying to stabilise the situation, and the arguments on which they rely: inside the Soviet Union they want to exclude the fundamentals of the régime from the enlarged area of free discussion. In international affairs they want to hold together the Soviet bloc, although in a looser and more equalitarian form (but with the U.S.S.R. still considerably more equal than anyone else) than under Stalin, and with the new name "the Commonwealth of Socialist nations".

The chief argument on which they rely to keep matters under control is the fear of being attacked by the West. This fear has grown strong again after the revival of the cold war as a result of Hungary and Egypt, the Eisenhower doctrine and the British Conservative Government's conversion to Mr. Dulles' strategy of 'massive retaliation' (now called 'reliance on nuclear deterrents').

With the help of this argument the Soviet leaders have been able to slow up and check, but not to stop, let alone reverse, the new forces. For they have neither the power nor the authority of Stalin, and lack his intransigeance. They are more intelligent and flexible, more exposed and readier to yield to pressure.

Stalin's almost mystical hold over the minds of Communist leaders in other countries has been broken. The present Soviet leaders, even if they wanted to, could not restore it and must resort to other methods to maintain the solidarity of the 'Socialist camp'. Either they rely on naked coercion, as in the case of Hungary, or they have to appeal to reason—that is, self-interest—generally fear of the West and/or of Germany, as in the case of Poland. And even when they go in for a policy of force they have to argue about and justify it as best they can in the face of searching criticism—they cannot simply impose their policy and official explanation by a *ukase* and treat all dissent as a crime, as in the spacious days of Stalin and the 'personality cult'.

Not being able to stop discussion by other Communist parties of their international policies, they are equally unable to keep people like the Yugoslavs and Poles from raising fundamental issues and making drastic proposals in the course of the discussion. Nor can they keep millions of people in the Soviet Union from listening-in to the great controversy, both literally and metaphorically.

The Soviet leaders can, for instance, hardly jam broadcasts and keep out newspapers, students and visitors of the most varied categories from the 'People's Democracies'. But from those sources and contacts large sections of the Soviet public are getting information and ideas that correct the one-sided views they hear officially.

Again, students and intellectuals are encouraged and supposed to study the works of Marx, Engels and Lenin. But with the measure of freedom they now enjoy to think about and discuss what they read, they can find food for unorthodox thought in the Marxist-Leninist classics, much as Protestants and Puritans found in the Bible during the Reformation and the English Revolution. By going back to the sources they can rediscover the European tradition of Communism, which after all originated in the West and to start with was in the grand tradition of liberal civilisation and humanism.

Possibly the semi-Asiatic, Stalinist twist arising out of Russian conditions and aggravated by capitalist hostility is so much part and parcel of modern Communism that it can no longer be ironed out without Communism perishing—or changing into something else under the same name. But there are some Communists even in the Soviet Union and many in the East European 'People's Democracies' who are, more or less consciously, pressing for a return to the European sources and original outlook of Communism.

The most potent source of change, however, is the vigour and development of Soviet society itself. The most striking recent example of this is the sweeping reform in the whole structure of economic administration, changing it from a unitarian to a federal system, that was announced at the end of March 1957.

I was given some idea of what was coming during my visit to Moscow in October 1956, as recorded in an earlier chapter. The Central Committee gave an outline of the new policy in its session of February 1957. But the breathtaking boldness and scope of what is nothing less than an economic and administrative revolution were first revealed when Khrushchev's report on the "further improvement of industrial and economic organisation and administration" was published on March 30th, 1957.

The report was issued in the form of a set of 'theses' for discussion. After that discussion raged in the columns of Soviet newspapers and reviews and at every level in the Party, Trade unions and economic, technical and administrative bodies of every kind, up to the final debate, amendment and adoption of the new scheme in the Supreme Soviet in May 1957.

The old unitarian system run from Moscow had become so cumbrous and involved so much waste and overlapping, Khrushchev explained in his 'theses', that it must be scrapped and something quite different put in its place. There were over 200,000 State industrial enterprises and over 100,000 buildings in various regions of the huge territory of the Soviet Union. To administer all this from Moscow was becoming impossible.

Khrushchev gave several examples of the waste, delay and duplication resulting from 'departmentalism' and 'vertical organisation'. That is, each industry, administered by one department or Ministry, would strive to be self-sufficient from the stage of raw materials and plant, components and accessories, such as nails, screws, nuts and bolts, up to the finished product. Thus, for instance, if a factory working under Ministry A needed nuts and bolts it would order them from another factory under the same Ministry, although that factory might be 2,000 miles away. And yet there might be a factory belonging to Ministry B, next-door to the factory placing the order, that was also making nuts and bolts—and transporting them too for thousands of miles to B Ministry factories that needed them and could not or would not order them from any neighbouring concern that was under another department!

Khrushchev did not mention that the mania for 'vertical organisation' and 'self-sufficiency' by each department was largely the effect of the centralised planning system backed by rigid requirements and harsh penalties for the slightest fault. Departments were simply told what their production quotas were under the State plan, and woe betide those responsible if they failed to fulfil them. They were afraid that if they had to depend on other departments there might be delays or failures in delivery through no fault of their own, for which they would nevertheless be held responsible. And so they preferred having under their own control, from start to finish of the production process, everything that they needed to fulfil their quotas.

Another drawback of the present system mentioned by Khrushchev was the bureaucratic conservatism it engendered. He gave the case of tough resistance put up by one department to switching over from caterpillar tractors to wheeled tractors, which were cheaper and quicker to make, used less raw material and were more efficient for most purposes. A third point was the excessive numbers of highly qualified technicians, engineers, etc., doing paper work in offices when they would be better employed in factories and mines, or building bridges, roads, houses and industrial plant.

In the new system the country is divided up into ninety-two economic units, based on the existing administrative divisions into counties, districts, autonomous republics* and 'Union' republics.* Sometimes an economic unit may cover only one county, but generally it comprises several, and may even take in the whole of a small republic. The criterion is the amount

* There are fifteen Union Republics, theoretically of coequal and sovereign status, in the Union of Socialist Soviet Republics. But some of these, such as the Russian Federal Soviet Republic (three-quarters of the whole Union) and the Ukrainian Soviet Republic, include 'autonomous' Republics in their territory.

and kinds of industry in the area, and the limits of the unit are fixed so as to make them of convenient size and character for planning and administration by a 'People's Economic Council', composed of directors of industry and representatives of Party, trade union, technical, economic and professional organisations, the county or regional or republican Soviet (i.e. elected authority), etc., in the area. Under the P.E.C. are the trusts and combines in which the industries of the area are grouped.

The People's Economic Councils will take over the industries in the areas hitherto run from Moscow, or by a Union Republic. The most important of the industries hitherto administered by the governments of 'autonomous' Republics will be handed over to the appropriate People's Economic Councils. Those purely local in character will be taken over by the corresponding local soviets (the equivalents of our urban, borough, district and county councils). The Republican Departments hitherto in charge of these industries will, like their all-Union counterparts in Moscow, be dissolved.

The Councils will also be responsible for seeing that the industries in their areas, so far as possible, pay their way, and for obtaining the necessary credits and raw materials and arranging, or at least approving of the arrangements, for delivering to and obtaining products from other economic units.

It is at this point that the all-Union State Planning Commission, whose powers are to be enlarged, comes into the picture: it is responsible for seeing that the plans for their areas worked out by the People's Economic Councils fit into the general framework of the over-all plan for the whole Union. Khrushchev's theses emphasise again and again that all the basic planning is to be done by the People's Economic Councils, but are equally emphatic about the co-ordinating and supervisory rôle of the State Planning Commission and on its over-riding powers to check tendencies to autarchy and fostering local interests to a degree harmful to the economy of the country as a whole. For instance, there might be an attempt to develop a closed economy within one area by developing local raw materials although it would be cheaper to obtain them from other areas, to start manufacturing various kinds of equipment already being produced in specialised factories, or using a greater proportion of available resources to satisfy local needs than the State feels it can afford.

Tendencies of this sort should be checked, say the theses, in the first place, by the public authorities (i.e. the elected soviets, that is councils, or republican parliaments, which have no powers of control except for purely local industries, but must be kept informed and consulted), by the trade unions, by the Party, and by economic organisations. But the State Planning Commission can also, through its statistical service, control of credit and over-all planning system, keep in touch with what is going on and take effective steps to confine local initiative within bounds compatible with the general plan.

Great emphasis is laid on the development and mechanisation of the statistical services at every level, culminating in a statistical committee attached to the State Planning Commission, on the ground that abundant, correct, up-to-date information is the life-blood of planning. Another body to be further developed and strengthened is a so-called "Engineering and Technical Committee" attached to the Council of Ministers of the U.S.S.R. Its function is to study all the latest domestic and foreign technical developments, publish its findings and see that they are brought to the attention of State enterprises and research institutes, so that they are in possession of the latest achievements of science and technology.

"It will be the duty of the Engineering and Technical Committee to see to it that all the latest discoveries of science and technology are incorporated in the national economy and to help the State Planning Commission and the People's Economic Councils to plan the development of the different branches of our economy in the light of the most up-to-date knowledge of science and technology."

The national plan, say the theses, must, in the interests of technical progress, pay great attention to applying new techniques at every level. The Engineering and Technical Committee will co-opt highly qualified scientists, inventors, engineers, and workers who have made valuable technical suggestions or discoveries and give them every facility and encouragement to work out their ideas.

The theses also lay great stress on bringing trade unions into the work of planning through the People's Economic Councils, and say that for this purpose many unions will have to be reorganised so as to get rid of too much bureaucracy and too many paid officials and give greater weight to the views of the rank and file. One of the jobs of the unions under this scheme will be to encourage inventors and 'rationalisers' of production among the workers. The greater rôle of the Party within each economic unit is also stressed.

The discussion, filling columns in the Soviet Press, that went on at every level up and down the country from the publications of the theses in March to the adoption of the great reform in May, was much freer and more real than usual. It revealed wide differences of view but a general desire for reform.*

Some of the suggestions made in the great discussion, however, went too far to be acceptable to the present Soviet leadership. Thus *Kommunist* condemned the idea of one contributor who proposed a scheme for a new kind of socialisation of

* An interesting sample of the discussion was an article in *Pravda* of April 12th, 1957, by a Soviet engineer (A. Markin) on the electrification of the country under the new scheme:

"Everyone who looks at a map of our country will be struck by the two enormous green spots—the West Siberian Plain and the pre-Caspian Depression with the Central Asian deserts. These territories are our chief reserves—future store-houses on a world scale. The time will come when Western Siberia will produce as much corn as the whole of the United States and the pre-Caspian Depression will become a world centre for raising cotton and sheep.

"Taking these future possibilities into account makes the proposals of some of our hydro-electric engineers totally unacceptable. They are suggesting the building of vast hydro-electric stations on the lower reaches of the Ob River, with reservoirs to give the necessary power that would flood an important part of the West Siberian plain. That would mean senselessly losing some of our richest forests and the mineral treasures of the area. According to the latest opinions of geologists we have in this area the greatest oil and gas deposits in the world. This can radically change our whole conception of the sources of power in Western Siberia. And in the Kolpashevo region on the shore of the Ob, one of the greatest iron ore deposits in the world was recently discovered and is now being surveyed." Mr. Markin goes on to suggest placing the proposed hydro-electric stations further south, where they could be combined with the irrigation of desert areas and would not flood any valuable land or mineral resources.

industry, taking it out of the hands of the State and introducing instead the self-government of factories and branches of industry. Another scheme suggested that the factory directors should be elected by the workers and other staff of the factory, instead of being appointed by the State.

These ideas, while what may be called the logical limiting point of the proposed reforms, would mean something like the Yugoslav system of workers' management in industry, and were condemned by *Kommunist* with the very phrase "anarcho-syndicalist theory" and the very argument (that this was what the "workers' opposition" proposed in the early '20s, when it was rejected by the Party on the proposal of Lenin) that was used in the polemics with the Yugoslavs, quoted in the previous chapter.

The discussion in the Supreme Soviet when the plan was submitted to it in May was also much more than a formality, and resulted in important modifications. In particular it was decided to retain transport and certain branches of heavy industry under central, all-Union Ministries, instead of turning everything over to the ninety-two Economic Councils. But in the main the great reform was adopted as outlined in Khrushchev's theses.

This reform has been described as the triumph of the technocrats over the bureaucrats. But in fact it is much more. It is a real and serious attempt to democratise the processes of production by giving more scope and influence to all those engaged in it, not only leaders of industry but also engineers, technicians, craftsmen, the trade unions and the Party. By 'federalising' the processes of production it cuts at the roots of the evils of 'vertical organisation' and 'departmentalism', and by introducing more play and democracy into the planning system it removes the motive for these vicious forms of organisation.

This reform will accelerate the process, which I saw at work during my visit to Moscow, whereby the workers, who are now far more numerous, better organised, educated and paid than in the past and have the right to change their jobs, are beginning to insist that the trade unions should effectively defend their interests and play the part assigned to them in Soviet

R

theory, but which they could never play in practice under Stalin.

The pressure of the workers through their Unions has already scored one important victory: it has nipped in the bud an attempt made by a so-called 'wages committee' under the chairmanship of Kaganovich, to increase productivity by widening the wage spread and raising the 'norms', that is, by demanding more work for the same or even less pay. There were many reports of protests and 'interruptions of work' ('the word 'strikes' would be regarded as indelicate in the best Soviet circles in referring to such phenomena) against this policy. Finally, the policy was reversed; the wages of the lowest categories have been raised so as to diminish wage spread. The productivity of labour is being increased, not by demanding more toil from the workers at the same pay, but by improving the technical equipment and methods of the factories. 'Stakhanovism' has been buried and the workers through their Unions and factory committees are to have a real say in fixing wage scales. "All this," wrote the trade union paper, *Trud*, "shows that the workers have obtained an effective share in shaping State policies."

Moscow papers from time to time report protests from rank-and-file Communists against the way the higher ranks of the Party are chosen and their demands to have more say in choosing them, through secret ballot elections [as now in Poland!] rather than selection. It is not surprising that *Pravda* rejects and condemns this 'demagogy' and 'irresponsibility'. What is significant is that these demands are being made—and reported.

These developments are creating something like an economic and administrative need, and ultimately a politically effective demand, for more freedom to discuss and disagree and speak one's mind on public affairs. Writers and artists have considerably enlarged the sphere within which they are free and are pressing for more. The controversy raging about Dudintsev's famous novel, *Not by Bread Alone*, in which the hero is one man struggling against the system, and the references from time to time in the Soviet Press to the immoderate indulgence of students in the dangerous but exhilarating pleasures of free speech, show that the ferment is working powerfully—also that the forces of Stalinism are fighting a tough rearguard action.

In the international field the Soviet Government have continued to take the initiative all along the line, although the moral effect has been lost and the political impact much weakened by their actions in Hungary: on November 17th the Soviet Government produced a bold and comprehensive scheme for reduction, limitation and control of ·armaments (including the aerial control demanded by the Americans within a zone covering the whole of Europe), and the withdrawal of foreign forces from the territories of Germany and her neighbours. The Soviet Government also offered to ban H-bomb tests, by any method acceptable to the other two powers also producing H-bombs. This was followed by the Soviet Foreign Minister's proposal for an agreement in the Middle East, based on the idea of an undertaking by the great powers to refrain from building up rival positions of strength in the area and to control the traffic in arms and provide economic aid co-operatively and not competitively. These offers were repeated and amplified in the spring of 1957. At that time too the Soviet Government produced a plan for all-European economic co-operation, including the development of atomic energy for peaceful purposes, under the auspices of the Economic Commission for Europe of the United Nations, that was a 'follow-up' of the proposals made to that body in April 1956. Later still, at the end of April 1957, came Bulganin's dramatic offer to the British Premier for a general settlement.

What do the present Soviet leaders want? As Khrushchev told the 20th Congress of the C.P.S.U. and has repeatedly said since, their ambition is to catch up with and surpass the most advanced capitalist nations in production per head of population and thereby to prove to the world the superiority of a Socialist over a capitalist economy. They really believe that it is this more than anything else that will convert the 'toiling masses' in the non-Communist world to Communism.

That view, of course, leaves aside the whole question of the political superstructure, or, rather, assumes that Soviet conceptions on this score will prove acceptable to other countries, whereas in fact they are being increasingly challenged even within the Socialist camp and have never had a chance in countries where democracy was a working reality to which the propertied classes were prepared to be loyal (as they were not in Italy, nor in France in 1934 or under Pétain and Laval, not to mention how they are reacting to Algeria.)

But in this basic belief the Soviet leaders have never wavered. Khrushchev, for instance, in his 'theses' of March 30th, 1957, on the great economic reform, pointed out that after the infant Soviet Union had repelled the armed intervention of the capitalist powers it bent all its energies to economic reconstruction, and that Lenin had said that "the battle all over the world is now being waged on this field. If we solve this problem we shall without doubt have won the final victory internationally. This is why questions of economic reconstruction are exceptionally important for us."

And, of course, the economic achievements of the Soviet Union really are extraordinary. Khrushchev, in his theses, pointed out that by 1957 industrial production in the Soviet Union was thirty times greater than in pre-revolutionary Russia forty years ago, and was four times greater than it had been in 1940. The metallurgical industry was 180 times greater than in 1930 and the production of electricity nearly 100 times greater. And this in spite of the fact that nearly eighteen of the forty years of Soviet rule had been wasted by the Civil War, intervention, the Second World War, and making good its devastation.

The national income per head of population between 1913 and 1956 had increased thirteen times [which of course does not mean that the standard of living has risen thirteen-fold!]. In pre-revolutionary Russia there were less than 200,000 specialists with secondary or higher education; to-day there are over 6 million. More than 50 million people are actually undergoing some course of instruction—that is, one in four of the whole population.

As late as 1928 there were only 98,000 engineers and technicians, whereas to-day there are more than 1,600,000. In 1913 the number of the scientific workers in all forms of scientific institutes, universities, etc., was a little over 10,000; to-day it is 240,000. Khrushchev gave even more startling figures for the changes in the backward parts of the Soviet Union, that is, the peoples who were in the tribal or nomadic stage, or sunk in Asian feudalism, at the time of the Revolution.

In a later speech Khrushchev said he and his colleagues were not given to boasting and admitted frankly that they were still behind the most advanced of the Western nations. But, he said, they were confident they would catch up. To judge from the report of the British Iron and Steel Federation's leading steel expert, Dr. Thomas Colclough, on the Soviet steel industry, after a visit to the U.S.S.R. in the summer of 1956, there seems to be substance in Khrushchev's claim. Dr. Colclough led a delegation of nine British experts on various aspects of steel engineering and production. They were shown the latest Soviet steel plants and were deeply impressed. These plants, said Dr. Colclough, "are equal in size and efficiency to any I have seen in the world, and in some respects they are in advance. They are getting striking production rates out of some of these works. Of course, they have picked the eyes out of the best practice in all other countries. Every member of our team was impressed by the men we met and the results they have achieved."*

Dr. Colclough suggests that the high levels of production and efficiency in the Soviet steel works he visited are due not only to the intensive application of accumulated Western experience, but also to the benefits of central planning. He points out that in 1914 Russian steel output was roughly 4 million tons, or 60 lb. a head of population—a typical figure for a backward agricultural community—whereas in 1960 the planned production will be 68 million tons, or 760 lb. of steel a head (as compared with 860 lb. a head for the U.K. in 1956).

In a report on management and labour in the Soviet steel industry, Mr. Campbell Adamson of Richard, Thomas and Baldwin Ltd. points out that differentials between labourers and skilled workers are nearly twice what they are in British and American steel-works, that output bonuses often account for nearly half the total wage, and that Soviet works directors enjoy greater authority and extremely high pay and allowances,

* Reported in the *Manchester Guardian* of April 26th, 1957.

and as a rule pay much less direct tax than their counter-parts in the West.

Productivity in 1955 was 57 tons of ingot steel per man-year, which is a little below the average British or German productivity and well behind that of American industry, which stands at 170 ingot tons a man-year. But because Soviet in-dustry is rapidly expanding the proportion of modern inte-grated plant is rising, and in the new steel-works great attention is being paid to automatic control devices and other technical developments. Productivity in the Soviet iron and steel in-dustry may therefore, says Mr. Adamson, surpass that of Britain in the near future (Khrushchev claims that this is already the case in 1957) and may even come within striking distance of the American figure.

Two first-rank American political correspondents, Joseph and Stewart Alsop, reported in the same sense when they wrote about the official impressions in Washington of the 20th Congress of the C.P.S.U. (*New York Herald Tribune*, Paris edi-tion, February 24th, 1956): "The Soviet rulers are now genuinely and absolutely confident of their position. . . . Observers on the spot, like [U.S.] Ambassador Charles E. Bohlen, and Soviet experts in this country, agree that this remarkable self-confidence was the real hallmark of the 20th Congress of the Soviet Communist Party last week in Moscow. As Khrushchev and his colleagues look about them, they can be pardoned for self-congratulation. Their home political base is wholly secure. They have in China a dependable and in-creasingly powerful ally. All Asia is leaning their way, as Paul Hoffman has just sadly warned, so that there is now solid basis for Khrushchev's boast that 'the majority of the popula-tion of our planet is on their side. As Trevor Gardner has also warned, there is not the slightest doubt that the Soviets are now threatening to surpass us, not only in missiles, but in the whole area of air-atomic power. Finally, the Soviet Union is now most seriously challenging the supposedly unchallenge-able industrial might of the United States."

This, of course, was before the Polish revolution and the Hungarian rising and the concomitant developments inside the Soviet Union. They have brought home the fact that the

Communist system and outlook, both as regards relations between Socialist states and internal arrangements, must change radically in the direction of more freedom and democracy or encounter great and increasing difficulties even within its own 'camp'.

On this point the conclusions of Joseph Alsop are worth recording, for they appeared in the *New York Herald Tribune*, March 8th, 1957, after he had spent some weeks in the Soviet Union on an extended journey that included Siberia, and had talked with very many people, including Khrushchev. Mr. Alsop is, of course, a firm supporter of the official policy of the United States and could best be described as an intelligent, honest and outspoken American imperialist who has no time whatever for Socialism, let alone Communism. But what he says tallies closely with the conclusions I arrived at after my own visit.

He starts by reporting what he said was the most useful advice he received in Moscow "from the most brilliant of foreign observers stationed there" [internal evidence suggests he meant U.S. Ambassador Charles Bohlen], who told him: "For God's sake, remember that this place isn't either *1984* or a banana republic. It isn't *1984* because it's a human society, maybe not a very nice human society, but still a human society, with its own built-in human problems. And it isn't a banana republic because in most ways this is a strong society, and it isn't going to be thrown by its problems—at any rate in the foreseeable future."

Mr. Alsop then proceeds to give the view of the situation he had gathered from what he calls 'the wisest Moscow analysts', as follows:

"The right way to see the ferment among the students and intellectuals is not as a central Soviet problem at the present time, but as the by-product of still another problem. This is the problem the Soviet leaders are trying to solve by their truly staggering planned shake-up of the whole Soviet industrial economy. In fact, it is the problem of running a high technical society.

"As has been suggested before in this series of reports, you can build a high technical society with the knout. Josef Stalin did just that. But you cannot develop, and expand, and amplify a high technical society with the knout. At a certain stage, all the key persons, industrial managers, scientists, technicians, engineers of all sorts, need a sense of being free to make decisions and communicate among themselves and assume responsibilities without danger of reprisal. That is the only way to go on building toward still higher goals.

"In some sense at least, this need for more freedom has been recognised and met by the Soviet leadership. There is more freedom to-day in the Soviet Union. And precisely because there is more freedom in general, the intellectuals and students, the two specially irrepressible groups throughout modern Russian history, have been thereby emboldened.

"In effect, they were given an inch. They took an ell. And now they are being pushed back to two inches, by exhortation and by disciplinary measures which have thus far been relatively mild if they are judged by the grim standards of the Soviet past. That is where the matter rests for the present.

"One has to say 'for the present', however, because of the very nature of this problem of freedom *versus* unfreedom. On the one hand, the régime would have to restore Stalin-style discipline in order to restore the chilly, universal silence of the Stalin era. . . .

"But, on the other hand, Stalin-style discipline cannot be easily restored, partly because there is no Stalin, but also because Stalinism's restoration would freeze Soviet society, preventing the great further growth of wealth and power and productivity that the leaders want. There is the dilemma. It is a long-range dilemma. It does not endanger the régime. But it quite probably—one is tempted to say almost certainly—means that in fits and starts, with many retreats as well as advances, this strange Soviet society will go on evolving as it has been evolving in the last four years."

Poland

Meanwhile in Poland the January 1957 elections were an overwhelming success. Those elections took place on the new electoral law and were the first relatively free elections the

Polish people had enjoyed for thirty-five years. Their success was largely due to the attitude of the Catholic Church in Poland.

The dangers facing the electorate and the Government were two: the first was that the electors would use their new right to pick and choose by voting for candidates who, while belonging to the People's Front and pledged to its coalition policy (there were a handful of independents, including Catholics, but they were all running on the programme of the People's Front) had been selected locally and were not among those approved by the National People's Front Committee, consisting of the leaders of the Communist, Peasant and Progressive Parties. For if they had done this a Sejm might have been returned that was dominated by non-Communists and local men better at reflecting popular feeling than understanding how far it was safe to go in the prevailing international situation.

Gomulka met this danger by his eve-of-poll speech in which he said bluntly that a vote for the top six candidates on the list in each constituency, or alternatively for the whole list of nine or more (which meant the top six being selected automatically for the available seats) was a vote for free Poland, whereas votes cast any other way might wipe Poland off the map. That was plain language, and it was understood.

The second danger was that the elections might be boycotted, particularly in the country. This was what the anti-régime and anti-democratic elements were trying to bring about, and would have disastrously weakened the authority of the new Parliament and Government. The Natolin group were covertly supporting both the boycotters and those who wanted to vote for locally selected non-Communist candidates.*

But before Election Day the priests in every parish urged their parishioners to vote as a patriotic duty, and themselves led their flocks to the polling booths to vote the official ticket. Parties of nuns, making the sign of the Cross, cast their ballots for the whole list, i.e. for the Communist Government.

The result was an overwhelming vote, averaging over 90% in both town and country, with most of the top candidates on

* So were, openly, the Voice of America and Radio Free Europe Polish language broadcasts. I listened to some of them at the time.

the coalition list getting in. That was the internal 'famous victory' of the Polish revolution, and meant it is now solidly anchored in the people.

But at the opening of the new Sejm one independent voted against the Government and made a speech saying that Cyrankiewicz's policy was too much like the generalities they had heard before, and he himself had remained Premier during the Stalinist period, and therefore could not be trusted. There was some applause on the Right, and in the public gallery, for this sentiment, and on the subsequent vote there were some abstentions as well as this sturdy independent's sole vote against the motion of confidence in the Government.

The same man voted against and roughly the same number (about a dozen) abstained two months later when the Sejm voted on Gomulka's declaration that the Government could not fulfil the promise it had made to meet all the wage claims of workers below a certain level. The demands the Government had received, he explained, were mostly justified, but they added up to a sum that would cause runaway inflation. And, on the other hand, they had been disappointed in their hopes of swiftly raising production by receiving credits and facilities from the West to buy raw materials and capital equipment, particularly mining machinery [in the United States the powerful die-hard Senator Knowland successfully opposed the Administration's plan to give such aid]. They must therefore tighten their belts and see it through.

Gomulka also had to take the Press to task for making what he considered to be perilously free use of its new-found political liberty. The Editor of the Party organ, *Trybuna Ludu*, who had published the full text not only of Tito's speech at Pula, but also of the drastic speech of Nenni on Khrushchev's secret report and his conclusion that the whole system was wrong in the Soviet Union and nothing less than thoroughgoing democratisation would do, was dismissed, and the old pre-October Editor reinstalled. There was trouble too when Sartre's indictment of Stalinism and other even 'tougher' articles by disillusioned French intellectuals were published by Polish reviews. The censorship, which had virtually ceased to function, is making itself felt again.

These developments have caused a furore of protests among students, writers and journalists, chiefly among the young, the so-called *wsciekli* (*les enragés*, literally 'the angry [young men]'). They accuse Gomulka of betraying the revolution and auto-Kadarising Poland. But the protesters are a minority even among the intellectuals and are regarded as irresponsible by the great majority, who glumly accept Gomulka's restrictions on liberty as a necessary evil in the present circumstances. It is generally recognised that these limitations on freedom are imposed mainly by the international situation and only secondarily and to a minor degree by the fear that freedom may get out of hand and threaten the foundations of Communist rule. "The latter situation we will take care of so soon as we are free from the international danger," said one of the fighters for more freedom to me. "But meanwhile we regard it as a patriotic duty to hold back a bit and do nothing to imperil the very real measure of freedom and independence we have won."

The Achilles heel of the new Polish régime is economic, not political. Everything depends on whether Gomulka can do something effective to better the lot of the people, and that depends largely on Western policy.

Yugoslavia

Yugoslavia too is having her troubles. Tito mentioned in his Pula speech that "events in Hungary have stirred up various elements which still exist in our country. They are not numerous, but they make a noise. Some of them would like to start some kind of trouble, hoping to get something out of it. I have never said that we have completely liquidated and re-educated all the Ustashy, Chetniks* and the die-hard defenders of the Vatican. I have always said that only the unity of the people will prevent them ever trying to start anything in our country. More than ever to-day we need the unity of our people and Party, but not because we are afraid that anything could

* Ustashy = Croat Fascists and collaborators under the Quisling Ante Pavelich. Chetniks = Serbian Royalists under Mikhailovich, who often collaborated with the Italians and sometimes with the Germans. See my *Tito of Yugoslavia* and Fitzroy Maclean, *Disputed Barricade*.

happen in our country such as has happened in Hungary. For after all our situation is very different. We shed our own blood to win our revolution through our fight for freedom, and we had a good house-cleaning at the time of our revolution, so that we are not threatened by any such danger."

This speech reflected some of the unrest in the country and the Party that existed before the Polish and Hungarian revolutions, but was greatly increased by them. In the beginning this discontent was directed against what was regarded as the Government's 'pussy-footing' over Hungary so as not to offend the Russians. Tito's Pula speech dispelled that feeling and strengthened the demand for more freedom within Yugoslavia so as to have a home policy that was in line with the principles and views expounded in Yugoslavia's foreign policy.

Djilas, in spite of his suspended sentence, kept on writing in the Western Press (he could not get an article printed anywhere in Yugoslavia) without pulling his punches. He had upset the Yugoslavs and created a delicate situation by his article in American and French papers at the very time Tito was negotiating in Moscow, in which he gave highly unflattering pen-portraits of the Soviet leaders, concluding that they could not be trusted.*

The Polish and Hungarian revolutions drew from him the comment, which again was printed widely in the West, that whereas Poland had struck a blow that was important to Communism, Hungary had struck a blow that was important for humanity. The Hungarians, he said, had made a clean sweep of Communism and shown that they wanted democratic Socialism. That was the fate that would overtake Communism everywhere. Compared with that the 'national Communism' of Poland, like that of Yugoslavia, although an advance on Stalinism, was of secondary importance. He also bitterly upbraided the Yugoslav leaders for their failure to protest against Soviet policy in Hungary and attributed this to their

* For this the Yugoslav Press denounced him bitterly, but no official action was taken. If nothing had been said the Russians might have concluded that Tito was playing a double game—negotiating with them on the one hand and letting the West know through Djilas on the other that he still regarded them with hostility and distrust.

being bound by their own bureaucracy and suppression of freedom at home.

He was arrested, tried in secret and given three years' hard labour. The authorities published the indictment against him, but not his defence. But they could not suppress Djilas's defiant declaration that he had ceased to be a Communist and was now a democratic Socialist. That has made him something of a hero and martyr in the eyes of many Yugoslavs.

Djilas was putting in crude, stark, black-and-white terms the dilemma confronting Communism everywhere: how far to go in political freedom without it being used to turn Communism into democratic Socialism and ending the monopoly of political power of the Communist Party, with no guarantee that there may not even be a partial return to capitalism.

The appointment, after Mosha Pijade's death, of Petar Stambolich, the Premier of the Serbian People's Republic, to take his place as President of the Skupshchina, marks the promotion of the man who is the head and front of the Yugoslav authoritarians, the strongest protagonist of firm Party rule and clamping down on any further demands for freedom. His appointment as well as the worsening international situation may be responsible for the Yugoslav leaders, in their joint declaration with a French Communist Party delegation in March 1957, veering back temporarily to the view that the Kadar Government should be supported "in the interests of the Hungarian people, peace and Socialism". In return they got the French Communists to endorse their views on equality, freedom and toleration of differences in the relations between Communist parties.

But the Yugoslavs have gone too far already to stop: they cannot go back on their great innovation of workers' management, and once they have gone that far they cannot in the long run resist the demand for political freedom and democracy, to make the views of the workers about economic and social planning effective at Parliamentary and Government levels.

This is not yet the case, in spite of official claims to the contrary, and the very interesting provision in the Yugoslav Constitution for an 'economic chamber' composed of representatives elected by associations of workers' councils. This body has not the right to initiate but may amend legislation passed by the Chamber of People's Representatives on social and economic matters within its widely-drawn limits of competence, with provision for joint discussion to overcome deadlocks.

A further development of this great experiment was the first National Congress of Workers' Councils of Yugoslavia, convened in Belgrade at the end of June 1957 after seven years' experience of the actual working of elected workers' councils and management boards. The Congress surveyed and drew the lessons from this experience and decided how 'producers' self-government' could be further improved and developed.

A five-year plan for agriculture was adopted in the spring of 1957, designed to raise production by one-third and ultimately to double the present output. The methods used are Government credits and technical assistance, large-scale investment in irrigation, the ampler supply of tractors and other agricultural machinery, greater use of artificial fertilisers and the fullest use and development of the general agricultural co-operatives, comprising about half the peasantry, as well as the collective farms (called producers co-operatives or Socialist farms in Yugoslavia!) which own about 10% of all arable land.

The more this policy succeeds in ending basic hostility to the régime among the peasants, because they enjoy rising standards of living, and in turning them into modern and co-operatively-minded farmers, the quicker the Yugoslav leaders will feel that it would be safe to advance toward further democratisation—and the greater the pressure will be from below for more democracy.

Nor will the Yugoslav leadership give up their campaign for freedom and equality in the relations between Communist Parties and Socialist States, for friendship and co-operation with social democratic and progressive movements everywhere and for a melting down of the rival blocs into the United Nations. The assumptions and attitudes behind this policy lay them wide open to the ideas and conceptions of freedom of the working class movement in the West and are increasingly difficult to reconcile with setting narrow limits to the development of democracy in Yugoslavia.

Last but not least, it should not be forgotten that Slovenia and Croatia are accustomed to Central European rather than Balkan standards, and that the Serbs, Montenegrins, Macedonians and Bosnia-Herzegovinians have centuries'-old traditions of sturdy independence and fights for freedom, reinforced during the partisan wars, that cannot be satisfied without more political democracy than the country enjoys at present.

Eastern Germany

Eastern Germany is very much an occupied country, with the heritage of Hitler and before that of the Junkers and Prussian militarism behind it. But here too national feeling and European standards and the impact of the Polish and Hungarian revolutions have set in motion forces that in the long run will prove irresistible. How far matters have gone is shown by the programme of a group of officials in the Socialist Unity Party (nominally Communist plus Social Democratic but for all practical purposes, Communist) that was smuggled out to the West when its leader, Professor Wolfang Harich, was arrested and sentenced to ten years' penal servitude for treason. Before his arrest he held the Chair of Social Sciences at East Berlin University, the most important academic post in East Germany. According to the indictment, he was the ringleader in a reformist movement widespread among East German intellectuals and Party members.

The programme is a terrific indictment of Stalinism and of the suppression of political freedom in Eastern Germany. Stalin's policy toward the People's Democracies, it says, had threatened to disintegrate the Socialist camp and provoked such resistance within the Soviet Union that it became necessary after his death to make sweeping concessions to the people. But the process did not go far and fast enough to prevent friction between the Soviet Union and the People's Democracies, leading to controversies, crises and to the events in Poland and Hungary, as well as to the clamping down of Stalinist repression on Eastern Germany after the Berlin riots.

The reformists in the Socialist Unity Party, says Harich's programme, want to be free to consider the ideas of Trotsky,

Rosa Luxemburg and of German Social Democrats, as well as the classics of Marx and Lenin. They want to study the experience of Yugoslavia, Poland, China and other countries. They want the Party apparatus to be democratised and the Stalinists to be expelled. They want an easing of economic and social policies both on the land and in industry. Above all they want to restore complete freedom of thought, and for the régime to make its peace with the Church, restore the reign of law, abolish the Security Police and secret trials, and vest supreme power in Parliament, with an electoral system giving the voters a real choice. Harich expressly says these views are shared by Polish and Yugoslav comrades with whom he discussed these matters, and owe a great deal to Georgy Lukacz, the veteran Hungarian Communist intellectual with a world reputation who was arrested with Imre Nagy but subsequently released.

The programme ends by coming out for the reunification of Germany on conditions that would ensure united Germany being Socialist, but democratic. It says the main political instrument of the working class in Germany will be the German Social Democratic Party, with which the Socialist Unity Party, completely purged of Stalinism, could and should co-operate closely and ultimately fuse.

The East German régime is, of course, uncompromisingly Stalinist, mainly in self-preservation against its own people. But it can get away with this only on the strength of the cold war and the presence of Soviet forces.

Western Communism

In the Western world the suppression of the Hungarian rising, coming on top of the revelations in the Khrushchev report, have had a shattering effect on Communist parties. In France and Italy the Communist Parties became strong under Fascism, the semi-Fascism of the Vichy régime and the Nazi occupation. But the Socialist-Communist alliance in Italy has split. There are grave dissensions in the Communist Party and it has lost 800,000 of its $2\frac{1}{2}$ million nominal membership. It looks as though the militant Marxist Social Democracy of the

Nenni Socialists will become the leading power in the Italian working-class world.

In France the Communist Party has lost some 50,000 of its 300,000 members and dissident groups are publishing semi-clandestine weekly papers full of drastic criticism and demands for democratisation of the Party, intellectual honesty and respect for the rights of free speech. The main reason the French Communist Party does not fall to pieces or revolt against its Stalinist leadership is the very real and growing danger of Fascism and civil war arising out of the Algerian war and the atmosphere engendered by the cold war.

In Britain, the United States, and the Scandinavian countries, where Communism is weak because democracy is strong (with an infusion in the United States of creeping Fascism and a faint flavour of the same even in Britain) and has never broken down as it did in France and Italy, the Communist Parties are negligible. But in them, too, dissident minorities are pressing vigorously for political reorganisation and respect for the rights of free speech and association, that would in fact turn them into left-wing Social Democratic parties.

Czechoslovakia

The Czech leaders have gone on abounding in loyal near-Stalinist declarations and polemics. But here too the pressure from below for more freedom is getting steadily stronger. The Government has yielded a good deal of ground already and its resistance would be still further weakened if the international situation were to improve.

Hungary

The wretched Mr. Kadar, on a visit to the Soviet Union, loyally thundered against 'national communism', which, he said, was the younger brother of Hitler's National Socialism and an enemy against which Communism must be defended. He accused Tito, Kardelj and Popovich of expressing views about the Hungarian rising similar to those of Mr. Dulles!

But at the same time he had to defend himself in Budapest against attacks in the Party organ, coupled with an apologia

s

for Rakosi, by Revai, Rakosi's right-hand man. These attacks of course would never have been printed if it had not been for strong Russian pressure and prompting. The incident shows how little some of the Soviet leaders have learnt from all that has happened.

Nevertheless, the Kadar régime and its Soviet masters have had to make considerable economic and social concessions to the peasants and the workers. The release of Georgy Lukacz is a concession in another field. And there is no sign of any considerable section of the Hungarian workers and intellectuals, let alone the rest of the people, turning back to Stalinism. On the contrary, the indications are that the Kadar régime could not survive the withdrawal of Soviet troops.

Roumania and Bulgaria

In Roumania the Communist régime is too weak to risk reforms. In Bulgaria the traditional pro-Russian national sentiment is so strong as to weaken revolutionary pressure. Neither country has had any experience worth speaking of of democracy, and in both Communism took over from neo-Fascist dictators and dependence on Soviet help is very great. But here, too, the same forces are operating and the same one-way process has been set in motion as in the other People's Democracies.

China

China is the equal and ally of the Soviet Union and conscious of her status as a companion great power. The Soviet alliance corresponds to Chinese beliefs and needs. Even if it did not it would still seem the lesser evil to the kind of treatment to which China is subjected by the West, under American leadership—boycott, exclusion from the United Nations, non-recognition, American occupation of Formosa and the Pescadores, and constant threats.

The Chinese are trying to pour oil on the stormy waters of the great controversy, but are somewhat handicapped as mediators by their dependence on the Soviet alliance and Soviet economic help. Moreover, whereas they are realistic and adaptable in working out their own solutions to their own problems inside China, they are apt to be doctrinaire and extreme in their international views, because their isolation cuts them off from first-hand knowledge and they depend largely on information from Soviet sources.

There is also something deeper. China's ancient civilisation had developed a unique society, ruled over by a god-emperor through his civil service recruited by examinations and separated by a gulf from the people. But this autocracy and bureaucracy were tempered by the very limited functions of the authorities, who did little more than collect taxes. There was not a Chinese State at all in the modern sense, as the Western powers found when they fell upon China in the spacious days of nineteenth-century imperialism. They had to force the Manchu Dynasty to assume functions which it had never dreamed of performing, and was not equipped to perform, and then took over those functions themselves and turned China into a semi-colony.

The European tradition of human rights and the value of the individual, stemming from Greece, Rome, the Renaissance, the English, American and French revolutions, the rights of man and so forth, was unknown to the Chinese tradition. The West to them meant the superior techniques and utter ruthlessness and treachery of foreign devils. The high civilisation of the old order in China rested on a very low valuation of life and unconsciousness of what we regard, at least in theory, as inalienable human rights.

The Chinese Revolution that began in 1911 with Sun Yat-sen, was even more comprehensive and profound than the Russian revolution. It was summed up in Sun Yat-sen's three principles—the equality of China with other nations, or national independence; the equality of all Chinese with each other, or democracy; the principle of the people's livelihood, or what we should now call the Welfare State, sustained by a Socialist economy. The Chinese have had to acquire a sense of nationhood transcending provincial loyalties and family loyalties; to instil a sense of citizenship and political rights into industrial workers and millions of toiling peasants, i.e. to make them stop being coolies and feel they are men; to emancipate women; in fact to make a State and modernise as well as revolutionise the whole of Chinese society.

Against this background, Communism has meant an actual advance in human dignity and sense of personal value and importance for the mass of the people, and the unspeakably childish excesses and follies of the brain-washing, blue uniforms, Party dictation about the choice of partners in marriage, and other interferences in private lives, did not clash with a sense of individualism and human rights as much as they would have done in the context of a different tradition. The Chinese are already out-growing this stage and evolving their own forms of 'Marxist-Leninist' Socialism adapted to their own unique civilisation.

The remarkable thing about this adaptation is that it is arriving along a Chinese road at much the same position as the Poles and the Yugoslavs. Mao Tse-tung's famous doctrine of "Let many (100) different flowers bloom and schools of thought contend" to justify cultural freedom, has been followed by the distinction he draws between disagreements within the people and quarrels with foreign or class enemies. The former, he insists, whether within the Party or between the Party and other Chinese, can and should be settled by discussion, reason and compromise. Attempts to settle them by authority result in hardening them into the antagonism of enemies and may lead to internal dissensions being exploited by enemies. In his secret memorandum adopted in February 1957 and published in June he carries this doctrine very far: The Chinese Party, he points out, have found room for patriotic Chinese capitalists in the new Socialist society they are building. (They have also offered Chiang Kai-shek a high post in the Government if he will rejoin the national fold, thus ceasing to be a foreign enemy or the agent of foreign enemies and becoming merely one of the internal problems of China to be dealt with by reason and compromise.) All this is very Chinese, and yet arrives at much the same destination as the Polish and other Communists who want to recover the traditions of European liberal civilisation.

There is one saying of Lenin's that one never hears in the Soviet Union amidst all the return to Leninism, and that is his remark that Czarist Russia had been the most backward of all the white nations, and when the revolution spread to other countries the Soviet Union would again be the most backward of the Socialist countries. Since then of course the Soviet Union has made gigantic strides in industrialisation, mechanisation of agriculture, the production of scientists and technologists, raising the standards of education and of living of its 220 million population. But all this has been achieved in isolation and evolved in the national tradition of Russia. There is a gulf of incomprehension between the present Soviet leaders and the minds even of most Communists in the People's Democracies, let alone between the Russians and the West, and Soviet methods when applied to the 'satellites' have proved a misfit.

For the European People's Democracies are in the European tradition and tend more and more to apply European standards of social and political judgment. Many Polish, Czechoslovak, Hungarian and Yugoslav Communists are much nearer to left-wing Marxist Social Democrats like Nenni, than they are to the Soviet Communists.

All this is partly overlaid and obscured in what the Russians now are calling the Commonwealth of Socialist Nations, because of the common security interests aroused by fear of the West, which bids these States cling together and accept Soviet leadership and protection. This fear also strengthens the Stalinist elements in the different Communist parties in their resistance to those who want more democracy and national independence. And of course the more the Stalinist elements and their cold war great power security policies dominate the group of Socialist States, the more they encourage the cold warriors in the West.

The impact of the policies of Western governments and working-class (i.e. Labour and Socialist) parties, has all along been, and continues to be, a first-class factor in the internal evolution of the Communist régimes and in the mutual relations of Socialist states. For this reason this book may fittingly close with a glance at "The West and Communism".

CHAPTER SEVENTEEN

The West and Communism

EVER SINCE the social revolution in Russia the policy of the governments of capitalist countries, whether democracies or autocracies, has, with variations of detail and some fluctuation and confusion, followed the same broad pattern, the classic pattern of ruling classes through the ages when faced by threats to the existing order: treat social unrest as due to infiltration and subversion by agents of the Kremlin and hence to Soviet aggression, and meet it by arms and alliances and policies of 'containment' and 'liberation' that work out as economic, political and even military interference in the internal affairs of other countries, in order to put down parties or Governments threatening the old social order and to prop up or restore régimes believed to be reliable defenders of that order. In Europe the Western powers have always tried to enlist Germany on their side in these enterprises.

After the First World War this policy failed to defeat the Russian Revolution, but did a good deal to promote and strengthen Stalinism. In Europe it did defeat the social revolution, but at the cost of promoting the spread of Fascism. Ultimately it made inevitable the wholly unnecessary second world war, which could have been averted again and again—but only at the risk of seeing the thwarted Fascist régimes overthrown by their peoples and Socialism spreading in Europe.*

* The reader will find chapter and verse for these allegations in my pre-war books, *Inquest on Peace, The Road to War, Why We are Losing the Peace, Between Two Wars?*; my wartime books, *Mirror of the Past* and *Mirror of the Present*; and the post-war books, *Can the Tories Win the Peace and How They Lost the Last One*, and *I Choose Peace*.

Notwithstanding its consequences, this policy was suspended but not abandoned when the Soviet Union was pitchforked into the war on our side by Hitler, and was resumed as early as 1943* (contrary to the popular belief that it was forced upon us by the bad behaviour of the Russians after the war). Stalin, of course, played into the hands of the Western cold warriors from the start and shared responsibility with them for the deadlocks and disagreements, the quarrels and mis-understandings, the arms race and the cold war that have brought us to where we stand to-day. But the history of Soviet-West relationships is a study in shifting shades of grey, not in black and white.

And now the time has come for a radical overhaul of our policies and agonising re-appraisal of their intellectual and moral foundations.

First, what are we up against? Rather less than one-third of humanity under American leadership pitted against rather more than one-third under Soviet leadership, with the rest of humanity sitting on the side lines. The H-bomb has merely underlined the fact that should have been obvious before, namely that it is morally and intellectually defective to believe that the ideological differences between these vast sections of humanity can be settled by force or the threat of force.

Moreover, to talk of one thousand million human beings experimenting with new forms of society, in terms of intel-lectually empty and emotionally charged *clichés* and abstractions like 'international Communism' or 'the Communist con-spiracy', and the rest of the vocabulary of compulsive obses-sion, springs from a condition of fanaticism, fear and hate that has nothing to do with political realism nor intellectual honesty nor moral integrity.

What is it we fear and hate? Do we really believe that the Soviet leaders want to impose Communism on the rest of the world by fire and sword? That is certainly the assumption underlying official Western policy, N.A.T.O. and all that. But there is not a shred of evidence for it, and it is in fact con-tradicted by the experience of forty years. So much so that the fact is even admitted in lucid intervals in the most

* See *I Choose Peace*.

surprising quarters. U.S. Vice-President Nixon, for instance, in a speech in Philadelphia on January 17th, 1956, pointed out that:

"Since World War II the Communist conspiracy has added 600 million people and a quarter of the earth's territory to the area which it dominates. The significant fact about this accomplishment is that the gains were made without the loss of a single Russian soldier in combat. What it adds up to is that the major danger the free world faces to-day is not defeat in hot war but defeat in cold war—a cold war in which potential enemies, undeterred by any moral restraint, use political, economic and psychological and other tactics which are just as effective in taking over territory as armed aggression—and much less costly. This is the way the Communist nations operate."

An even more surprising witness is Mr. J. Foster Dulles himself, who at a N.A.T.O. conference in Paris in December 1955 made the same point as Mr. Nixon. But he claimed that whereas the Soviet Union, since the death of Stalin, had gone in for economic and political action and showed no signs of reverting to policies of force, it had in the first few years after the war sought to achieve its aims by violence. In saying this he flatly contradicted his own statement at the third National Conference of Churches and the World Order on March 8th, 1949: "So far as it is humanly possible to judge, the Soviet Government, under conditions now prevailing, does not contemplate the use of war as an instrument of its national policy. I do not know any responsible high official, military or civilian, in this Government, or any government, who believes that the Soviet Government now plans conquest by open military aggression."

That too is the emphatic opinion of the man who is regarded in the United States as the leading authority in the Diplomatic Service on the Soviet Union, namely, Mr. G. F. Kennan, former head of the Policy Planning Staff of the State Department and former U.S. Ambassador in the U.S.S.R. In a book published in September 1954, entitled *The Realities of American Foreign Policy*, he pointed out that the Soviet Government had never used war as an instrument of national policy, and relied on other means for the spread of Communism in the world.

In the *Reader's Digest* of March 1950, Mr. Kennan gave the reasons why this is so: "Stalinist doctrine does not demand war. On the contrary, it teaches that eventually capitalism will fall largely of its own weight, i.e. as a result of the 'inner contradictions' which the Communists believe it embodies. They see the rôle of Communism as one of hastening the collapse of capitalism and assisting, as a midwife, at the birth of the Socialist order." But they "regard this as primarily the task of the native Communists in each country, and not of the Soviet Red Army.

"There is nothing in Stalinist doctrine which would make it necessarily the main responsibility of the Soviet Union themselves to overthrow capitalism everywhere by direct military action. This premise would actually seem illogical and improper, from the Communist point of view; for it would imply that capitalism, in the absence of such an attack, would be basically sound and capable of coping permanently with its own 'contradictions'. But this is exactly what good Marxists do not believe. . . . Political expansionism by means short of war has been the real Soviet programme since the conclusion of World War II. During this period the Soviet Government has not taken one inch of land by outright military aggression."

This analysis, of course, like Mr. Dulles' and Vice-President Nixon's, is vitiated by the assumption that Communism is synonymous with some kind of conspiracy and action by the Soviet leaders and the spread of Soviet power and influence. This ignores the whole social basis of Communism and most of the facts set forth in this book.

But it does bring us back to just what it is that the West fears and hates. Is it the crying evils of tyranny, oppression and the Police State in Communist countries? But the cold war and the arms race aggravate those evils. And those who are most fanatically determined to go on preparing for war and regard compromise and negotiation as appeasement are mostly those who were appeasers if not friends of Hitler and Mussolini and supporters of Franco before the war. To-day they are totally indifferent to tyranny and dictatorship among the nations in the American camp.* Indeed, the record suggests that from the point of view of official Western policy there is no objection to tyranny, dictatorship and the evils of the police State, so long as they are exercised on the side of preserving the old social order.

In other words, what Western Governments find really fearful and hateful in the Communist one-third of the world is not so much the fact that countries which have never known democracy have so far failed to develop it in the conditions of revolution complicated by the cold war, and have instead produced some pretty horrifying police régimes, but the fact that they are trying to build a new society. And of course, to those whose real concern is to preserve the old social order even at the cost of the values of liberal civilisation and even if it means courting the destruction of the human race, the prospect is terrifying enough: for these new societies have enormous vitality. And those who are building them are sustained by a power of faith that cannot be matched in the West. Moreover, their planned Socialist economies have scored successes which measured against the conditions previously prevailing in those countries outstrip anything capitalism can accomplish. Their experiments in combining all this with the power of the workers through their trade unions to take a hand in determining their

* Cf. Representative Thomas B. Curtis in the *U.S. Congressional Record*, February 18th, 1955: Mr. Curtis said he had asked for information from the reference service of the Library of Congress and on the basis of the information received could assert that "There are seventy-one countries outside the Iron Curtain which we erroneously refer to as the 'free world'. Of these seventy-one nations, forty-nine are . . . dictatorships or close oligarchies, and the majority cannot even pass under the term 'benevolent' dictatorships. Of the remaining twenty-two nations most of them truly have some claim to the adjective 'free' as far as their political governments are concerned, but certainly as far as the economic government of several of them is concerned, it is oligarchic and a small percentage of the nation is living off the backs of the other 99%." This leaves out the colonies in the 'free world': since the war 76,000 people have been butchered in Madagascar to keep the island loyal to its colonial status in the *Union Française*. A great deal of indiscriminate murder and torture as an official system has been going on for a long time in Algeria as part of the policy of 'pacification'. Then there is the little item of the 40,000 Kikuyu in concentration camps, Cyprus, British Guiana, and so forth.

own conditions of life and work and the planning of their society, even the management of industry through their elected representatives, suggest a whole new range of possibilities. If these things can be married to political freedom, democracy and what we understand by the rights of man and the rule of law, the old order will indeed be subjected to a formidable, nay irresistible challenge.

But let those who are beset by such fears, take heart: the standards of living of the Western Democracies are still so much higher, their political traditions are so much richer, and they have gone so far in solving the problem of a just balance between the rights of the individual and the needs of society, that we have nothing to fear from the countries of the social revolution, if what we care about is to preserve and enlarge the values of humanism and liberal civilisation.

If what we want is to help these régimes to reform themselves, to experience a new birth of freedom, the future is ours. But if what we are trying to do is to destroy the new societies so as to preserve the old social order, the best we can hope for is failure and the worst, death, universal death, the extinction of the human animal because it was too stupid and too wicked to live.

What all this means in terms of analysis and policy is the theme for another book. But perhaps this book could fittingly close by propounding certain propositions or maxims on which we in the West might meditate with advantage before making up our minds about what to do in face of Communism in transition, in a world where man's destructive power has outrun his capacity to survive.

In June 1947 the official organ of the Vatican, the *Osservatore Romano*, published four remarkable articles by its veteran Editor-in-chief, Count Giuseppe della Torre. Analysing the world situation he concluded that just as 150 years ago there was a counter-revolutionary coalition led by Britain against revolutionary France, so to-day there was a counter-revolutionary coalition led by the United States against revolutionary Russia. In such a conflict there was in no true sense a clash of conflicting principles of ideology and civilisation, but only a struggle between great powers using ideologies to mask their national interests, with right and wrong mixed and distributed on both sides and no issue which could not and should not be settled by negotiation and compromise. With war everything would be lost, and there was not much left to lose after two world wars, whereas with peace everything could be regained. Communism had originated in Western Europe a century ago and would go on whatever happened to Russia. It was impossible to kill an idea by force, even the idea of Communism. "Whatever may be the positions or opinions we hold about Communism, as an idea and in practice, as a philosophy and morality, as economics and politics, to-day and to-morrow, we cannot and we must not, if we wish to remain civilised and Christian, imagine that we can overcome or modify Communism by force, with the blood, anguish, violence, misery and barbarism of war" (June 26th, 1947).

Mr., as he then was, Churchill's famous speech at Fulton, Missouri, on March 4th, 1946, with President Truman on the platform, that was, so to speak, the West's declaration of war in the cold war (which in fact had been going on in various forms ever since the Russian revolution and was only partially suspended even when we and the Soviet Union were allies in the Second World War) called for the combining of the military power of the United States, the British Commonwealth and Western Europe to halt the spread of Communism, which he identified with Soviet aggression. That has been official Western policy from that day to this.

But *The Times* leader of March 6th, 1946, commenting on it, is worth quoting to-day: it condemned Winston Churchill for his assertion that Communism and Western Democracy were 'irreconcilable opposites dividing or attempting to divide the world between them to-day' because, it said, this was an assumption of despair that failed to recognise two important points:

"The first is that there are many forms of government intermediate between Western democracy and Communism, and some of them may be better adapted at the present stage of development to the requirements of Eastern Europe or of the Middle or Far East. The second is that, while Western democracy and Communism are in many respects opposed, they have much to learn from one another—Communism in the working of political institutions and in the establishment of individual rights, Western democracy in the development of economic and social planning.

"The ideological warfare between Western democracy and Communism cannot result in an out-and-out victory for either side. The issue will be determined neither by clashes of eloquence nor by clashes of arms, but by the success of the great nations in dealing with the problems of social organisation in the broadest sense which the war has left behind it."

The third proposition was stated in the following words by General Douglas MacArthur, American and United Nations C.-in-C. in the Korean war and at that time the darling of the right wing Republicans and head of the preventive war school in the United States, in a speech at Los Angeles on January 26th, 1955.

"The agony of the cold war is kept alive by two great illusions. The one a complete belief on the part of the Soviet world that the capitalist countries are preparing to attack them; that sooner or later we intend to strike. And the other a complete belief on the part of the capitalist countries that the Soviets are preparing to attack us; that sooner or later they intend to strike. Both are wrong. Each side, so far as the masses are concerned, is equally desirous of peace. For either side war with the other would mean nothing but disaster. Both equally dread it. But the constant acceleration of preparation may well, without specific intent, ultimately produce a spontaneous combustion....

"When will some great figure in power have sufficient imagination and moral courage to translate this universal wish for peace—which is rapidly becoming a necessity—into actuality? It is the leaders who are the laggards. The disease of power seems to confuse and bewilder them. Never do they dare to state the bald truth that the next great advance in the evolution of civilisation cannot take place until war is abolished.

"This idea has always been dismissed as impossible by every cynic, pessimist, and swashbuckler in history. But that was before the science of the past decade made mass destruction a reality. The argument was that human character has never reached a theoretical development which would permit the application of pure idealism. In the last two thousand years its rate of change has been deplorably slow compared to that of the arts and sciences. But now the tremendous and present evolution of nuclear and other potentials of destruction has suddenly taken the problem away from its primary consideration as a moral and spiritual question, and brought it abreast of scientific realism. It is no longer an ethical equation to be pondered solely by learned philosophers and ecclesiastics, but a hard core one for the decision of the masses whose survival is the issue."